NICE
GIRL

NICE GIRL

THE STORY OF KELI LANE AND HER MISSING BABY, TEGAN

RACHAEL JANE CHIN

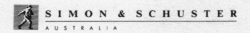

SIMON & SCHUSTER
AUSTRALIA

NICE GIRL
First published in Australia in 2011 by
Simon & Schuster (Australia) Pty Limited
Suite 19A, Level 1, 450 Miller Street, Cammeray, NSW 2062

A CBS Company
Sydney New York London Toronto
Visit our website at www.simonandschuster.com.au

National Library of Australia Cataloguing-in-Publication entry
Author: Jane Chin, Rachael.
Title: Nice girl: the story of Keli Lane and her missing baby, Tegan/Rachael Jane Chin.
Edition: 1st ed.
Subjects: Lane, Keli. Lane, Tegan. Missing children – New South Wales – Sydney.
Newborn infants – Crimes against – New South Wales – Sydney. Victims of crimes –
New South Wales – Sydney. Absence and presumption of death – New South Wales
– Sydney. Criminal investigation – New South Wales – Sydney. Trials (Murder) –
New South Wales – Sydney.
Dewey Number: 364.155092

ISBN: 9780731814961 (pbk.)

Cover design: Ful-Vue Pty Ltd, Sydney
Internal design and typesetting: Midland Typesetters, Australia
Printed and bound in Australia by Griffin Press

The paper used to produce this book is a natural, recyclable product made from wood
grown in sustainable plantation forests. The manufacturing processes conform to the
environmental regulations in the country of origin.

For my husband, David

CONTENTS

Author's note   ix

1   A strange case   1
2   Going for gold   15
3   The in-crowd   33
4   Happy birthday, Keli   45
5   Do you love me?   67
6   Tegan   77
7   A third baby arrives – but where is Tegan?   87
8   Crying in the chapel   107
9   Manly police station drops the ball   117
10   No longer a secret   129
11   Release the hounds   165
12   Murky waters   181
13   Robert Lane takes the stand   189
14   Duncan and his family take the stand   199
15   Keli's friends keep the faith   215
16   Sandra Lane takes the stand   223
17   Uncertain conclusions   237
18   Piece by piece   249
19   The murder trial begins   261
20   Keli's lies: sad or sinister?   279
21   Justice for Tegan, agony for the Lanes   293

Acknowledgements   309

AUTHOR'S NOTE

While this book is written in a highly narrative style and some scenes have been fictionalised, all details including dates, names and events have been drawn directly from the transcript of the coronial inquest into the suspected death of Tegan between 2004 and 2006, news clippings, press releases, first-hand observation of the 2008 police dig, first-hand observation of Keli Lane's 2009 arraignment, first-hand observation of every day of the 2010 murder trial and each day's court transcript.

Keli Lane's children are not named in this book, with the exception of Tegan. A pseudonym has been used for her fourth child. The names of the fathers of her children have also not been used or have been changed.

Some quotes from court transcripts have been edited. In particular, the opening and closing addresses of both the defence and the Crown have been heavily edited, with every attempt made to convey the intended meaning.

Rachael Jane Chin

1

A STRANGE CASE

It's 2006, and Senior Constable Epstein is driving out of the cavernous car park under Glebe Morgue, an anonymous brick building on Parramatta Road, one of Sydney's busiest thoroughfares. On the passenger seat beside her is a folder containing a few sheets of neatly typed paper, the results of a search she has done of the unknown and unclaimed children and babies in the state's morgue records. Epstein is on her way to present her findings at the Westmead Coroner's Court, where a long-running inquest is in its final stages. Her instructions were to see if a female born in September 1996, who was at least two days old at the time of death, is among them. As strange as those instructions sounded, Epstein instantly knew what she was about to be involved in. The case of this missing child has been in the papers and on the TV for over a year. It's the mystery of Tegan Lane.

The suspicious deaths of children usually make the news,

and those that make the news are almost always solved. They come with sad regularity, a reminder of the madness that happens in far-flung suburbs and towns no one has ever heard of. There are some human monsters who hurt and kill children for pleasure, but most crimes towards children, especially at the hands of those who are supposed to protect them, are a result of desperation, of pathetic incompetence and of hopeless, downward spiralling lives. These are the perpetrators who appear on the nightly news, rough and unkempt, shielding their faces from photographers by pulling their tracksuit tops over their heads. Broken families, broken lives, nothing to be proud of. The background stories to the crimes are the same: drugs, unemployment, a family well known to welfare authorities and police.

But as Senior Constable Epstein knows, an even harsher reality is that some people who kill children, even their own, are never caught. Not many get away with it, but a small number do. The details of the bodies of the anonymous dead children, infants and toddlers whose parents have never reported them missing sit neatly documented in the morgue's system. These unspeakable crimes may go unpunished, but the morgue never forgets the nameless children.

Epstein has found two unidentified children, but neither of them are Tegan. Her body cannot be found, but Tegan has been missing for so long that police hold very little hope of her being alive. In the case of missing children, normally suspicions fall on the person who last saw the child alive, but Tegan's case is unique. Senior Constable Epstein, like a lot of people in Sydney and the rest of Australia, has seen pictures of Tegan's mother, Keli Lane, on the evening news. Police say she is the last to have seen Tegan alive, but Keli simply doesn't look like the kind of person most imagine would be involved in a suspected homicide, let alone the suspected homicide of a newborn child.

Keli and her family are typical, solid, middle-class Australian stock who could easily be mistaken for solicitors in their neat navy suits and ironed shirts as they enter the Westmead Coroner's Court. Keli's father, Robert Lane, who has sat beside his daughter every day of the hearing, which has been held for several weeks spread over the past year and a half, sometimes carries an umbrella, while Keli herself carries a shiny, plain handbag. Nothing about the Lanes is flashy, cheap or in need of repair. But the family's middle-class respectability only highlights the confusing strangeness of this case.

Driving towards the small car park at the rear of the Westmead courthouse, Senior Constable Epstein passes a group of waiting TV cameramen and newspaper photographers outside the main entrance. She enters via the back, but she knows she isn't the one they are waiting for. Their target is already inside. The courtroom is furnished with nondescript carpet and swivel chairs. Keli sits behind her barrister with her ankles demurely crossed. She is a big, pretty girl in her early thirties. Today she is wearing a conservative navy suit with flat, ballet style court shoes. She is tall, her shoulders are broad and she has straight, chin-length blonde hair. Her clear complexion doesn't need much make-up. Her father, Robert, who is in his mid fifties, sits by her side. He is lean but not skinny, with broad shoulders and an erect posture. Robert is an ex-athlete, just like Keli. His white-grey hair is cut short and his skin is slightly ruddy.

As normal as Keli appears to be, she is someone with a disturbing, hidden past. Keli gave birth to Tegan when she was twenty-one years old and living at home with her parents. Rob and Sandy, as they are known to their friends, Keli's brother and her long-term boyfriend at the time, Duncan Gillies, claimed they knew nothing about Keli's pregnancy or Tegan's birth until police and other authorities investigated the case years later. They said Keli hadn't looked pregnant, even when her pregnancy had reached full-term. Those closest to her said that, like some women, Keli's body didn't grow into a typical pregnant shape and this meant she was able to keep Tegan's existence hidden from them.

The fact that Keli was able to hide her pregnancy from her nearest and dearest was remarkable in itself. What made her concealment astonishing was that, at the time, Keli was an elite water polo player who spent many hours each week in her swimming costume. Keli somehow managed to keep up a physically demanding training schedule throughout her pregnancy, revealing her body for public scrutiny several times a week. When it was time to give birth, Keli took herself to a hospital on the other side of the city and did it alone without any support. Two days after her secret birth, Tegan disappeared without a trace. And only hours after Tegan's disappearance, Keli was sitting at a wedding beside Duncan, completely composed, as if nothing out of the ordinary had happened.

When the authorities discovered Tegan's birth and disappearance, Keli told many stories about what happened the day her daughter vanished, all of them different. By the time the matter came before the coroner she had settled on the following version of events: Tegan's father was a man with whom Keli had a brief affair while she was in a serious relationship with Duncan. This man was angry that Keli had fallen pregnant. Nonetheless, after checking herself out of the maternity ward two days after giving birth, Keli handed Tegan to the baby's father in the hospital car park. Present at the handover was this man's mother and his de facto partner who, for some unknown reason, was happy to take custody of a child born of an affair conducted behind her back. Keli claimed to have seen Tegan one final time several months after she had handed her over.

But besides Keli's word, Chief Coroner John Abernethy, who has presided over the long-running inquest, has found no evidence to support this story. The man whom Keli claims to be Tegan's father has never been found, despite an extensive police search. There were no blood samples taken from Tegan because Keli checked out of the maternity ward before they could be done, and since leaving the hospital in her mother's arms, no single rebate for a doctor's appointment, school attendance record, name change application or passport for Tegan has been found. Keli's friends and family also have no clue where Tegan might be because they had no idea she even existed until they'd been told by police, eight years after her birth and disappearance. There wasn't even a birth certificate for Tegan until Abernethy ordered one for her in 2005. The child had simply vanished into thin air. But despite this, and despite not having had any contact with her missing daughter for ten years, Keli insists Tegan is alive.

As the coronial inquest unfolded, the media revelled in Keli's strange story. 'MY GIRL IS NO KILLER', 'I DIDN'T KILL TEGAN' and 'CORONER TELLS KELI TO SEE A SHRINK' the newspaper headlines shouted. The huge black words framed pictures of Keli Lane, her father and other members of her family as they walked with their arms linked, jaws clenched and eyes cast downwards, weathering the storm of jostling photographers together. When Keli's family took the stand early on in the hearing, they declared themselves satisfied with her explanation as to what happened to Tegan, refusing to entertain the possibility that it could be a lie. While police think Tegan has been the victim of foul play, the Lanes believe Tegan might still be alive somewhere, living in childish innocence of the huge, nationwide search for her.

And while Tegan's birth and disappearance threw a cloud of suspicion over the Lane family, in the public gallery of the coroner's court that suspicion very quickly turned to sensation once the full, shocking extent of Keli's secret life was finally revealed. Incredibly, Tegan was one of three babies Keli had secretly carried to full term while living at home.

The first child was born two days shy of Keli's twentieth birthday in 1995. The next year, in 1996, Tegan was born. Then, three years later, Keli's third child was born. As with Tegan, the other two pregnancies and births went unnoticed by Keli's parents and boyfriend. And while this was strange enough, even stranger was the fact that, for her first and third children, Keli had arranged for their legal adoption. Why Tegan was singled out and treated so differently from her siblings was an unsettling question. In fact, the coroner's court had never seen a case like it before.

There is no suggestion of strong religious beliefs as an explanation for Keli's behaviour. Her parents knew she was sexually active, as most young women are once they hit their late teens and early twenties. While things may have been different in her mother's day, girls of Keli's age are no longer expected to be virgins when they marry. Certainly, it would have been socially unacceptable for Keli to be promiscuous, but she was in a long-term relationship with her boyfriend, Duncan. Keli had other boyfriends before and after Duncan, but not a huge number of lovers. But while falling pregnant by accident is not unusual, doing so three times is, especially when the use of reliable contraception is normal. Nobody likes the idea of having an abortion, but the option is there if everything else fails. Someone like Keli simply didn't have to have a baby if she didn't want to.

So why did she give birth, apparently in secret, three times? Was she trying to trap Duncan into marriage? Was she acting erratically due to the pressures of elite sport and trying to keep up with her high-achieving peers? Was she mentally ill? In the grip of a personality disorder? Or was she in deep denial about something terrible in her life, something so horrific that giving birth in secret was easier than dealing with it? As the hearing stretched on, there were plenty of theories but no one knew the answer. Besides trying to understand why Keli would go through with three pregnancies, her ability to conceal those pregnancies – and births – while sharing a home with her parents and a bed with her boyfriend was something no one could comprehend.

'How could the mother not notice her daughter was pregnant? They were living under the same roof!' women across Sydney and the rest of Australia asked each other over the evening news. 'How could the boyfriend not know she was pregnant if he was having sex with her?' men asked themselves. But there they were on the stand, the Lane family and Keli's ex-boyfriend, claiming under oath to know nothing about Tegan or the two other secret children.

The search for Tegan has been far and wide. Police have used the media to reach out to the wider public, but still there is no clue as to where she is. Chief Coroner John Abernethy's duty is to decide whether Tegan is in fact dead, despite the absence of a corpse. If he decides she is, he also has to indicate whom the police should charge with killing her. His task is proving to be a difficult one. The hearing has now been running off and on for over a year, almost all of the evidence has been heard and still there is no clue as to where Tegan is or what happened to her. There was no choice but to have Senior Constable Epstein search the records of unnamed corpses in the morgue just in case Tegan is there.

Coroner Abernethy sits behind his bench looking down on the bar table where the lawyers stand, behind whom sits Keli and her father Rob, who is there to support her while the details of her strange history of secret births is aired for all to hear. Across from Keli and Rob is the witness stand. The journalists sit in the small public gallery behind Keli at an angle so they can see the side of Keli's face. When they aren't watching her, the journalists sit with their heads bent, pens jerking across pages, noting as quickly as possible everything each witness says.

Senior Constable Epstein enters the witness stand. The counsel assisting the coroner stands and reads out her statement from the bar table. The barrister for Keli Lane sits on the right hand side.

'You say in paragraph six that you looked for records for a body or bones which could be those of Tegan Lane either as an infant or a child,' asks Keli's barrister.

'Yes,' replies Senior Constable Epstein.

'So when you say a child, what age group were you specific-ally looking for?'

'I suppose any age from 1996 to when I searched, so I suppose that's up to an age range of about ten.'

'Were there any children's remains that weren't allocated to a known death?' the barrister continues.

'There were a couple of children, but they were believed to be other persons.'

The barrister pauses before going on. 'How old were those children?'

'There was a boy aged approximately two and there's an unknown Asian female baby,' Epstein answers bluntly.

Even though the barrister knows the results of the search it's still startling to hear it out loud. He's spent many months trying to throw doubt over claims that Tegan is dead. It's easier to do when such an act is seen as unthinkable. His job has just been made harder by the acknowledgement of the deaths of the other babies in such a matter-of-fact manner by this dutiful police officer.

'That unknown Asian female baby is not identified?' he asks.

'Yes, still not identified. It was dumped at a hospital,' Epstein replies.

The barrister asks one or two more questions, pressing home the fact that since this dead baby is not Tegan, there is still some chance that she is alive.

Coroner Abernethy listens, his face cast downwards. Then he questions Epstein about the meticulous care taken each day with the state-wide body counts. 'In fact, Senior Constable Epstein, your daily primary task is to receive every day of the week the fresh documentation representing the fresh dead in the catchment area of the Glebe?'

'That's correct.'

'And a similar process occurs here at Westmead covering the western suburbs of Sydney, where there are police like you whose job is to receive the fresh documentation at the time the bodies are booked into morgues?'

'That's correct.'

'And elsewhere around the state are there similar processes?' asks the barrister, feeling the need to take control of the questioning.

'Elsewhere around the state, deaths are similarly reported to coroners and booked into morgues, but there aren't usually specialist police to handle the processing of them. They're generally done at the police stations,' Epstein answers.

Despite this enormous daily effort, no clues as to where Tegan might be found have surfaced. Abernethy looks glumly at his list of remaining witnesses. He has already heard from so many, but none have been able to help him find Tegan. Keli will be the last witness to take the stand, but Abernethy holds very little hope of her saying anything that will help solve this case.

The coroner looks up and surveys his courtroom. The majority of journalists present are young women in their twenties and early thirties, the same age as Keli's friends and acquaintances who have given evidence in this court, confused and clueless as it was. Keli's friends' attitudes ranged from bewildered to defensive on the witness stand. Some have known her since she was at primary school, others had partied with her on the weekends over the years and many had played competitive water polo with her. All of them came across as credible witnesses who were at a loss to explain what had happened.

The journalists are sent by their bosses to cover many of the days of the hearing. Together they have listened to witness after witness speak about their part in Keli's extraordinary double life. The effect has been surreal. Keli's friends, the witnesses who took the stand, and those who reported what they said seem strikingly similar. They all wear plain, modest, well-made clothing. Everyone has natural looking hair; there are no outlandish colours or cuts. Women with long hair have it drawn back into simple ponytails. Both witnesses and journalists probably date or have married other professionals working their way up in the world. They have the same kind of ambitions and drink at the same sort of bars, even if Keli's friends drink in Manly while the journalists drink on the other side of the harbour. It's very possible the two groups have friends in common.

Despite the confusion demonstrated in the stand about Keli's other life there is one opinion shared by all the witnesses. Without exception they hold the Lanes in high esteem and describe Keli as a good and faithful friend. Even though she had obviously lied a number of times in very serious circumstances, nothing could convince them that she had done anything to harm Tegan. The disturbing nature of this case hasn't caused them to doubt the decency of her or her family.

It's fair to say this loyalty has made things difficult for police and the coroner in their search for the missing child – it seems none of Keli's family or friends have demanded she tell them what happened to Tegan. The Lanes have been given a terrible time by the media, but the public show of support by Keli's friends has been helping them through the siege. Keli's friends seem like a moat outside the wall of silence the Lanes have erected around their daughter.

Abernethy looks at the short, spiky-haired counsel assisting him as she quietly sorts through papers in her manila folders. Behind the scribbling journalists sit a handful of pensioners, court enthusiasts with time on their hands, watching the drama unfold with their own eyes before watching it again on TV. Abernethy knows the TV crews that he despises are waiting outside. Like the court reporters, they've been there for many days of the hearing, staked out near the double glass doors that open to the short concrete path to the car park, ready to pounce on Keli and her father as they walk to their car once the day's hearing ends. The Chief Coroner shakes his head. This has been one of the most frustrating cases he's ever heard. A baby is probably dead, the mother is sitting right in front of him and there is nothing more he can do to shake the full story out of her.

Keli's account of what happened the day Tegan disappeared, despite being wildly improbable, cleared her of any criminal wrongdoing – at least for the next five years. But in late 2009 Keli would be charged with the murder of her missing baby. She would never stop claiming Tegan was still alive. Her family never spoke about the subject, but they had Keli's lawyers publicly confirm their ongoing support for Keli and her story as they prepared for Keli's trial for the alleged murder of Tegan in mid 2010. But in the coronial inquest at Westmead between 2004 and 2006, there was simply nothing – and no one – to prove Keli's unconvincing story wrong.

In fact, nothing will ever shake Keli, not even the trial for Tegan's murder five years later. Keli had given birth among strangers, determined her three secret babies wouldn't leave any trace on her life. If it hadn't been for the sharp eyes of a child welfare officer who pulled the scant records of each anonymous birth together three years after Tegan's birth and disappearance, this picture of Keli's secret side would never have emerged. It's taken over four years for a rough sketch to make its way to the Coroner's Court, and it will take another five years and thousands of hours of police time until the full picture of Keli's secret side is revealed in the Supreme Court of New South Wales.

Right now in the Westmead Coroner's Court, Keli's family and many close friends are standing steadfastly besides her, blindly loyal despite the shock of her secret babies. But Keli's stubborn silence as to what really happened to Tegan will mean that, in the years to come, she will repay their loyalty with chaos and heartbreak beyond their wildest imagination.

2

GOING FOR GOLD

To understand where Keli Lane comes from you have to catch the ferry to Manly.

Thousands of people from all over Sydney, the rest of Australia and overseas make the trip from Circular Quay, Sydney's main ferry hub, to the seaside suburb when the weather is fine. Every half-hour a new stream of visitors dressed in thongs and shorts pour into the large, two-storeyed ferries. Many make a beeline for the seats on the open top deck.

Within minutes of pulling out of Circular Quay, passengers have the best possible view of the Sydney Harbour Bridge, its full length stretching before them. They see what the world sees when the New Year's Eve fireworks are broadcast on television. Awestruck visitors are then treated to an equally perfect view of the Sydney Opera House on the other side. As the ferry makes its way east along the harbour, both landmarks slide into view side by side. Tourists click their cameras furiously to catch the picture perfect profile, which slowly diminishes in size as the ferry carries its passengers over the blue water.

The profile of the entire Sydney CBD skyline then comes into easy view. Apartment towers, mansions and trees crowd the surrounding landscape as the ferry moves towards the heads where the harbour meets the open ocean. Sailboats and motorboats race along as the breeze blows strands of hair around the passengers' heads. The cliffs of North and South Head and the rougher waters of the ocean mark the point at which the ferry turns north towards Manly. The city and its haze of pollution disappear from view behind a hill covered with trees.

There is a holiday feel at the Manly Ferry terminal. Passengers leaving the ferry pass crowds of sunburnt and sea salt covered day-trippers waiting to travel back to Circular Quay. Those who have just arrived walk through the terminal, past the doughnut and ice-cream stands and spill out onto the paved area outside. Immediately ahead, across the road, is the Corso, Manly's main strip of shops, which leads directly to the suburb's massive beach.

If any of the thousands of daily visitors decided to turn left and walk up the street rather than cross to the Corso, they would soon walk past a brown brick police station. If they kept walking a few more metres and then crossed the intersection with Sydney Road they would reach Manly Oval, home of the Blue Marlins rugby team. On every second Saturday between March and September the oval hosts a first-grade club rugby match. Some players are tall and strapping, others are short and nuggety. Big front-rowers wrap white and black tape around their heads so their ears aren't ripped and scarred so much in the scrum. Men on the sidelines stand with their fists shoved into their pockets, yelling encouragement and abuse.

In the stands and on the sidelines there are usually several good-looking girls, aloof with their long hair and big black sunglasses. These are the players' girlfriends, or at least girls who want to be. They rarely yell out, preferring to clap to show their support. They spend a lot of time talking among themselves and ignoring everyone else, including those on the field. Landing a top rugby player as a boyfriend is a serious business. Beneath the make-up and clothes beat the hearts of keen political animals. While it may not look like it to the untrained eye, the softly spoken competition in the stands is just as fierce as the physical contest on the field.

This is part of Manly's sunny, prosperous local stronghold and the residents like it that way. Here, sport and surf life-saving clubs reign supreme. Trips on the ferry or over the Sydney Harbour Bridge to the Sydney CBD are unwelcome interruptions – Manly likes to keep a little bit of distance with the rest of Sydney. Over the years Manly and many of the seaside suburbs nearby and further north have morphed from working class to upper middle class. But the fundamentals of the Northern Beaches, known by all as the 'Insular Peninsula', remain the same. Change may take place all over the rest of Sydney but, here, residents don't want anything to disturb their piece of paradise.

Unless you were born and bred here, locals will consider you as just another one of the passing parade grabbing some time in the sun. It's said, only half jokingly, that to be accepted as a local in Manly you have to have been wheeled down the Corso to your first Manly football match in a pram. By this test, Keli Lane is a Manly local through and through. She was certainly in a pram when she was taken to her first Manly football match. What's more, her dad was coaching the team.

Robert Lane moved his wife Sandra, their four-year-old daughter Keli and toddler son from Wheeler Heights to a house on the border of Manly and Fairlight in June 1979. The Lanes wanted to be closer to the Manly Rugby Union Football Club where Rob had been made the first-grade coach three years earlier, and to the Manly Police Station, where Rob, who was a police officer, hoped to be transferred to. It was also handy to be closer to Manly Hospital, where Sandra, or Sandy as everyone called her, worked in administration.

These days, buying an average house in Manly or Fairlight costs well over a million dollars, making both suburbs among the most expensive in the Northern Beaches and Sydney in general. Rob has never been a wealthy man, but back when he moved into the area, Manly and its surrounds were far more working class. Rob bought his new home from a mechanic for $68,000, a price he could afford on his wages as a young constable. He already had strong ties to the beachside suburb. Less than a decade earlier he'd been a first-grade player with Manly himself, giving his all for a chance at the big time. In the 1960s he made the selection squad for the national team, the Wallabies. However, that was as close as he got, and he was never chosen to pull on the gold jersey.

By the mid 1970s, when Keli was born, Rob was at a crossroads. Realising that he wasn't going to get to the very top of union, he tried his hand at rugby league. Of course, league was every bit as competitive and Rob was again destined to be one of countless talented sportspeople to not quite make it to the professional ranks. Knowing when to call it quits is never easy, no matter how much an elite sportsperson has achieved, but Rob had entered his mid twenties and had a young family so it was time to think about the long-term. Boyhood dreams have to end sometime, even when they're agonisingly close to coming true.

However, Rob was determined to stay a part of the rugby world. The Blues rugby club, along with the Manly Surf Lifesaving Club and the Steyne Hotel, were the key meeting places for the area's leading businessmen, social and political figures in the 1970s, as they still are now. At that time Manly was run by a group of men known as the Bower Street Boys. These businessmen and politicians had strong links to the Manly Rugby Union Club. One of their number, Ian MacDonald, a key organiser for the Liberal Party, was the deputy president. Another Bower Street Boy, Brian Cox, himself an ex-Wallaby, was the father of two first-grade players. These Manly big shots never strayed too far from the prestigious glow of the club, which boasted many players who represented Australia. This heady mix of elite sport and local heavy hitters meant many ordinary club members centred their social lives around club barbecues and award nights. After all, it was the place to be seen.

Would the Lane's entrée into this exciting world be over now Rob was no longer a first-grade player? Rob wanted to somehow still be a part of it all. And just as the writing was on the wall about his playing career, along came his chance. In 1976, local legend and former Australian representative Anthony 'Tony' Miller had been the first-grade coach for Manly for several years. However, Miller had fallen out with senior club management and in early December he was unceremoniously dumped from the management committee along with four other club officials. Club president Peter Bradstreet was happy for Rob Lane to step up from coaching the minor grades to coaching the top team. Rob stood unopposed to replace Miller and was duly voted in.

Lane quickly set about repaying Bradstreet for backing him. In his first season as coach, Rob took the Blues the closest they had come to winning the prestigious Shute Shield for many years. With Rob as coach from 1977 to 1979, and again in 1981 and 1982 (Rob was dumped in 1980, but regained his position again the following year) the team made the semi-finals every season, reaching the finals twice and the grand final once.

These were heyday years for the club, and the role Rob 'Moose' Lane played in that success meant the right sort of people knew who he was. The Lanes weren't wealthy, but because of Rob's success they were right in the centre of Manly's social whirl. Their house was the place to party in the late 1970s and early 1980s, especially after a home game. Sandy established herself as a social queen bee, deciding who was invited to party with Manly's rugby elite and who was left out in the cold. The wives and girlfriends of players knew that they had to have Sandy's approval if they wanted to be accepted into the club's inner circle, and Sandy relished her power.

However, despite Rob's achievements, the club was hungry for more. It wanted the New South Wales championship, the Shute Shield, something the Blues hadn't won since 1950. While Rob was clearly one of the club's most successful coaches ever, the near misses were becoming too much to bear. No longer content with runners-up trophies, club president Bradstreet and the rest of senior management decided it was time for drastic action.

In 1983 Robert Lane was dumped as coach and replaced by someone who wasn't a local. Incredibly, the man who was to relegate Rob Lane to the sidelines, Alan Jones, wasn't only an outsider, he had never been a first-grade rugby player.

At the time of his recruitment as the new Manly coach, Jones was two years shy of beginning his career as a radio broadcaster, an occupation that continues to make him one of the most powerful people in Sydney to this day. Jones had come a very long way through the sheer power of his personality and a remarkable ability to make friends with powerful people.

Rob's ego was certainly in for a battering. Jones promptly managed to deliver to the club its heart's desire – the Shute Shield. President Bradstreet was euphoric. 'There are two types of people in this world – those who play for the Manly Rugby Union Club and those who wish they play for the Manly Rugby Union Club,' Bradstreet boasted over the microphone at an end of season function. The celebrations continued, with the mayor of Manly organising a street parade and a ball held in honour of the players at the Manly Pacific Hotel.

Jones's victory for Manly had opened the way for him to become the coach of the national team, the Wallabies. As quickly as he came, Alan Jones left. Despite the speed of his departure, even the most one-eyed Manly diehard couldn't honestly blame Jones for making the jump.

The next two years were a dramatic fall from grace for the Blues, who failed to make the semis for two seasons in a row, and Rob Lane's years in the wilderness continued. But with typical unwavering determination, he refused to give up trying to get back into the action. The Blues trained on Tuesday and Thursday nights, after which the players would come inside the clubhouse for a beer. Propping up the bar most nights would be Rob Lane, talking to the fathers of first-grade players. While Rob liked a drink, he wasn't there to get drunk – he was there to talk about club business, putting in the hours with others in the know, week in and week out.

His efforts to stay in the loop over those years paid off. In early December in 1986 the club decided to re-appoint Rob to his beloved first-grade coaching position. One of Manly's most successful coaches was back in the saddle. Anticipation about what Rob Lane could do with the talent-rich Blues was regularly discussed in the pages of the local newspaper, the *Manly Daily*.

The 1987 season began well for the team, with wins against major rivals making them early leaders in the competition. Rob, who had a reputation as being stern, gruff and slow to hand out praise, was reported as 'purposely not going overboard on his side's good start to the season'. But by June, even Rob couldn't hide his enthusiasm. Having beaten Sydney University in the previous match, the Blues followed with a win against arch-rivals Randwick. 'It was a great performance for our boys to grab the points,' an uncharacteristically delighted Rob was quoted as saying.

However, the wheels fell off. The Blues stopped winning and by the end of August it was crunch time. The Blues couldn't afford to lose any more matches if they were to reach the semi-finals. In the week leading up to the match Rob dropped the first-grade captain, a highly risky move in terms of team morale. It didn't work. Manly lost and Rob was under no illusions about what management did to coaches who didn't perform. He decided to jump rather than be pushed. Rob explained to the *Manly Daily* he had recently been promoted at Manly Police, where by now he had been working for a couple of years, and his kids were on the cusp of becoming teenagers, so he was considering his future as coach. In the first week of December Rob withdrew his nomination for the position of first-grade coach, removing the need for any public showdown with club management.

Rob's strategy of falling on his sword was the right one. His ability to acknowledge political realities, even at a time of huge personal stress and disappointment, allowed him to bow out on top. 'Over the years Rob has excelled himself as a player, administrator and coach and he is highly regarded at Manly and throughout the world of rugby,' club president Bradstreet was quoted as saying in the *Manly Daily*.

Rob Lane, the local copper, had secured his status as a senior statesman in the club. For years to come he would be an influential sounding board for other coaches, selectors and heavy hitters, making and breaking the careers of players. More importantly, the elite social connections his position with the club had afforded him and his family remained firmly intact. Rob was local royalty.

Meanwhile, his daughter Keli was growing up.

Keli Lane had shown great sporting ability since she was very little. The whole family were members of the Manly Surf Lifesaving Club, and Rob had Keli doing beach sprints almost as soon as she could walk. She grew up being the apple of her father's eye and in return she was Daddy's girl. He regularly took her to footy training sessions when he was coaching. Being around her dad and the players bought out the tomboy in six-year-old Keli. Her frequent outbursts of locker room swearing shocked some but made others laugh. She was precocious and assertive, happily playing roughly with little boys as well as having lots of girls as friends.

By the time she was a teenager Keli was on the road to becoming an elite athlete. The sport she excelled at was water polo. She played for her school team, MacKellar Girls High, in the state-wide public schools competition along with a girl named Melinda Black whom Keli had known since primary school and fellow budding water polo star and school friend,

Lisa Berry. Keli also played with another school friend, Kati Holt. Kati wasn't keen to play beyond high school, but she was one of Keli's closest friends. Keli, Melinda and Lisa also played in the combined New South Wales's high schools Under 15s competition and in 1990 they all travelled to the Sunshine Coast to play against the Queensland Under 15s team.

Also playing for the New South Wales Under 15s was a girl named Taryn Woods. Back when he was young, Rob Lane had tried his hand at water polo and played a few games against Taryn's dad, David Woods. And while Rob's first-grade football-playing career faltered, David went on to represent Australia in water polo in the 1972 and 1976 Olympics. Now, some fifteen years later, the two families were again united through sport. Taryn played for her dad's old water polo club, Balmain. Not long after the Under 15s tournament in Queensland, Keli, Melinda and Lisa joined the Balmain Water Polo Club with David as their coach. Together the girls would go on to play in the Under 16s competition and for the Australian Schoolgirls team, touring Canberra, Albury and Melbourne in 1992.

The Balmain Tigers' saltwater pool headquarters, the Dawn Fraser Baths, is a ferry ride away from Manly, a couple of stops west of Circular Quay, past the Opera House and the Sydney Harbour Bridge. Players warm up by swimming laps of the tidal harbour pool. Then, barely stopping to rest, they practise their passes and throwing, treading water while holding balls high above their heads. They face each other in pairs to push on each other's shoulders or place their hands on each other's heads to dunk one another, all the while in water too deep to stand in. No one except the supremely fit can complete one of these demanding training sessions, which last for an hour and a half. Elite players, even those as young as fifteen, spend at least ten hours a week in the pool, often training twice a day. On top of that they do a couple of weights sessions each week and other cardio training.

Top water polo players are almost without exception tall and well built, and both the men and the women players have broad shoulders, strong legs and plenty of stamina. Women players are typically at least 170 centimetres tall and weigh between 70 and 80 kilograms once they hit their late teens and early twenties. While some players are slender, most have classically powerful builds. It's not a sport for waifs. Besides demanding very high fitness levels, players have to be physically aggressive. After all, water polo is a contact sport. During games players block each other, grab onto limbs and try to push each other down like footballers on a field. Illegal under water dirty tricks and fights can make the game rough if not properly controlled. Keli had always been suited to the game – she could swim, tread water, block opponents and pass the ball with the best of them. As a schoolgirl and throughout her playing days her favourite position was driver, one who swims quickly to take a pass or to get to the ball in the water and to drive in towards the goal and shoot. She also showed her toughness as a defender.

As far as school went, Keli was an average student who aimed to become a physical education teacher. Partying and sport were far more important to her than books, and both made her very popular. She quickly got a reputation for being able to drink as much as the boys. She always had plenty of team-mates to hang out with and her family's very extensive network of friends meant she grew up with lots of kids around Manly, seeing them every weekend on the beach, at the pool, at barbecues and at footy games. Her boyfriend Aaron, whom she started seeing when she was about fifteen, wasn't just some guy. He was an elite kayaker she had met at the Manly Surf Lifesaving Club who wanted to compete in the Olympics and who had come up to Sydney from Victoria to train. Besides training, Aaron – who was the same age as Keli – was doing his trade apprenticeship.

Neither Aaron nor Keli was ever going to be a doctor or a lawyer, but their status as young sports stars meant they went to all the right parties and plenty of kids wanted to be friends with them. Keli had grown up accustomed to being able to throw her weight around, just like her parents. She was good fun to be with if you were in her clique but disdainful towards those who weren't. Accustomed to getting her way, Keli was often haughty and had a bit of a temper, but because of who she was – Rob 'Moose' Lane's daughter – kids learnt to just put up with it. They had to if they wanted to be part of the sporty crowd.

As golden as life looked for Keli, not everything went to plan. Near the end of 1992, the year she toured with the Australian Schoolgirls team, seventeen-year-old Keli discovered she was pregnant, despite being on the pill. Like countless other teenagers before her, Keli learnt the truth after using a home pregnancy test she had bought nervously at the chemist. She told only Aaron, and for four days the two young lovers talked about what they should do, before making the decision that hundreds of thousands of teenagers make: Keli was going to have an abortion.

The clinic was in the city. Aaron offered to take her there but Keli decided she wanted to go alone. Aaron dropped her off at Manly Wharf instead, watching her join the huge crowd boarding the ferry. He was waiting for her when she came back later that day, watching her walk past the souvenir shops and doughnut stands. He walked up to her, hugged her and she burst into tears. He led her somewhere quiet, where they sat together until she could face going home.

Over the next year things started to unravel between Keli and Aaron. One day when he was on beach patrol a suspected drowning of a six-year-old boy was radioed in. Aaron and some other surf lifesavers went out and found the boy, dead, on some rocks frequented by fishermen. Aaron had to wait with the tiny corpse until the rescue helicopter arrived. He was deeply disturbed by the experience and he felt the surf club didn't do enough to help him cope with that awful day. Soon he found himself spending less and less time on the beach. Keli felt for him, but the surf club was a big part of her and her family's life, so as Aaron drifted out of the scene they went their separate ways.

Meanwhile, Keli's water polo ambitions were as strong as ever. In March 1993, Keli, along with fellow Balmain team-mates Taryn and Melinda, played for New South Wales in the national Under 20s championships. Other members of this team were Lisa Berry, who had by now moved to the Sydney University club, her older sister Suzanne, and a girl named Bronwyn Mayer, another girl who played for Balmain who also happened to be Taryn's cousin. New South Wales won the championship, and several of these girls, including Keli, were among the twenty-two players selected from the whole competition to train in an Australian junior women's development squad.

However, despite Keli's success in being picked for this squad, several of her contemporaries were already starting to pull ahead in the race to the top. Joining her older sister Suzanne at Sydney Uni, Lisa Berry was now a part of the team to beat in the state as it boasted the greatest number of players already selected to play for the Australian senior team.

Also that year, Taryn was selected to play for the New South Wales senior team while Keli was not. Like Lisa, Taryn could have joined Sydney University if she'd wanted to, but given her family history with Balmain, the club her brothers also played for, she was happy to stay and be coached by her dad. While Keli was considered a solid contender for senior teams in the years to come, Taryn and Lisa's sporting careers would leap ahead.

Men's water polo had long been an Olympic sport at the time, but women's wasn't. For decades the Australian water polo community had been thinking of ways to lobby the International Olympic Committee to include women's water polo, and it was a long held ambition to succeed in time for the 2000 Olympics. In September 1993, when it was announced that Sydney would host the 2000 Games, Keli was among those burning with ambition to be there representing Australia. But in the meantime, there were many more years of punishing training and competition to come.

At the beginning of the 1994 rugby season Keli had just turned nineteen. As always, she was spending a lot of her spare time at the Manly rugby club, and this year she noticed a guy who had recently joined and played fourth grade. Duncan Gillies was a country boy who grew up in Yass, a doctor's son. He also came from a sporting family, with two of his three brothers playing professional rugby league. He was tall, strong and lean with dark brown hair. Keli was impressed. The guy she had dated for a few months since breaking up with Aaron played in Duncan's team, but things between them were winding down. Not long after Duncan joined the club it became clear he was destined to quickly jump into the top grade, and Keli liked guys who aimed for the top of their sport. The night before his debut game with Manly's first-grade side

Duncan and Keli had their first date. Duncan had spoken to Keli's old boyfriend about whether he minded – after all, he was a team-mate, and it doesn't do to date someone else's ex-girlfriend without asking first – and there were no problems there: the other bloke said he was on the way to getting back together with his long-term girlfriend anyway.

Keli's driving ambition and love of a good party were attractive to Duncan. They were both young, fit and out for everything life could give them. They began a sexual relationship very soon after that game, falling into bed almost every day. The parents of nineteen-year-old women don't exactly celebrate their daughters having sex, but they usually choose not to know or calmly accept the reality. Keli's mother had been allowing Aaron to sleep over with Keli in her room, especially when Rob was overseas coaching. Rob hit the roof about it when he first found out, but got used to the idea of his little girl not being so little anymore. For most parents facing this dilemma, it certainly helps if the boyfriend is someone they like, and Duncan was the sort of young man with whom the Lanes wanted Keli to have a future.

However, although Keli was attractive, she didn't fit the mould of pretty footy trophy girlfriend, and holding onto a first-grade footballer wasn't going to be easy for her. What Keli did have, however, was Rob Lane as her father. Given his influence, it wouldn't hurt the career of an ambitious footballer to date his daughter. All of the Manly players knew who Keli's father was. She never had to spell it out. Duncan started to spend a lot of time with the Lane family, staying over at their house a couple of nights a week. After Thursday night training Duncan would often eat at the club, have a few beers and then sleep over at the Lane's house. He would often do the same on a Saturday, especially after the fortnightly home games played at Manly Oval. Otherwise Duncan was living with a mate in and around Manly, moving from one rental property to another every few months. Keli would spend a couple of nights a week at his place, too.

Soon, more changes in Keli's bedroom were about to take place. About three months after Duncan and Keli started dating, Keli began sharing her room at home with one of her water polo team-mates. Stacy Gaylard was a Queensland player whom Keli had met during the Under 15s junior tournament on the Sunshine Coast four years earlier. They'd kept in touch and, two years later, over the summer of '92 –'93, Stacy stayed with the Lanes for a fortnight. By mid 1994 Stacy decided to move down to Sydney to further her water polo career by playing for Balmain and the Lanes invited her to live with them. This was all part of Rob and Sandy's ongoing support of Keli's sporting ambitions.

In January, a couple of months before she met Duncan, Keli, Taryn and some of the others played for New South Wales in the Under 21s national championships. Sandy Lane was team manager, travelling with Keli and her team to Brisbane for the tournament and staying on when Keli was chosen to play for the Australian junior side against New Zealand afterwards. Keli's team-mates noticed that Keli and her mother didn't seem to have a particularly warm relationship, a view shared by Keli's Manly friends. But nonetheless Sandy was there, doing her bit for her daughter and the team and Keli needed the support of her parents as the task of making it to the top of water polo wasn't getting any easier. In 1994 Taryn and her cousin Bronwyn were selected for the Australian women's senior team but Keli wasn't. However, the disappointment just made her more determined to make the leap up from the junior teams and join them.

Keli and Duncan's relationship grew amid a hectic schedule of training, matches and work, with Keli working part-time at a surf shop and Duncan and his brother Simon running a tree-lopping and lawnmowing business. Keli had also begun an arts degree with the University of Newcastle, but after a few semesters she dropped out. Keli and Duncan spent a lot of time with their large circle of friends, many of whom were rugby and water polo players, surf lifesavers and schoolmates at pubs, parties and the Manly surf club.

These were golden days for the Lanes. Sandy, who doted on Keli's younger brother, still enjoyed her status as a social queen bee, Keli was dreaming of sporting glory, and by this time Rob was Sergeant at Manly Police and in charge of the foot patrol. As his was a desk job, it was Rob's habit to take a walk down the Corso at lunchtime to stretch his legs. It was only a twenty minute walk, but not for Sergeant Lane. Shopkeepers and shoppers alike constantly stopped him for a chat, making his lunchtime walk an hour-long round trip. He knew everyone and everyone knew him.

However, there was a secret in the Lane household, a secret that would cast a huge shadow over the Lanes in years to come. Nineteen-year-old Keli was pregnant again.

3

THE IN-CROWD

As Keli's secret child grows inside of her, Keli's life appears to go on as normal. It's a Saturday night at the height of summer and she is out with her friends at the Steyne Hotel in Manly. Keli stands with a drink in her hand. Around her are her friends, talking to each other between sips and the occasional cigarette.

Kati and Melinda are there. So are Alison Cratchley and Natalie McCauley, Manly girls who have known Keli since they were little. Some of the others are footballers' girlfriends, like Charmaine, who met Keli through Melinda. She has been dating John, one of Duncan's team-mates, for about as long as Keli and Duncan have been dating. The only girl in the group who isn't a Manly local is Stacy, the water polo player from Queensland who is staying with the Lanes. The girls are all dressed in jeans, strappy sandals and cotton tops, gently perspiring in the heat. On any given weekend these girls and their boyfriends might choose to drink at the skiff club, with its views of the sailing boats moored in the harbour. They also might end up at the rugby club or the surf club. It doesn't really matter where they go. The action is wherever they are.

The boys, mostly surf lifesavers and rugby players, stand in their own group near the bar. Among them is Duncan, out for a big one after his game today with John and some other team-mates. Another bloke standing with them is Brandon Ward, who plays in the club's minor grades. Brandon is a very old friend of Keli's despite being eight years older. Rob Lane was best friends with Brandon's dad until he died several years earlier. Brandon's parents, especially his mum, were fixtures at Sandy Lane's parties in the late seventies and eighties, so Brandon and Keli grew up together despite the age gap. Melinda met Brandon through Keli and now they are dating.

Keli shoots glances at Duncan, but he doesn't notice. He's concentrating on what his mates are saying, laughing and shouting comments when he can get a word in. None of the girls bother to approach the boys to get their attention. They know they'll wander over when they want to. Then the tables will turn and it'll be up to the girls to decide whether they feel like laughing with them, ignoring them or even giving them a hard time. Right now the night is young, so Keli and the other girls buy rounds for each other and get drunk.

'Oh, thanks,' says Keli as someone hands her a drink. 'To be honest I already feel a little tipsy from the two I've had already. Our match today really tired me out.'

It's hot, but Keli doesn't have to worry about her make-up slipping since she doesn't use much. With her fresh face and blonde hair she is pretty enough, but she hasn't been looking her best lately. She has put on weight, making her jeans look a little tight, and her top isn't completely covering up the bulge around her waist.

Around the pub young women with long hair, tight clothes and bags slung over their bare shoulders are being ogled by men both young and old. A girl saunters by in heels and low-slung jeans, showing a glimpse of her G-string.

Keli smirks at Alison. 'I wonder who she's going home with tonight?'

'Take your pick!' snorts someone in their group, and they all snigger.

Keli and her friends wouldn't be caught dead dressed like that. After all, they don't have to put it all on display to be close to the most sought after men in Manly. No self respecting girlfriend shows too much flesh on a night out, even if she has the body for it. Trying too hard to look sexy is a dead giveaway that you aren't taken seriously by your man. Besides, tight clothes have never been an option for Keli. Her ten or more hours of intense physical training a week would make most girls lean like a greyhound, but Keli simply isn't built like that.

The passing girl is certainly getting some attention, even though she pretends not to notice. A guy with skinny arms and a pot belly curls his hands around his eyes like binoculars and follows her trail with an exaggerated lunge. The girl bristles slightly, rolling her eyes at her friends. Keli's group are not pleased to notice they are standing close to their men. The boys have noticed this girl and her clique, and while they won't be obvious about it, it's not as if the footy players and the surf lifesavers are above that sort of thing. They can be the most boorish drunks in the room when the mood takes them. Sometimes one of them will stand behind a girl and leer over her head to his friends, who are laughing at her discomfort. If she is standing with her back to them a couple of the boys might stare openly at her, discussing her body as if they are judging livestock at a country fair.

Duncan's mates can get away with more than most men. They are by far the best looking guys in the place. Tall, muscular and tanned, they stand out among the younger guys and those whose office jobs have put them on the road to seed. But as the top dogs in that pub it wouldn't do to look as though they are following the lead of some low level runt, so for now the presence of these girls stirs no comment. Duncan gently pushes past the hot young thing and she smiles at him. Girls with come-hither smiles come and go from the arms of sportsmen every week and footballers' girlfriends hate the attention their men get – but it comes with the territory. Even Charmaine, a slender ballet dancer who looks and acts exactly like a trophy girlfriend should, has to keep a jealous eye out for rivals. It's not easy being part of the in-crowd.

Besides dressing like a proper girlfriend, Keli's confident exterior is enhanced by serious sporting credibility. Being Rob Lane's daughter means lots of people approach her to say hello when she is out for a drink. Some want to stop and chat about footy, just like the old guy approaching her right now.

'You're Rob Lane's daughter, aren't you?' he says by way of introduction, holding a half-finished beer.

'Yes, that's right. I'm Keli.'

Keli's friends turn and talk among themselves as this man delivers his views on the Blue's back row. Keli stands and nods, polite as always, waiting to get back to her friends. It's hard to stop some blokes once they get started, but fortunately this one is quite brief.

'Well, pass on my regards to your father,' the man says after his one-sided conversation.

'Will do.'

Keli finishes her drink, looking around the pub over the top of her glass. Her hair is dry and brittle from the endless hours in the water, although playing in the salt water at Balmain is better than playing in chlorinated water as far as hair-care issues go. Melinda and Kati look at their watches. It's getting close to midnight. The boys are still keeping their distance, horsing around and trading jokey insults. Stacy is perched on a nearby bar stool. She's laughing, happy to be part of it all.

The noise gets louder as drinkers from other parts of the Northern Beaches make their way to the Corso. Many of them head for the pub next door, which is hosting the finals of a swimsuit contest for a lads magazine. Local beauty queens are strutting around in next to nothing under hot lights and on sticky, beer soaked carpet. It's hardly glamorous, but there are plenty of contestants.

It always gets rowdy on the Corso. Several months earlier, when Keli had just started seeing the bloke before Duncan, there was an ugly incident. It was a Saturday night and, as usual, everyone was pretty drunk. Keli and her boyfriend were standing on the Corso kissing when Aaron stumbled nearby. He had been drinking heavily when he saw Keli.

'You're a slut, Keli!' he yelled at the top of his lungs. 'You're a fucking slut!'

Some plain-clothed policemen nearby quickly walked up to Aaron, telling him to cool it. He started to mouth off at them, too, so within a few seconds his hands were cuffed behind his back and he was taken to the station. Before too long Aaron drifted right out of the Manly scene altogether. It wasn't as if the policemen hauled off Aaron as a favour to Rob Lane's daughter, although there were plenty of times they would help Keli and her mates out of a scrape. Usually they would find one of her crowd drunk somewhere, phone their parents and ask them to come and pick them up from the station. Manly has a drinking culture. It wasn't unusual for young constables to be sent to the Steyne Hotel to drag out roaring drunk senior coppers and help them get home.

The story of how Keli's old boyfriend from the surf club got drunk and yelled abuse at her had made the rounds, but it was only one of the thousands of bits of gossip that flew around Manly every week. Alison wonders what the boys are saying tonight. Recently she'd heard of one particularly nasty story doing the rounds. It was about Keli. Alison watches Keli from the corner of her eye, noticing that she does look thicker than usual around her middle, just like the surf lifesaving guys had said the other weekend at the skiff club. Keli has never been a thin girl, though, certainly not by Manly beach standards. That she is fit and strong is without question, and she certainly isn't ugly; quite the opposite, in fact. But those boys don't care. Nothing but physical perfection is good enough in their eyes. Any girl who puts on weight is fair game for abuse.

Alison can't remember exactly who told her, but some of the boys have started a rumour that Keli is pregnant. It makes Alison so mad. She knows what it's like to be on the receiving end. Exactly the same thing was said about her a little while ago when she put on a couple of kilos. No one ever came forward to ask Alison if she was pregnant; she just found out one day that this was what people were saying. It wasn't true, of course, and she doubted any of the boys who started or spread that rumour seriously believed it. They just wanted her to know that they weren't happy having a fat girl hanging around. Here's Keli, a champion in her own right, and all they can say about her are nasty lies. They are such bastards sometimes. Alison's younger sister plays water polo and looks up to Keli. A lot of the younger girls do. But that just doesn't matter to the boys.

Alison wonders whether Duncan has heard the rumour. Either way, she decides she isn't going to raise it with Keli and risk spoiling her night. Alison glances quickly from Keli's feet to her waist, then to her face. So she isn't thin, so what? Alison hates Manly's toxic ways sometimes.

'Do you want another drink?' Keli asks, noticing Alison's gaze.

'Yeah, all right.'

The crowd gets bigger and louder as the night wears on. Some of the boys stagger over to their girlfriends, while some make drunken passes at other girls nearby. Duncan moves over to where Keli leans over the bar. He stands next to her, talking into her ear as she tries to get the attention of the bar staff.

Keli makes it known that she isn't in for a really big night and is considering going home. Duncan considers whether to crash at Keli's place or to go home to the share house he's living in now. It's a sure bet that there won't be anything in the fridge for breakfast at his place. Stacy waits for Keli and Duncan to work out what they want to do. She's happy to stay out after playing her match today, but since she's living with Keli she'll have to fit into her plans.

'Come on, Keli, don't be a piker,' Stacy thinks to herself.

Keli and Duncan finish talking. He gives her a kiss on the cheek, turns around and walks off towards his mates. Keli approaches Stacy, Alison, Kati, Natalie and Melinda with two drinks in her hands. Charmaine has already gone home.

'Here, Alison. Sorry, I didn't get you guys anything.'

'No worries,' Stacy replies, looking around at the bar to decide if she will bother fetching one.

'Is Duncan staying at your place?' asks Kati as Keli hands Alison her drink.

'No, not tonight,' Keli says, hitching her bag on her shoulder.

Despite repeating how tired she is, Keli stays for another hour. Duncan comes back and stands with his arm around her shoulders. The boisterous crowd pushes this way and that. Beer is spilt, the laughter gets louder and people start to slur their words. At one o'clock in the morning Keli tells Stacy it's time to go home. They can walk home if they really want to – it only takes about 20 minutes from the Corso. However, sometimes the prospect of the uphill climb after a night out is too much.

'Let's catch a taxi,' Keli suggests once they're outside.

The ride home only takes a few minutes, so Keli and Stacy don't bother talking. Once inside the front door they creep to Keli's room, careful not to wake the rest of the family. Keli changes out of her clothes in the dark while Stacy goes to the bathroom. Keli's clothes are too tight for her and she won't be able to wear them if she gets any bigger. It doesn't take much for Keli to stack it on. The minute she stops exercising she gets heavier. Summer was normally her thinnest time of the year because it coincided with water polo season, but keeping slim has always been a struggle. And because of the secret growing inside of her, Keli's struggle is more than anyone can guess. The nasty rumours about her are true. Keli is nearly seven months' pregnant.

There is enough light coming through the window for Keli to keep changing in the dark without it seeming a little weird if Stacy walks in. Keli can slip between the covers in an instant if she needs to quickly cover herself. After a few minutes Stacy enters. Keli is already in her bed, seemingly asleep. Stacy changes in silence, looking at Keli curled up under the sheets.

The Lanes have really helped Stacy financially by inviting her to stay with them since she first moved to New South Wales. Also, Keli's father is such a big deal in Manly that hanging out with Keli gave Stacy immediate entry into the social elite. The women who dated footballers didn't try to push her out because of her links to the Lanes. Being near some of the players is a real experience. Duncan's big-time rugby league brothers occasionally came out with them. Stacy could feel the eyes of starstruck onlookers on nights like that. Full-grown men would practically swoon when these young guys were near.

But while Stacy enjoys the scene she's ready to move out of the Lane's home. Sleeping on the makeshift bed in Keli's room is comfortable enough, but she misses having her own space. And Keli is very sensitive about privacy. Stacy has no problem with that, but being someone's guest twenty-four hours a day is never relaxing, and she has been one for months. Recently Stacy found somewhere else to live and she broke the news to Keli that afternoon after the match. Keli was very neutral in her response, simply asking Stacy to let her know when she wanted to leave. Although she was a little surprised by Keli's response, Stacy didn't think Keli was hurt or being rude. It's Keli's way to be a little cold sometimes. She has heaps of friends, but she's naturally somewhat stand-offish. Quite of few of Keli's friends are a little sycophantic towards the Lanes, and Keli sometimes seems more accustomed to having people do as she says rather than having heart-to-heart chats.

As Stacy settles into bed, Keli lies in the dark, wide awake. The mask she so convincingly wore that night, the one that had Duncan, her friends and everyone else she knows believing she enjoyed herself at the pub, is gone. Instead, Keli is staring into the darkness, alone with her thoughts. Next to her Stacy falls asleep.

What was going through Keli's mind? Those around her don't know. Years later, when Keli is questioned by police and her actions are examined by a coroner, judge and jury, it's *never* really clear what she is thinking. That night at the pub, was she worried whether anyone felt her belly? Plenty of people pressed against her in the crush of the crowd. Did Keli wonder if any of them suspected anything?

The water polo match that day must have been a huge drain on her energy. Keli would have copped her share of the usual underwater kicking and shoving with only a swimming costume between her and those clawing hands and thrusting feet. She would have had to tread water and swim up and down the pool as if everything were normal. Only a week or so earlier she'd come back from touring with the New South Wales's junior women's team to Perth for the national championships and had taken to wrapping herself in a towel while walking around the pool deck to cover her growing belly. She'd also had to avoid a trip to the beach with the rest of the team while they were over there. But while she'd been able to cover herself up outside the pool, what about when she was in it? And what if something had happened during one of the games – if she'd gone into premature labour? Would she have been left alone in the water, surrounded by a huge cloud of blood and a crowd of horrified onlookers?

At least Keli had been able to get home that night. Duncan's home match was the perfect excuse to go out in Manly. Otherwise she would have found herself in a Balmain pub on the other side of the harbour trying keep up with her team-mates drink for drink. Those girls took pride in how hard they could party, and Keli was known for partying the hardest of them all. Drinking in Manly also meant Keli could sleep in her own bed rather than staying the night at Taryn's or Bronwyn's house, where she and other team-mates often crashed after a big night in Balmain. As Taryn's father was the coach of Keli's team it was very important to Keli's career that she and Taryn and Taryn's cousin, Bronwyn, remained close friends. Staying the night at either of their places was good for that bond, but Keli's belly had grown so much that if she wanted to keep her pregnancy secret it was better for her to stay in Manly.

Did Keli's thoughts turn to Duncan as she lay awake? He was so close to making it as a footballer – either union or league – just like his two brothers Simon and Ben, who both played for the Canterbury Bulldogs, a premier rugby league team. His brother Ben had made it as a professional at twenty-three. Simon, the superstar of the family, had made it when he was still a teenager. Was Keli worried that Duncan hadn't paid as much attention to her that night as he normally did? It was unusual for him not to stay over at her place after a home game, but then again she had left the pub earlier. Did Keli realise lots of people were gossiping about how heavy she looked? Being Rob Lane's daughter had its advantages, but no footy player was going to stay with a fat girlfriend forever.

Being Manly, everyone knows everyone's business and Keli's friends could count the number of lovers she'd had on one hand. Besides Aaron and the guy she'd dated briefly before taking up with Duncan there hadn't really been any others, except for maybe one sneaky one-night stand that only her very closest mates knew about. Everyone knew she was really serious about Duncan but they weren't at all certain if he felt the same way. The first flush of sexual excitement always fades and Keli and Duncan had been dating for several months. Would they become a solid couple that year or go their separate ways? And what would happen if their sporting careers really took off?

As Keli lay awake that night, though, she would have known one thing for certain: she was going to give birth to a baby, and soon. And that baby could change everything.

4

HAPPY BIRTHDAY, KELI

Ten years after that summer, at the coronial hearing at Westmead, Keli's old friend Alison is in the witness box.

'Manly can be a very toxic place,' she remarks. 'If you put on a little bit of weight, the next thing you're accused of being pregnant. That's something that's happened to me in the past, so I dismissed those rumours.'

Keli cries noiselessly while she listens to Alison give evidence. Behind her journalists take their rapid fire notes.

There were so many rumours about Keli over the years. Alison also once heard that Keli had gone up north with her mother to have a baby. Alison can't remember exactly when she'd heard it, so the police and the coroner can't determine whether that particular rumour was going around at the time Keli gave birth to her first child, her second — Tegan — or even her third.

'Could you have heard two different rumours at two different times?' asks Keli's barrister.

'Yeah, definitely.'

'But you really can't remember the details?'

'Honestly, I can't remember.'

'And you've obviously turned your mind to it, knowing what this case is about?'

'Absolutely. I mean, if I could help Keli I would.'

Keli's barrister is satisfied he has made it clear it wasn't unusual for nasty rumours about young women being pregnant to circulate in Manly. 'You obviously hold her in very high esteem,' he concludes.

'Yeah, definitely.'

Keli gives Alison a grateful smile. She, along with many others, is publicly stating in the witness box that, despite all that has happened, she is still Keli's friend.

However, no one is any wiser as to why Keli kept the pregnancies and births of her three children secret, including her first child in 1995. All that can be observed by anyone in the courtroom is that there are no smiles from Keli for Duncan when he recalls the time he told the then seven months' pregnant Keli he had been unfaithful.

It's near the end of summer in 1995 when Keli and Duncan stand in the backyard of her parents' house. Keli, uncomfortable in the hot sun, has tears running down her face.

'I'm just being honest with you,' says Duncan, his hands thrust deep in his pockets.

Keli swivels on her heels and turns her back to him. He remains still, watching her. Thankfully they are alone. Duncan waited until her family had stepped out before he broke the news, but Keli is clearly in no mood to notice this one small dignity. Her head is in her hands, absorbing what he has just said to her. He has betrayed her. No – worse – he has humiliated her. She presses the heels of her hands into her eye sockets. Duncan feels awkward, but the agony is hers. The words with which he began his confession still hang in the air:

'Look, something happened at Freshie.'

Duncan was talking about the Freshwater Surf Lifesaving Carnival. Keli knows it well. Every Australia Day long weekend, from early in the morning to late in the afternoon, Freshwater Beach, just north of Manly Beach, is overrun by lifesavers. The sixpack stomachs on the guys, the narrow waists and sun bleached hair of the girls and the powerful thighs of the older competitors mark them out from the ordinary beach-goers who are relegated to the margins of the beach.

Surf lifesavers and their supporters set up folding chairs and eskies along the length of the sand dunes under twenty or so club tents. At the water's edge are wooden surf boats, which take up to eight people to lift and carry from the car park. Officials dressed in broad brimmed hats, shorts and long-sleeved shirts stand among them, along with competitors waiting for their race. At the crack of the starter's pistol oarsmen push the great boats into the surf, jump in and pull at the oars in unison to ram their way through the waves. They row out past where the waves break to buoys floating in the sea, turn around and make their way back into shore, racing to the finish.

Usually Keli would go to watch her friends compete, but not this year. She desperately needed some rest, even if for just one day. For months she'd been struggling with the exertions of her club water polo games. Also, the heat of the sand and the sun, even if she sat in the shade of one of the club tents, would be too much to bear in the final trimester of her pregnancy. People expected her to be at the carnival and the party afterwards, so she'd made up some excuse explaining why she couldn't go. Duncan decided to go without her.

After the competition finishes, the sun goes down and the drinking begins, and this year was no exception. People shone with the day's excitement and Duncan was feeling good. Anyone who was young and beautiful enough to be invited to the party was there. Keli's mate Taryn made the trip from Balmain to celebrate. She was such a star, already having reached the pinnacle of her sport and been chosen to represent Australia. Like Keli she was a big, strong girl, but Taryn was leaner with a beautiful face framed by soft blonde hair. She was widely considered a catch, and that included Duncan. He'd love to score with someone like her. Taryn and Duncan stood together at the party laughing over many beers. Before too long both of them were drunk, not that anyone else was sober. Duncan leaned in and kissed Taryn; Taryn was far drunker than she realised and didn't push him away. To her horror, she woke up in his bedroom a few hours later, realising everyone at the party had seen the kiss. Duncan decided to tell Keli straight away before she heard it from someone else.

Now his hands remain in his pockets, his eyes on the ground. He and Keli are locked in tense silence, each with their minds racing. He is almost defiant as he waits for her reaction to his confession. Of course, he gets a lot of attention from other girls. Plenty throw themselves at him but Duncan almost always says no, which is a lot more than could be said for some of the other footballers. It's a reality a proper footy girlfriend has to come to grips with if things are going to work.

Until recently Duncan was confident that Keli's ambition to play for Australia meant he was safe from any real pressure to settle down for a few years yet. Duncan knows Keli truly understands the price athletes pay to make it to the top. It was one of the things that attracted him to her in the first place. He thought her own ambitions meant she would be a fellow traveller who would be there to enjoy the good times and to give him the space he needed to achieve his dreams. Back in the heady first few months of their relationship they talked about a future together, but in a general sense. He certainly hadn't proposed and Keli had no reason to think they were destined to walk down the aisle anytime soon.

Duncan still has fun with Keli, but his attraction to her has been cooling, and Keli seems to be more serious than ever about their relationship. There are some obvious reasons why Keli wants to settle down with him. It cannot be denied that Duncan is very good looking. Like Aaron, Duncan is never going to become a doctor or a lawyer, but he already runs a business with his brother. Mix in his footy ability and Duncan is a guy with a bright future. Keli's parents can see that, and they are keen for the two families to develop permanent ties.

Another large part of Keli's desire to settle down with Duncan is because of who his brothers are. Keli tells all her friends about any time she spends with them. She has also found out that Duncan and his brothers are friends with the sons of head Canterbury coach Chris Anderson, a superstar of league in the 1970s and 1980s and now on the cusp of coaching the Australian test team. These are the sort of connections Keli and her dad dream of. While Keli has ambition and a life of her own, Duncan knows she would love for them to be engaged, and Keli is a girl who is used to getting what she wants. Those rumours about Keli being pregnant haven't gone away, although these rumours are behind Duncan's back. No one has actually come up to him and asked him if Keli is pregnant. Even if they did, Duncan wouldn't be worried because he knows she's on the pill – not only for contraception but to allow her to skip her periods so she has fewer interruptions to her training.

What Duncan does know right now, standing in the sun after confessing that he cheated on her, is that Keli looks fat and bloated. Here he is, a first-grade footballer with a blimp for a girlfriend. It's beginning to raise a lot of eyebrows. He still has feelings for Keli – despite his wandering eye – but things are getting rocky. Still, even if he wanted to break up with her there is one huge consideration standing in his way: her father, Rob Lane.

It's been eight years since Keli's dad was a first-grade coach, but that doesn't mean he no longer has clout. Quite a few Wallaby selectors originally came from Manly, Warringah or the widely-feared and resented Randwick. They tend to watch games played by their old clubs and it's no secret that they are heavily influenced by the powers that be in those clubs as to which players should be considered for the gold jersey. Being an acknowledged senior statesman of the Manly club means Rob still has some influence over who gets attention from the selectors. Sure, he doesn't have the ear of the selectors like Steve Williams, Peter FitzSimons or the Cox brothers do. These men were Manly players who went on to become big name Wallabies, and everyone looks up to them. Rob Lane may have coached some of these guys, but he isn't in their league. Nonetheless, it would be foolish to dismiss Rob as a man who quietly stands in the shadow of these men. The last thing Duncan needs is Keli's dad campaigning against him because he broke his daughter's heart.

It's an understatement to say that 1995 is going to be crucial for Duncan. He is now twenty-three years old, and both his brothers Ben and Simon had made it as professional players by this age. Duncan wants to join them at the top so badly. He has already come a long way. Playing first-grade for Manly is a big achievement in anyone's book, something to distinguish him from most footballers, let alone ordinary blokes. But as amazing as last year was, playing club rugby isn't enough for him anymore. As far as union goes, the next step for him is to become a Wallaby, the ultimate achievement.

Being selected to play for Australia is a long shot for even the most talented players, and Duncan knows he isn't a star. Only a handful are chosen to join either the Wallaby squad itself or the emerging Wallaby squad for each position. Duncan plays at fullback or centre, two glamour-boy positions. There are a couple of players who are front line contenders to play both positions and he isn't one of them. Right now, Duncan is just another face in the chorus line of hopefuls fighting tooth and nail for the tiny number of spots available.

Duncan also knows Keli's dad could really help him or hurt him if it turns out that rugby league is the way to go. League scouts regularly poach talent from the prestigious but amateur union game and they make no secret of their presence in the stands at union matches; in fact, they're rarely unwelcome. Coaches contact them all the time about players they know aren't going to make it to the Wallabies but could make a living playing professional footy. Rob Lane is definitely a man who knows how to put those wheels in motion.

With all these thoughts in his head, Duncan holds his tongue. A lot of footballers cheat on their girlfriends, and dumping a girl was seen as more serious than being unfaithful. If she calls it off he'll look a little better in the eyes of their friends once the story makes the gossip rounds.

Keli doesn't yell at him, or rant and rave. She is clearly upset, but a wave of determination seems to have welled up inside of her. She turns back to face Duncan.

'You're not getting away from me that easily,' she says.

There is no emotional hug of relief or promises to never do anything so hurtful again. Duncan simply walks out through the gate, gets into his huge F100 truck and drives home.

Not long afterwards the phone rings. 'Keli, it's Taryn. Look, this is really embarrassing and I feel terrible, but I kissed Duncan last night in front of everyone. I am so sorry. Nothing else happened, I promise. I feel so stupid.'

Keli is angry at first, naturally, but she calms down as Taryn explains everything, including her drunken decision to fall asleep in his room. They have been friends for much longer than Keli has known Duncan and Taryn can be trusted. Keli says she believes her and hangs up. But it isn't necessarily relief that Keli may be feeling. Perhaps she's feeling that, once again, she has been outclassed by Taryn. Perhaps Keli sees that in Duncan's eyes she's the runner-up prize. Or perhaps that Duncan is happy for all the world to think he slept with her, including Keli, but Taryn didn't want him, even when she was drunk.

Standing quietly, Keli remembers what time it is. Regardless of the blow she has just received she has to gather her strength and go to water polo training. No matter how rotten she might feel, missing training simply isn't an option if she wants to play for Australia. When Keli arrives at the Dawn Fraser Baths, Melinda is poolside.

'Hi Keli,' says Melinda as her friend walks towards her. Taryn is already in the water, treading water while passing the ball to others in a circle. Taryn looks up and smiles and Keli smiles back. Taryn is relieved to see everything is OK between them. However, Taryn, Melinda and the other girls can't help noticing how huge Keli looks. Keli's size couldn't be ignored when they all went to Perth earlier in the month, nor can her strange new habit of walking around wrapped in a towel when everyone else simply struts around in their swimmers. Some have gone so far as to guess she might be pregnant. Keli isn't looking good, that's for sure. Maybe that's why Duncan is happy for everyone to think he cheated on her.

Keli lets her towel slide and quickly jumps into the water. The coach watches Keli's performance from the sidelines. Like everyone else, David can't help noticing how heavy she is. He wonders how her weight is going to affect her performance in the upcoming club championships.

'You indicated in your statement that you never spoke to Keli about the rumours that she may have been pregnant for obvious reasons. Why did you not speak to her about that?' Keli's barrister asks David Woods, her old water polo coach, at the coronial hearing.

'Well, being the coach of a women's water polo team, it's a bit of a knife-edge thing, talking about pregnancy with an eighteen- or nineteen-year-old. It's not a good place to go,' David answers, reflecting on the period that was the pinnacle of Keli's elite athletic career, but only the middle of Keli's long, fruitless struggle to make it into the Australian senior team.

'So were these rumours persistent or was it just something you heard?'

'It wasn't persistent. It was mentioned a few times and I just kind of thought about it and . . . Well, if she was pregnant, I thought her mother probably wouldn't let her play, so I didn't think it was an issue.'

'So you never spoke to Keli about her being pregnant?'

'No.'

Despite the coach's private concerns about Keli's weight, she is playing well. There were a few missed morning training sessions, but after some stern words from David she seems to be back on track.

The day of the club grand final arrives: Balmain versus Sydney University. Keli's parents, Duncan, one of his brothers and Duncan's mother, Julie, come to watch Keli play. So does Brandon, who has come to watch Melinda play alongside Keli. Balmain puts up a good fight but loses. Keli plays a good game and Duncan says he is proud of her. After the match the whole team, David the coach, Duncan, his brother and mother, Melinda, Brandon, and everyone else's supporters, except for Keli's parents who can't stay, go to a pub in Balmain to celebrate the end of the season and the end of David's time as coach of the women's team.

A couple of hours into the evening, after the sun has gone down, a few of Keli's team-mates notice Keli is missing. One of them asks David if he has seen her, but he hasn't. Duncan, his mum and brother are still in the pub, not looking too concerned, so Keli's friends think nothing more of it. In fact, Duncan doesn't realise Keli is missing until the next day. Once he does he makes a few calls but still can't find her. Despite this, Duncan isn't that concerned, even when he doesn't hear from her for several more days.

But as will be revealed fifteen years later in the Supreme Court of New South Wales, a few hours after playing in the club finals, Keli started having contractions. While she was at the pub her contractions became so strong she slipped out and took herself to hospital. A few hours after that, surrounded by strangers, Keli gave birth. Incredibly, Keli's mother Sandy, her father Rob, her boyfriend at the time, Duncan, his mother Julie, a nurse with several decades' experience, and Keli's best friends Melinda and Brandon, had no idea that Keli, who played water polo in front of them that day, was carrying a baby at full term.

Keli lies in a bed in the King George V Memorial Hospital's post-natal ward in Camperdown. Along the corridor are other women lying in beds surrounded by flowers, cards and teddy bears. Everything is clean and neat. Nurses calmly attend to newborns while answering the garbled demands of frantic family members who burst through the doors. Little children run in circles and play hide and seek, fuelled by the nervous excitement.

Keli lies quietly, a few sobs surfacing now and then. There are no flowers or cards near her bed. She hasn't had any visitors or phone calls since she checked in and she isn't expecting any now that her baby has been born. A nurse passes and smiles. Keli's loneliness has been talked about. Some have never seen a woman give birth without the support of any family or friends, but the more experienced nurses know it happens from time to time. It's not common, but it's far from unheard of. The staff look upon her with curiosity and kindness. The consensus is that Keli is polite and good natured, one of those new mums who hates to be a bother. There is nothing odd or off-putting about her to explain her situation. They decide that, whatever the reason for her being alone, she is a nice girl and they feel sorry for her.

However, feelings of pity have turned to deep concern. It's been an hour or so since Keli gave birth and she has started to cry uncontrollably. Tears and swinging emotions are normal in the maternity ward as oceans of hormones wash through new mothers, but Keli's distress is unsettling. Lying in her bed, unable to stop the sobbing that shakes her whole body, Keli is falling apart. The soft words and hand holding of the nurses have no impact. Keli is unable to tell any of them why she is so distressed. It's quickly decided that Debbie the social worker is needed.

Debbie walks to Keli's bedside and sits down. She will sit there for as long as it takes for Keli to work out the words that will let her get a handle on the pain. Eventually Keli is able to utter her torment out loud.

'I want to put my baby up for adoption.'

Keli sobs again but Debbie is relieved. She knows the dam has burst and the emotions will now drain away.

She puts her hand on Keli's shoulder. Not many babies are put up for adoption these days. Back in the 1970s it was several hundred in New South Wales each year, but now the numbers are tiny, maybe seventeen one year, eleven the next. Vast improvements in contraception and the abandonment by authorities of policies that put pressure on young single mothers to give up their children for adoption are key reasons for the dramatic drop in numbers. Of course, a young, single, educated woman in her twenties like Keli would have been a prime candidate for abortion. About one in every four pregnancies in Australia is terminated, totalling an estimated 80,000 a year. Keli's choice to go ahead with an unwanted pregnancy is unusual. She is silent as to her reasons why.

Debbie thinks about what to do now. Keli needs to choose an agency quickly so that someone with detailed knowledge of adoption procedures can come in and get the wheels in motion. There are four agencies that deal with adoptions in New South Wales. There is the Department of Community Services; Anglicare, which is connected to the Anglican church; and Centacare, which is connected to the Catholic church. The fourth, Banardos, usually deals with the adoption and fostering of older children. Debbie explains the options to Keli and asks her to think about which one she wants to approach.

Now breathing normally and dabbing her eyes with a tissue, Keli explains why she can't look after her child. 'I'm an elite water polo player. In fact, I'm due to play for Australia soon.'

Debbie looks at Keli's arms and torso. She certainly is a particularly strong looking girl.

'I also want to play for Australia in the 2000 Olympics,' Keli goes on. 'Women's water polo isn't an Olympic sport yet but we're doing all we can to change that.' At this point Keli begins to cry gently again. 'I can't look after my baby and train for the Olympics at the same time.'

Debbie decides not to ask Keli too many more questions. The adoption agency worker will ask plenty when she comes tomorrow. Before Debbie leaves, Keli makes an unusual request. 'I need to leave the hospital tomorrow night. I need to go out without my baby.'

Debbie looks at Keli. 'What do you mean?'

'I need to speak to the baby's father, Duncan, about the adoption,' says Keli. 'He and I moved to Sydney from Perth three weeks ago. Perth is where we both grew up and met each other. We moved here so Duncan could further his footy career,' Keli says. 'My parents still live in Perth.'

Debbie, having only Keli's word to go by, accepts her story, even though Keli's parents at that moment are only a forty-minute drive away.

'Duncan is the only person I know in Sydney,' Keli adds quietly.

'I'll see what I can do,' Debbie replies.

Keli chooses Centacare to be the agency for her baby's adoption. The next day a case worker pulls up a chair beside Keli's bed. After introducing herself, she begins to probe Keli about the baby's father and her family.

'Duncan and I had been living together for a year in Perth when I fell pregnant,' Keli tells the case worker. 'It wasn't planned. My parents know about my pregnancy and they're disappointed in me. As soon as I found out I was expecting I knew I wanted to put my baby up for adoption because I didn't want to have an abortion and I'm not ready to be a parent. Besides that, I want to study and pursue my water polo career. Being pregnant was the reason why I wasn't selected to play for Australia last year.'

'And you are playing water polo here in Sydney?'

'Yes. In fact I have been selected to play for Australia in Canada this year.' In a few weeks' time Keli will indeed be selected to play for Australia's junior side. Keli adds she might be away for twelve months.

'And you also aim to play for Australia in the 2000 Olympics?'

'Yes.'

The next day is Keli's twentieth birthday. Resigned to the fact that no one is going to visit, call or send any presents, the nurses have bought Keli a birthday cake. They keep it in the staff fridge, waiting for the right moment to bring it out. Keli has also been granted a gate pass, meaning the hospital has agreed to take care of Keli's baby for a certain number of hours during the night while Keli goes out. The hospital rarely grants this privilege, but it's decided that Keli is a special case. It isn't often that a lonely new mother has to speak to her partner about putting their baby up for adoption on her own birthday. Keli's pass begins in the early evening, so the nurses will surprise her with the cake in the afternoon.

At the arranged time, a small group walk her towards the kitchen. 'Happy birthday, Keli,' they say cheerfully, determined to overlook the awkwardness.

Surprised and a little embarrassed, Keli manages to be gracious. 'Thank you, how lovely.'

A silent breath of relief passes through the nurses. Despite everything, she is able to make them feel good about trying to brighten her day. Keli doesn't eat much cake, but that doesn't matter. The group stands around her, eating and smiling before they have to go back to work on the ward.

Keli gets ready for her night out. She expresses breast milk as she has been taught and then dresses. By 6 pm she has left. Keli returns as planned the next morning, but it seems her meeting with Duncan has not gone well. 'I don't know if I want to involve Duncan in the adoption,' she tells the adoption agency case worker. 'It was my decision not to have an abortion. It was my decision to give birth and it is my decision to put my baby up for adoption.'

The case worker has learnt from experience that secrecy is part and parcel of most adoptions. There are situations where the father is genuinely unknown, such as in the cases of sexual assault by a stranger. However, even when the father is known, the private dramas that surround the birth often mean the mother doesn't want him in the picture or to even know his child exists. 'I know this is difficult, but we need to contact Duncan if his name is to be on your baby's birth certificate.'

Keli sighs again. 'I'll give you an address where he can be reached,' she says.

The case worker outlines what will happen. Keli will go home alone and the child will be placed in short-term care. Keli will then need to give her written consent for her baby to be adopted. After signing she will then have a window of thirty days to change her mind. If she still wants to go ahead at the end of those thirty days the child will then be taken out of foster care and placed with the adoptive parents. Several months after the placement the adoption will be finalised by an order of the Supreme Court.

'Now Keli, even if you go ahead with the adoption that doesn't mean you have to cut off all contact with your baby,' says the case worker. 'There was a time when adoption was kept a secret and mothers lost all contact with their children, but not anymore. In fact, we encourage you and the adoptive family to keep in contact at a level that everyone feels comfortable with.'

Keli looks at her with searching eyes.

'That is something that will sort itself out. Swapping letters and photos is a good start,' the case worker adds.

Keli's breasts feel heavy. It is time to feed the little one. The nurses bring the baby to her, watching her gently hold the child. She has no problems producing milk. It has been a couple of days of high emotion but Keli has been feeding her baby throughout. Not long afterwards Keli checks out of the hospital alone. Her baby is taken into foster care awaiting final placement with the adoptive parents.

The club water polo season has ended but the national championships are yet to be held. Keli's fellow Balmain teammates haven't seen her since the club grand final three weeks ago. One morning, while those who have been selected to play for the New South Wales senior team are finishing their practise session, Keli appears. She has lost a lot of weight, her stomach is flat and she is wearing a two-piece swimming costume.

'Hi Keli,' says Lisa, noticing Keli is no longer wrapping herself in a towel around the pool.

Keli hasn't been selected for the senior state team, but she has been selected for the junior side. She and the other girls are now in the last year of being able to play in both junior and senior competitions, so she will go to the nationals with them in a couple of weeks time. Before she sets off for the nationals, Keli is invited to visit her baby in foster care. An experienced staff member of the agency watches Keli hold her child. She takes a photo of the two together.

'We are having real problems contacting Duncan,' she says as Keli coos at the little face looking up at her. Normally a father would tell the agency loud and clear if he didn't want to know about the child or the adoption process. The adoption agency staff hear all sorts of reasons why fathers don't want to be involved. Denial, reconciliations with estranged wives, callings to the priesthood – they were all just excuses, but she wasn't there to judge. Still, there hasn't been a single response from Duncan, not even a curt 'go away', which is most unusual when the name and contact details of the father are known. There have also been a number of meetings that Duncan was supposed to attend to discuss the adoption. Keli said that he told her he was coming but failed to show up. It gets to the point where an extension on the foster care agreement has to be organised. At one meeting where Duncan doesn't turn up, Keli is very angry.

'The club have sent him over to Scotland to play in a

competition. It's a nightmare. They don't care about me and I'm beginning to think he doesn't either,' she says. Tears well in her eyes as a new consent form is typed to allow the adoption to go ahead in his absence if necessary. However, the agency needs to keep trying to contact Duncan, so they ask Keli for his address. Keli gives them one.

For a few weeks the agency are unable to contact her. Keli is competing at the nationals. On top of dealing with the secret adoption of her baby she is trying to impress the Australian selectors. Yet again, after the nationals Taryn and Bronwyn are selected to play in the Australian senior team while Keli isn't, but she doesn't walk away empty-handed. As she'd hoped, Keli is one of thirteen girls selected to represent Australia in the world junior championships in Canada.

Keli calls the agency to say she has been interstate and will be back the next day. She also tells agency staff that she and Duncan have separated temporarily. 'He said he doesn't want to speak to me until I clean up this mess,' she cries. The next day when she appears at the agency she is still upset. 'I'm not receiving any support from Duncan. He says I tricked him by telling him he wouldn't have to be involved in the adoption. Everything is so out of control. I feel I've let you guys here at the agency down.'

'Keli, you've done everything you can,' a staff member tells her soothingly. Keli gives them an address she says is for Duncan's mother, where she claims she is staying now that she and Duncan are separated. She also gives staff an address for her parents in Western Australia and a phone number for Duncan. Keli tearfully chooses her baby's adoptive parents from profiles provided by the agency. The staff hand her the baby's hospital wrist-band and tag for her to keep as they talk about arranging an access visit so Keli can see her baby in foster care. They also tell her they have sent a letter to Duncan.

With the world junior championships looming Keli's training regime intensifies. Three mornings a week, between 5.30 and 7 am, the team trains at Homebush, which is the site of the upcoming 2000 Olympic games. Three afternoons a week, between 6 and 7.30 pm, the team trains in Balmain. On top of that there is weight and fitness training.

Meanwhile the wheels of the adoption keep turning. Agency staff still have no success getting into contact with Duncan, who Keli says is now back from Scotland. They call the number she gave for him, but the man who answers says no one named Duncan lives there and that the address they are talking about isn't the address for that phone number. 'Oh, that's just Duncan's house-mate lying for him,' says Keli. 'I've been in contact with Duncan. He just doesn't want to be hassled.'

Over the next month Keli visits her baby in foster care twice. She brings flowers and talks excitedly about how lovely the foster family is. She tells them she wants to see them again before she goes to Canada. 'I might not be back for twelve months,' says Keli, adding that she hopes this doesn't interfere with her seeing her baby settle in with the adoptive parents. At the third foster visit Keli weeps when she sees her baby. Afterwards she tells the adoption agency staff how things are going with Duncan and her own family.

'Duncan wants me back, but I'm not sure I'm interested,' she says. 'I told my parents why we've broken up. Dad phoned Duncan and called him a coward for not supporting me. Mum might call you while I'm away in Canada. They've just moved to Sydney for my brother's final year at school. It feels great to have them around.'

The day Keli is to meet her baby's adoptive parents arrives. 'These are for you,' says Keli nervously as she hands the mother a beautiful bunch of yellow roses. The adoption worker stands nearby as Keli faces both parents, the father cradling her baby in his arms while the mother inhales the perfume of the roses. 'They are gorgeous, Keli, thank you,' she says as both she and Keli burst into tears. Keli wipes her eyes, takes a deep breath and then smiles at her baby. 'This is for you, little one. It's from your daddy, Duncan,' she says as she waves a little stuffed toy. The new father takes the toy and holds it close to the gurgling infant.

The adoption worker smiles, glad that this difficult time is going so well. The agency has finally been able to get in touch with Duncan. For a while there it looked like their letter was never going to get through to him. It had been sitting in the Harbord post office after an unsuccessful delivery attempt when, much to everyone's relief, they were told that the letter had been collected. While he isn't here today, it's lovely to see he is thinking of his baby. The emotion of the meeting is intense, so the adoption worker discreetly steps in after a suitable time and leads Keli out of the room. Once alone, she hands Keli photos of her baby and a copy of the adoption papers. 'Come and visit us before you leave for Canada, Keli,' she says, and Keli promises she will.

'How do you think the meeting with the new parents went?' the adoption agency worker asks Keli when she comes in a couple of weeks later.

'Oh, it went so well. They are going to be such a great family,' Keli enthuses, looking fresh and full of life.

'Good,' replies the agency worker, adding the adoption is currently being formally finalised by the Supreme Court.

Before Keli leaves, she makes a special request. 'Could you

keep the photos and papers here for safe-keeping?' she asks, handing over her copy of the adoption papers and the photos of her baby. The agency worker is a little surprised, but she takes them. 'OK, we'll keep them in the filing cabinet. You can come and get them any time.'

Keli walks out, beaming. After all that pain and emotion everything is now going to plan. Of course, she'd lied when she told nurses and the adoption agency that she and Duncan had just moved to Sydney from Perth. And the addresses she had given them for her family, for herself and for Duncan after the fictitious breakup were all false, too. On top of those lies, Keli took careful steps not to let any cracks show in the story she had told the adoption agency. In fact, Keli – not Duncan, as they thought – had picked up the agency's letter from the Harbord post office. She simply told the post office workers she was picking it up for her boyfriend and they let her sign for it. Keli had bought the little stuffed toy. Duncan didn't know a thing.

With nothing holding her back, one of Keli's sporting ambitions is realised. The world junior water polo tournament in Canada is a roaring success. Keli's team wins silver, an outstanding achievement for Australia. Keli calls home to tell her parents about the medal. She is elated and so are Rob and Sandy.

Keli seems to radiate confidence when she comes home. She looks great, too. One day, not long after her triumph in Canada, she walks into the kitchen where her father and Duncan are deep in conversation – or at least her father is talking while Duncan listens carefully.

'Campese is still going strong. He'll be in the team for a couple of years yet. You've got no hope against him,' her father says while Duncan nods in agreement. Rob sees his daughter and smiles. Keli smiles back. 'You're looking beautiful, Keli,' he says. 'Don't put all that weight on again.'

Keli's shoulders drop. The smile on her face becomes frozen. She stutters as the breezy response she'd planned to say gets stuck in her throat. Her father and Duncan look on mutely as Keli's skin flushes a deep red. She tries to busy herself with something in the kitchen but her hands are shaking. Before long, she rushes out. Rob and Duncan look at each other and laugh with surprise, shrugging their shoulders at the mysteries of women.

5

DO YOU LOVE ME?

'Go Taryn!'

It's late 1995. Keli sits in the stands, yelling support for her friend. All around her are other players from Balmain and the Australian men's team.

It's the women's finals of the World Championships and every player in the stands wishes they were in the pool. Australia is playing the Netherlands, holder of five world championships. The noise bouncing around the walls of the Homebush Aquatic Centre, the dampness of puddles underfoot and the smell of chlorine has been part of their lives and dreams for so long.

Keli wanted to be selected for the senior team, to represent Australia at the very highest level, but she wasn't. Most of the players from the Australian junior team didn't get this chance. Taryn and Bronwyn were the only Balmain players to be picked. 'That's elite sport for you. That's how tough it is at the very top,' older players would say. But just because something is true doesn't make it any easier to deal with.

The triumph of Keli's team's silver medal in Canada is overshadowed by the drama unfolding in the pool right now. Australia scores a goal. Keli and the others erupt into cheers, lost in the moment. They love the game, always have and always will. At full-time the dream has become real. The Australians are the new world champions. The feeling in the stands is euphoric. 'We're off to celebrate!' someone announces as the yelling and hugs subside. Keli follows the crowd to the pub.

She stands with the Australian women's team, laughing and joking. But things have changed over the last few months. Keli is no longer part of the elite, and while she's close to the inner circle, she's not a part of it. Keli is now one of the friends and well-wishers standing around the team. There is a constant crush of people pushing against her, threatening to separate her from the champions.

Keli moves towards the bar and stands still for a few minutes, waiting to grab the attention of the staff. She has a self-conscious look on her face. Her expression turns to relief when she sees Duncan emerge from the crowd.

'Hey Duncan, can you buy me two beers?' she yells out over the din. He nods assent. She gestures to him again. 'Do you need me to help carry the drinks?' Again he nods. Keli gestures back, happy to alert everyone that her boyfriend Duncan, the up-and-coming footballer, is here.

'Hey 'Roids, how are you?' someone asks, calling Duncan by the nickname he has earned from bulking up so much. The crowd around the Australian team opens to allow them in. 'Going to join your brothers at Canterbury are you?'

'Well, it's looking hopeful,' he says with a knowing smile on his face. Everyone leans in to listen. A lot of them know

Duncan's brother Simon was made captain of the Canterbury side earlier this year. The presence of one of the Gillies brothers, along with the newly crowned world champion water polo players, is making the front bar buzz. Keli hands around the beers while Duncan holds court. It's a big night and everyone gets pretty drunk. Keli is laughing with her old team-mates, the beer fuelled noise swirling around the boisterous groups of men and women. At the end of the night Taryn asks Keli if she would like to stay at her place rather than drive all the way home.

'I'll just see what Duncan wants to do,' Keli says, looking over her shoulder for him.

'I think he's left already,' says one of the girls.

'Yeah, thanks for saying goodbye, Duncan,' Keli jokes, rolling her eyes.

Her team-mates don't say anything, tactfully trying to avoid her gaze.

It's early 1996 and the club water polo season is in full swing. Taryn and Bronwyn are now established members of the senior Australian team. They have also been headhunted to play for European teams, leaving the others to contemplate their futures as they swim lap after punishing lap of the pool.

Lisa, having played for the New South Wales senior team and being part of the silver-winning Australian junior team in Canada, decides to quit competitive water polo. Melinda pulled out some time ago and Stacy is considering making this her last year of competitive water polo. However, this year Keli is selected to play for the New South Wales senior team for the first time. It's an Olympic year, and while women's water polo is yet to be included as an Olympic sport, girls like

Keli, who are still putting in the training to make the grade, have stars in their eyes.

'OK, partner off,' calls out the new coach. The training session grinds on for another hour.

There is so much for Keli to be excited about. She's going to start studying at the Australian College of Physical Education in January so she can become a physical education teacher. Also, just a couple of months ago Duncan was offered a contract to play rugby league for Canterbury, the club his brothers play for and the one Simon captains. The money for his first professional footy contract isn't huge – after all, Duncan isn't a going straight into the premier league – but it's a decent income for someone not quite in his mid twenties, the sort of money that other guys his age usually get slogging it out in an office. Buying a house is a priority for Duncan, and he bought one just before Christmas 1995. He isn't going to be one of those footballers who blows all his money and then retires with nothing to show for his playing years except good yarns and lots of injuries.

Duncan's new place is so handy for Keli's training sessions at Balmain. It's in Gladesville, only a fifteen minute drive from the pool. It's also much closer to the college where she is studying than her parents' place in Manly. 'Not a bad effort for someone who began playing first-grade footy two years ago,' said Keli, squeezing Duncan on the arm when he told her family about his new place. The house is a pleasant weatherboard house with very tall trees standing behind it. Keli tells all her friends that Duncan's brother Simon and his wife live directly opposite, with both homes facing each other over a slightly dipping intersection. Keli's star is rising again in the pool and her connection to Duncan gives her Manly friends entrée into the world of elite football outside of their beachside suburb. She tells people about how she and Duncan went to his other footballer brother Ben's '95–'96 New Year's Eve party. This year Keli and many of her friends will turn twenty-one. It is going to be a year of partying hard every weekend.

Keli spends as much of her precious spare time at Duncan's place but it's clear she wishes it was a lot more. Now that Duncan doesn't train in Manly, Keli has to travel to his new home to spend time with him. Between training and studying she's pretty busy, but she manages to stay over at his place at least once a week. It might be simpler for Keli if she just moves in, but even if that's what she wants, it doesn't seem like Duncan is going to ask her to anytime soon. He's in no hurry to end his bachelor life.

On Valentine's Day Duncan has a surprise for Keli. It's a green Hyundai, a little run-around so she doesn't have to use her mother's car anymore to get to his place. Duncan hasn't actually bought it for her. It's a hire purchase he got a good discount rate for from a sponsor of his team.

Duncan's oldest brother, Dougall, who doesn't play footy, and a mate move into Duncan's new house to help pay the mortgage, but two more tenants are needed to make things work. In April 1996 an American water polo player named Juan moves in. He won't be there all the time as he'll travel back home to the US throughout the year, but Duncan doesn't mind, so long as the rent keeps coming in. Ben Anderson moves in, too. Ben is the son of Canterbury coach Chris Anderson, who looks set to follow his father's footsteps as a premier league player. Both Ben and Juan work for Duncan and his brother Simon's tree-lopping and lawn-mowing business. It's hard physical work that starts early in the morning and ends just before footy and water polo training. Duncan keeps the mowers and tree-lopping equipment in his shed and piles of cut wood in his backyard. During the week the boys all fall into bed not long after coming home at around 9 pm and having something to eat. Saturday night is the night for drinking, and Keli joins in with gusto.

Also in April, Keli turns twenty-one and her parents throw a party for her in their big backyard. Keli celebrates with Duncan, her water polo team-mates and her close-knit crowd of life-long friends: Melinda, who is still dating Brendon; Kati, and Natalie – who Keli gave a speech for at her twenty-first party the year before. Other Manly guests include Charmaine and John, as well as the guy Keli saw before she started seeing Duncan, and his long-term girlfriend, and Alison, who is beginning to be viewed as a bit of an outsider by Keli's inner circle as she spends less time in Manly these days.

Everyone knows Keli and Duncan as an established couple, despite the whispers about Duncan fooling around that have been circulating for a while. Both sets of parents are happy that Keli and Duncan are together. Duncan and Keli visit his mother Julie, who lives a few hours' drive north of Sydney at Blueys Beach. Duncan doesn't spend as much time with Keli's dad Rob these days. As he no longer plays for the Manly Blues he doesn't come over for dinner after matches or training. But no one in Keli's family takes Duncan's absence personally. He's a professional footy player now, and they know what it takes to stay at the top.

As exciting as it is to have both her own and Duncan's sporting careers take off, Keli finds the time to pursue her goal of becoming a physical education teacher. At college she becomes friends with Lisa Andreatta, who is a couple of years younger than Keli. Both are willing to give any sport in the college curriculum a go, as long as it isn't dancing or gymnastics, and they both like to have a drink and a laugh. Keli introduces Lisa to her other friends and they soon regularly hit the pubs of Manly together. Before too long Lisa hears the rumours about Duncan playing around with other women. She doesn't particularly like Keli's boyfriend, but she knows Keli loves him. Lisa wouldn't bother with a guy like him, but for the sake of the friendship she keeps her opinions to herself.

Besides making it into the New South Wales senior team, 1996 holds another major milestone for Keli. In August she lands a job coaching water polo part-time at a prestigious private school, Ravenswood School for Girls. The sporting facilities at this school are incredible. Keli coaches water polo in an indoor twenty-five metre pool. Above it is a sprung floor gymnasium with stadium seating for about a hundred people. There is also a large grass oval that serves as a hockey field and four or five tennis courts. Keli's parents would never have been able to afford to send her to a school like this, and the same is true for most of her water polo buddies. Everyone is duly impressed. Keli is keen to make a good impression at the school. Her skills as a coach are quickly recognised, earning her a mention in the school's 1996 yearbook.

Keli is treated like a big deal in Manly and along the Northern Beaches, but she is merely one of the crowd on the other side of the Harbour. It's a reality that Keli has problems recognising, and at times her arrogance annoys her Balmain teammates. The drunken kiss between Taryn, one of the queens of the water polo set, and Duncan a year and a half ago is still making things awkward. Duncan still maintains they had sex, although most people believe Taryn's side of the story. However, Keli can hold her head up high when she goes to Taryn's twenty-first birthday party with Duncan in August. She has her new job at Ravenswood to talk about and the knowledge she has finally made the state senior team. Maybe a spot on the Australian team and a ring on her finger are only around the corner.

Keli wants Duncan all to herself, but his reputation as a ladies' man is still hanging around. Juan, the American housemate, along with everyone else, knows not to say anything about the rumours in front of Keli. Now that Duncan is a professional footy player he has more licence to do what he pleases than ever before. It's clear that Keli is deeply in love with him and doesn't want to let him go but many are surprised that they're still together. Putting aside the whispers of Duncan's unfaithfulness, Keli is putting on weight again. Juan notices just how big she is one day when he sees her in a red bikini at the pool in late 1996 after coming back from the US. He isn't the first. Rumours about her being pregnant again have been circulating around Keli's Balmain team-mates for months.

Earlier that year, when Taryn was taking a break from her commitments in Italy and her overseas tours with the Australian team, she was training with the Balmain team. While treading water, Stacy, the Queensland girl who'd stayed with the Lanes two years earlier, told Taryn that Keli had started wearing her tracksuit over her swimmers, only taking them off just before getting into the pool. Other girls said that it reminded them of Keli wrapping herself with a towel before and after training during several months in 1995. Sure enough, as Taryn and Stacy watched from the corner of their eyes, Keli slipped out of her tracksuit and slid straight into the water in a way that suggested she was trying to hide her body. With their goggles on, Stacy and Taryn dived under the water to look at Keli's body. Once they surfaced, they looked at each other and nodded in agreement.

'She looks like she's pregnant.'

'Yep.'

And just like the year before, the rumours are true. Keli is pregnant again.

6

TEGAN

It's 3.40 pm on 11 September 1996. Keli walks alone through the doors of Auburn Hospital, grinding her teeth. The expressionless mask she has worn all the way to the hospital drops as she passes through the doors. She tells staff she is nearly a fortnight past her due date and her back pain is close to unbearable. She is admitted and quickly led to a bed. Keli chose this hospital because they don't know her here. Just as with her other pregnancies and her first baby, Keli can't go to Manly or Mona Vale hospital as her mother, Sandy, would be sure to find out.

Auburn is a suburb in Sydney's south-west where newly arrived immigrants live. Its main shopping streets are lined with shop signs written in a mixture of Chinese and Arabic characters. Asian shopkeepers dressed in shorts and t-shirts stand in doorways while women dressed in burqas and African men dressed in sandals and tunics walk by. It's a peaceful place.

Its main mosque is not one of those reputed to attract funda-
mentalist followers like some in neighbouring suburbs and its
doors are open to anyone who wants to enter. But the likelihood of anyone from Keli's life in Manly or even the water
polo scene visiting here are next to zero.

The month before, even though Keli was heavily pregnant,
she went to Taryn's twenty-first birthday bash and partied
hard. She hasn't slackened off the pace in other areas of her
life either, having started her part-time coaching position
at Ravenswood and her training as part of the New South
Wales senior team. She's still studying at the Australian
College of Physical Education, but plans to defer her studies
for a semester or two soon. The fact that she has a great job
and ambitions to be selected for the Australian team will be
adequate explanation for the postponement of her studies to
those looking at the shiny exterior of her life. But behind it is
the fact that she is about to give birth, and once again she
is going to do it in absolute secrecy.

Keli isn't booked in to give birth at Auburn, so the medical
staff ask who is looking after her. Keli tells them she is under
the care of a midwife who originally was going to help her
have a homebirth. Staff wonder why the midwife isn't with
her. As a rule, homebirth midwives are very possessive of their
clients and consider sending one to hospital to be a huge failure
on their part, leading most to overcompensate by obsessively
ringing to check up on their clients and repeatedly turning up
to the hospital to hover over them. But Keli's midwife hasn't
called and is nowhere to be seen, so a nurse asks Keli for her
phone number. Despite her complaints of pain and her claim
she is overdue, Keli is not in labour. Medical staff attend to
her pain and she leaves hospital that evening, but reappears
at 7.15 the next morning, Thursday 12 September, asking to

be induced. Keli nominates her friend Kati as someone the hospital can call in an emergency, as well as Duncan.

There are problems making contact with Keli's midwife, a woman named Julie Melville. A nurse calls repeatedly to get Keli's antenatal results, which normally include screening tests for blood clotting problems, rubella, hepatitis B and other key dangers and information needed before a birth. She uses the number Keli has provided, but no one answers and there is no message service: the number is not in use. Frustrated, the nurse makes a note of what has happened. Preparations are being made for Keli's baby to be induced while staff continue their hunt for her absent midwife. Now, the nurses notice that Keli has no family or friends calling her. They start to make gentle enquires why as she is taken for a CTG.

'Oh, my partner is a professional footballer,' Keli tells them as they monitor her contractions and the unborn baby's heartbeat. 'He's overseas playing at the moment. That's why he isn't here.' Keli sighs. 'It's tough being with him, really tough.'

Just before 8 pm on Thursday 12 September Keli gives birth to a baby girl. There are problems with the placenta and Keli loses a litre of blood during the delivery, but otherwise all is well and the baby is healthy. The doctor and attending nurses note that the infant was probably thirty-eight weeks' gestation at birth, arriving roughly a fortnight before the due date, rather than overdue as Keli had claimed. However, thirty-eight weeks falls into the medical definition of a full-term pregnancy, and the medical staff were satisfied that the baby was full-term before inducing Keli. A tag with the name 'Lane' is taped onto the newborn's back and a band with the name 'Lane' is taped around the baby's wrist.

On this day there are four births, including Keli's. The maternity ward is full of new mothers recovering in its twenty-four beds. The new mums come from all over the world – China, Sri Lanka, Lebanon, Fiji, Vietnam and Tonga. Keli is one of only two white women in the whole ward. But while Keli and her daughter are wheeled into a shared room to recover, the other white woman is lying alone, sedated in a private room. Her baby was born dead.

The new mum Keli will share a room with has been there for a few hours before Keli and Tegan arrive. She notices the young woman with blonde hair and her baby in a hospital bassinet when she gets up to go to the bathroom in the early hours of Friday, 13 September. She tries to make eye contact but Keli turns away. When the young mum comes back from the bathroom, the curtain between her bed and Keli's is drawn. It remains drawn all day as her husband and then an army of brothers, sisters, parents, cousins and in-laws visit her and her new baby. She doesn't see anyone visit Keli or her daughter.

The next day at the busy nurses' station the phone rings. It's Ryde Hospital. The call is about a patient named Keli Lane, who attended Ryde Hospital hours before she arrived at Auburn and a couple of times before that seeking pain relief and to be induced. According to their records, she is now admitted in Auburn Hospital. The nurse who answers the phone brings up her file. The caller from Ryde Hospital comments that making contact with Keli's midwife is a matter that needs to be chased up.

'Right,' answers the nurse, making a note. She can see from the file that Keli had originally wanted a homebirth, but that her midwife had sent her to hospital. The nurse notices that Keli was admitted to Auburn the day before, when she wasn't on duty. She concludes that Ryde Hospital, where Keli sought to be induced before coming to Auburn, is simply letting Auburn know that they are already trying to chase up Keli's oddly slack midwife, who hasn't bothered to call either hospital yet.

Meanwhile, Keli and her new baby are recovering in the maternity ward. A social worker who used to practise as a midwife approaches Keli to see how she is going. Keli sits upright in her bed breastfeeding her baby as they chat generally about her family. Keli occasionally gets a bit teary, but that's nothing out of the ordinary for new mothers. The nurses have told the social worker that no one has visited or called Keli. She chats to Keli about what arrangements she has made once she leaves the hospital.

'My boyfriend's name is Duncan Gillies,' Keli tells the social worker. 'He's currently overseas, as are my parents. Mum and Dad are back on Tuesday, and Duncan will be back on Wednesday. I've got a friend to stay with me until then. In about three months' time Duncan, the baby and I will move to London. We plan to live there for a couple of years.'

'What unfortunate timing,' the social worker thinks to herself. During her many years of experience here and overseas she's seen too many women give birth without any friends or family by their side. It isn't common at Auburn Hospital, but it certainly happens. 'At least this new mother has family,' she thinks. It seems Keli is a perfectly nice young woman who has been unlucky enough to give birth when none of her loved ones could be by her side. Aside from the loneliness, the nurse can see nothing wrong with Keli. There are no obvious signs of depression. Still, it's unusual to have absolutely no one visit or call. In any case, Keli seems happy and confident, so the social worker feels there is nothing more for her to do. Keli's plans and the lack of family support at the time of birth are noted on Keli's file.

Keli makes it known to the nurse running the ward that she wants to be discharged the next day, Saturday 14 September. A lot of new mothers don't like being in hospital – they can't sleep and they don't like the hospital routine – so Keli's request to go home as soon as possible is not unusual. Being fit and young, Keli is recovering quickly from her birth, so preparations are made for her to leave. Besides checking up on her recovery, staff also hand Keli some paperwork to fill out. Consent for a blood sample to be taken from her newborn plus a letter from medical staff to Keli's midwife are left on her bedside table.

The morning of her planned departure comes. The ward clerk presses upon Keli a blue book for her daughter's upcoming health checks as well as birth registration, Medicare and social security forms. 'You must fill out the Medicare form now. We'll send it in for you,' says the clerk as she hovers over Keli. 'You'll need to post the other forms yourself.'

Realising the clerk isn't going to leave until she has a completed Medicare form, Keli picks up a pen and fills it out. In the space for the baby's name Keli writes 'Tegan Lee Lane'. Satisfied, the clerk takes the completed Medicare form and leaves the others on her bedside table. Keli now waits for a doctor to give her and the newly named Tegan their final physical examinations. Doctor Chen comes by to examine Tegan before lunchtime. Keli's medical file shows she is fine. He carefully examines the infant for any abnormalities, and finding none he declares the baby and mother fit for discharge. As soon as she is given the all clear to leave, Keli collects the documents on her bedside table, picks up Tegan and walks out of the hospital.

Her exit is swift and she doesn't stop to speak to anyone, not even the nurse whose job it is to note Keli's discharge on her file. The nurse realises Keli and her baby have left when she finds Keli's bed and the baby's bassinette empty, and the paperwork and all of Keli's belongings gone. Keli doesn't have a baby capsule. No one came into the hospital to take her home and she didn't ask anyone to call her a taxi. She had quietly slipped out of the hospital, her newborn daughter in her arms, without any of the nurses seeing her.

Baby Tegan was due to have a blood sample taken that morning for what is known as a Guthrie test, which checks for congenital illnesses such as cystic fibrosis. This is what the consent form, left with Keli, was for. Also yet to be done before Keli left the hospital was the final weighing and identification of her daughter. The nurse had spoken to Keli about these things the day before when Keli made her request to leave. However, the nurse did also say that once her baby had been examined by the doctor and deemed medically fit for discharge, Keli was officially free to go.

The nurse's eyes run over the file. Keli's midwife, a woman named Julie Melville, would have to organise for the Guthrie blood test to be done. The nurse calls the hospital closest to the home address Keli has given them to arrange for a follow-up home visit by a hospital midwife in a couple of days to make sure the test and the other checks are carried out. The nurse finishes making her notes, closes the slim file on Keli and Tegan Lane and continues her busy day.

At 4 pm that day a groom stands at the front of a church in Manly waiting for his bride.

All the guests are assembled, chatting quietly and waving to each other. The groom knows he is expected to wait for a little while, but they had agreed that she wouldn't be too late.

Nonetheless, standing in front of such a crowd of family and friends naturally makes him a little jittery. What if by some horrible chance she decides not to show up? He knows this isn't going to happen, but he's nervous anyway.

Like every other couple they know, Wally and Di are spending a small fortune on their wedding video. It happens to be a beautiful sunny day. Earlier, the videographer took shots of the beach, even aerial shots over Manly, before taking footage of the guests taking their seats in the church. As the camera pans around it captures two of those guests, a young man and woman walking hand in hand down the aisle. The couple then sidle down a pew and stop to face each other, the man looking directly at his partner as she slides a pair of sunglasses up over the top of her hair, before they sit down.

The young man is Duncan. Unlike what Keli had told the nurses at Auburn Hospital forty-eight hours earlier, he is not overseas. He has been out of Sydney, but only as far as Yass, his hometown, where he has been playing in a country rugby tournament. He has made a special return trip to Sydney to be at the wedding today, managing to squeeze in a game of golf that morning. The young woman next to him, looking calm and collected in her white suit and heels, is Keli. He and Keli have been invited to the wedding because the groom used to be one Duncan's rugby coaches before Duncan made it to the professional ranks of league. The bride knows Keli, too, having babysat her once or twice when she was a kid. Nevertheless, even though the invitation was made out to both Keli and Duncan, they were really only invited because of Duncan, despite the power of the Lanes' social pull in Manly.

Not only has Keli arrived without Tegan, it's as if her daughter doesn't exist. There are no hints or clues that, two days earlier, all alone and on the other side of the city, she had given birth to a baby. There is also nothing to show that, since leaving the hospital that same morning with her infant daughter, Keli had travelled for over an hour before arriving alone at her parents' house. There is only Keli's calm demeanour as she waits for the marriage ceremony to start. For now she is simply another guest at another wedding in Manly, about the third this year within Keli and Duncan's group of friends. But as all of Sydney and the rest of the country will learn nine years later, somehow, during the past few hours, baby Tegan, whose name Keli wrote for the first and final time on the Medicare form she'd filled out that morning, has disappeared, never to be seen again.

Two days later, on Monday 16 September, the phone at the nurses' station in Auburn's maternity ward rings.

'Oh, hello, it's Keli Lane here. I gave birth last week.'

The nurse looks up Keli's file. 'Ah, yes. You are due to have a visit from the home visit midwifery service in the next couple of days. It's just to make sure the heel-prick blood sample is taken from the baby for an important routine test, to check the little one is feeding, weeing and pooing OK –'

'Yes, look, could you cancel that home visit? My homebirth midwife is going to take care of all those things,' says Keli.

The nurse agrees, but is perplexed. Midwives in charge of homebirths often take care of all the postnatal care, but she has never experienced a midwife leaving it up to her client to ring up the hospital to cancel a routine home health-service visit.

'All right, Keli, I'll pass on your request,' answers the nurse and hangs up. 'What an appalling midwife that woman has,' she thinks to herself.

7

A THIRD BABY ARRIVES –
BUT WHERE IS TEGAN?

As far as the people in Keli's life can tell, Keli ends 1996 on a high. She is invited to Duncan's brother Ben's wedding, yet another sign his family see her as part of Duncan's future. She and some of the other guests party hard that night, drinking until 5 am before stumbling home. There is also a lot of talk about a renewed push to have women's water polo included in the 2000 Olympics. The next four years look so promising for Keli.

But in 1997 things start to go wrong in the pool. Keli plays for Balmain in the club finals, helping her club beat Sydney University to take the premiership in the women's competition for the first time since 1974, the year before Keli was born, but it isn't enough to take her to the next level. She is dropped from the senior state side. Keli also isn't chosen for the FINA Women's World Cup. Once again she finds herself sitting poolside while Taryn and Bronwyn play for Australia that year. In October it's announced that women's water polo is going to be included in the 2000 Olympics. Keli is thrilled at the news. She isn't invited to the official announcement like the members of the Australian team are, but she tells Duncan and her friends she aims to compete in the Olympics. Soon after the announcement, the Australian Institute of Sport selects a squad of Australia's first women's water polo Olympic hopefuls. Keli misses out. The coaches and selectors do not consider Keli to be an Olympic contender, but Keli refuses to give up. She writes a letter to the College of Physical Education asking if she can take a year and a half off from her studies so she can concentrate on making the Australian team.

Duncan's professional league career also fails to take off. After being dropped from the premiership competition to the Metro Cup competition during his first year playing for Canterbury in 1996, he isn't offered another contract in 1997. It's clear Duncan isn't going to make it like his brothers Simon and Ben. Like many players at the end of their elite footy career, Duncan looks overseas for his last few playing opportunities. Through his old coach at the Manly rugby club he secures a tour with the New South Wales union side to Scotland in October and November 1997. It's a success, and in early December Duncan leaves again for Scotland to play in a local team for three months. After the disappointment of his brief league career, Duncan is pleased to discover he is still a sought after first-grade union player. During his three months in Scotland he plays in a Five Nations International tournament against Ireland. He's also asked to play for the Australian B-grade Sevens side in Fiji in mid March in 1998 before returning to play for the first-grade Manly side for the 1998 season.

Just before Duncan leaves for Scotland for the first time in 1997, he and Keli attend the wedding of Charmaine and John. The bride and groom met at the Manly rugby club, just like Keli and Duncan, and had dated for the same length of time. But marriage is not on the cards for Keli – in fact, Charmaine and John's wedding will be one of the last times she and Duncan go out together as a couple. Once Duncan takes off overseas they keep up the façade of a long distance relationship for a little while but it's wishful thinking on Keli's part.

While playing in the Five Nations International tournament Duncan meets a pretty, slim, curly-haired woman named Karen. When he comes back to Sydney in March 1998 for a few days before taking off to play in Fiji he tells Keli he has met someone else. He doesn't tell her that he is bringing his new girlfriend back to Sydney in a few months' time, but once the rugby season starts and Duncan comes back to play for Manly, everyone notices the new girl on his arm.

Keli is devastated and she tells her friends about her broken heart. Some of her old friends, like Kati, and her newer ones, like Lisa whom Keli met at the Australian College of Physical Education, never liked Duncan much. In their eyes he is arrogant and always out for number one. But they really like Keli and are happy to listen to her sorrow, even though both privately think Keli is well rid of him. Keli also tells a colleague at Ravenswood about how she has to go to Duncan's house to retrieve her things, one last unhappy chore to mark the end of his love for her.

On top of losing Duncan, 1998 sees more stagnation in Keli's water polo career, although Keli is determined not to admit it. She plays well for Balmain in the club competitions, and is picked for the senior state side, but once again she fails to make the Australian side. After years of training most days a week, even when so many of her peers had given up, Keli still hasn't made it to the top. Still, Keli refuses to stop trying. Her studies remain on hold as she prepares for the national tournament in Noosa in February 1999, her final chance to make the Australian team. Keli, playing for Balmain, is knocked out of contention in the first round of the selection process at the Noosa nationals. While Taryn and Bronwyn are selected, Keli flies back to Sydney dejected. Her Olympic dream is over.

Keli's closest friends, Melinda and Kati, are full of sympathy for Keli. 'What a rotten year you're having,' says Kati as they sit in the pub, helping Keli drown her sorrow. 'First Duncan does the dirty and now this.'

But despite Keli's heartache, all three can honestly agree that Keli's job is fantastic. Keli loves being part of Ravenswood, and she can now direct all her energies towards the school and finishing her studies. Keli also has her busy Manly social life to distract her. Melinda and Brandon are getting married and Keli is to be a bridesmaid. She throws Melinda a hen's night in the Lane's backyard, with guests such as Kati making it a night of fun for her and Melinda's closest mates. On the big day, Keli stands for photos among the flowers arranged by Charmaine, and walks down the aisle partnered by groomsman and Charmaine's husband, John. Her friends sitting in the pews quietly observe that Keli has gained a lot of weight. They know she's no longer training six or more times a week. But Keli is still getting over losing Duncan and her chance to be an Olympian, they reason. Surely she deserves a break from trying to be perfect.

Keli's size isn't only noticed at Melinda and Brandon's wedding. One night at the surf club, Duncan's mother, Julie, sees Keli. Julie notices Keli is wearing a miniskirt, a poor choice considering Keli's thicker than usual waist. Julie hesitates for a few seconds before approaching her. Duncan and Karen are also having a few drinks at the club, so saying hello is going to be awkward. Keli ignores Duncan and the girl he left her for and focuses on telling Julie about her wonderful full-time position at Ravenswood.

But Keli's heartbreak over Duncan and not making the Olympics is just the tip of the iceberg. There is a huge secret in Keli's life in 1999, one she doesn't tell any of her friends or family. The bulge under her bridesmaid's dress and her miniskirt is another unwanted pregnancy.

Keli pushes her luggage into the overhead locker and takes a seat. In February she'd flown to Queensland surrounded by nervous Olympic hopefuls, but this time she flies alone.

Once again Keli has discovered she is pregnant well past the three-month point. In fact, as she sits on the plane waiting for take-off, Keli is six and a half months' pregnant. Keli doesn't want to give birth a third time, so she is taking action. Days before boarding the flight she booked herself into an abortion clinic in Brisbane known throughout Australia for performing second trimester terminations. She told the clinic that by the time of her appointment she'll be twenty-four weeks' pregnant, right on the cut-off point beyond which even they won't be able to help her.

Keli catches a taxi from the airport to the clinic, sitting silently in the muggy Queensland heat. Whether Keli realises she is over twenty-five weeks' pregnant or not, the doctor quickly discovers the truth when he examines her.

'I'm sorry Miss Lane. We cannot carry out the procedure,' he tells her. Keli has no choice but to catch the plane home, knowing that once again she will have to give birth.

A couple of months after her failed attempt to have a termination, Keli begins to prepare for the birth. Keli turns up at a hospital unannounced. However, unlike her first two births, Keli has been to this hospital before. It's Ryde Hospital, where three years earlier she had received some treatment for pain and tried unsuccessfully several times to have Tegan prematurely induced.

Just like the others, the arrival of her third baby is set to be a lonely affair. 'I'm living in London and I've flown out to give birth here in Sydney,' Keli tells admission staff to explain why she is all alone. 'Both of my parents and my partner, Duncan, are still in London.'

Staff punch Keli's name into the hospital computer. The details of Keli's earlier visits to the hospital and the fact that she gave birth at Auburn Hospital come up on the screen. 'So this is your second child?' the nurse handling Keli's admission asks. 'In 1996 you had a baby at Auburn Hospital, just after presenting a few times here?'

'Ah, yes. My daughter is here with me in Sydney,' Keli says cheerfully. 'She flew out with me, but no other family members.'

'Right,' says the nurse, noting Keli's answers, which will be read out in Tegan's murder trial eleven years later. 'Now, do you want to breastfeed this baby?'

'I'm not sure,' says Keli. 'I have no problems breastfeeding. I breastfed my daughter for six months, but I haven't decided if I want to do it again,' she says.

'OK. Now, who has been looking after your prenatal care?'

'The Royal Women's Hospital in Brisbane.'

A week passes before Keli comes back to Ryde Hospital. Nurses call the Royal Women's Hospital in Brisbane, but after extensive questioning and searches there is no record of a Keli Lane there. Nonetheless, soon Keli calls Ryde in the early hours of the morning to say she is going into labour. She arrives and within a few hours gives birth. The baby is healthy and there are no complications. Keli is teary afterwards but that is normal for any new mum and staff are not concerned. The day after the birth, Keli cuddles and breastfeeds her newborn happily in her hospital bed.

Since early December in 1996, about three months after Tegan's birth and disappearance, Keli has owned a mobile phone. Back then they were rare but by 1999 they are more common, though still a status symbol. Keli always has hers with her, and being in hospital after just giving birth is no exception. The day after the birth, with her new baby sleeping beside her, Keli sits upright and makes a call. It's to her friend Lisa.

'Hi there,' says Keli casually. 'What are you up to?'

'Oh, not much,' says Lisa, completely unaware of where Keli is calling from or that she has just had a baby. 'Hey, I'm going to buy new luggage for the trip.'

'Yeah, I might, too,' answers Keli. She and Lisa are going on a six week holiday in the UK and Europe together, beginning in December. They are going to meet up with Kati and some old family friends of the Lanes. 'Maybe something with wheels.'

Having finished her chat about holiday plans with Lisa, Keli hangs up. She now has to make a very serious call. Keli wants to put her newborn baby up for adoption as quickly as possible. Rather than spending time talking about her decision to a nurse, Keli decides to call an adoption agency herself. She calls Anglicare, a different adoption agency to the one she used four years ago for her first secret baby. Adoption worker Virginia Fung answers Keli's call.

'I want to put my baby up for adoption. The baby's father left me when he found out I was five months' pregnant,' Keli tells Virginia in a quiet voice. 'I live in London but I flew out to Australia to have my baby. I'm all alone and I have to go back to London to work at the end of the month.'

Virginia calls a social worker who works for Ryde Hospital who quickly goes to Keli's bed. Through her tears, Keli tells the social worker that she's finding it hard to be away from her family in the UK. She also doesn't want any of the staff at the hospital to know she's putting her baby up for adoption because she fears they will judge her. As Keli wants to leave the hospital without her baby this is impossible, but the social worker assures her everything will be done as discreetly as possible.

The next day Virginia is by Keli's bedside. 'I found out I was pregnant at five months, immediately before I told Duncan,' says Keli, naming her ex-boyfriend as the father, even though they've been broken up for over twelve months. 'Not that it makes any difference. I couldn't ever consider having an abortion,' Keli says. She also says her parents know about her baby and are ashamed of her.

Virginia doesn't know about Ryde Hospital's record of Tegan's birth. In the murder trial in 2010 the hospital social worker will claim she left a message about the details of Tegan's birth for the Anglicare case worker but, for whatever reason, Virginia doesn't know Keli has given birth before at this point. And Keli says nothing about Tegan, nor her first baby, nor her failed attempt to have this third baby aborted. Before leaving, Virginia brings the social worker to Keli's bedside to quietly help organise Keli's departure from the hospital as soon as possible and to arrange for her newborn to be left in the hospital's care. Later that day, Virginia is by Keli's bedside again just to make sure she is OK.

'I so wish I was able to keep my baby, but I can't,' Keli cries.

Keli leaves Ryde Hospital in a hurry, not waiting for a standard antenatal blood test to be taken. Her newborn is admitted into the hospital nursery awaiting collection by the adoption agency, which will organise the foster care of the little one while the adoption process is completed. Before the baby is picked up the next day, Keli visits and cuddles her infant in the hospital nursery, tears rolling down her cheeks. She leaves gifts for the foster parents.

Virginia is always careful to note every little detail about her cases. In her records for that day she writes:

Keli describes her baby as perfect. It is evident that Keli loves her little one. Baby roomed in with her after the delivery . . . An early discharge nurse will visit Keli at home tomorrow for postnatal check up . . . Keli stated she was more concerned about her baby's wellbeing than her own. It is so clear that she has bonded strongly with her newborn. I inquired whether she would like to consider keeping her child, but Keli feels at the present she is unable to care for a baby the way she would like to. Since Keli found out about the pregnancy she did not want to have a termination as she feels her baby would be able to bring joy into someone's life.

In the meantime, nurses attempting to check that Keli is recovering well from the birth discover the phone number and address of the house where Keli said she was staying with friends are false. One midwife knocks on the door of this address, which is Duncan's old place in Gladesville. In 1998, Duncan sold the house to his brother Simon and now a friend is living there as a tenant. All the hospital midwife knows is that the man who answered the door said Keli hadn't lived there for eighteen months. Virginia meets with Keli at the adoption agency and tells her what the nurse was told when she knocked on the door, but Keli insists the address is correct. She tells Virginia the people staying at the house are friends of friends who hadn't seen her prior to her admission to hospital. Later that day Virginia tries to call Keli on her mobile, but it's switched off.

From that time onwards Keli makes herself very hard to reach. Virginia, too, quickly realises the landline phone number Keli has given her is false. Keli starts to leave messages on Virginia's message bank at work after hours, usually to cancel meetings with very little notice, and when Virginia calls Keli on her mobile number at the times when Keli has requested she calls her, it is again mostly switched off. After a couple of weeks Virginia is able to arrange an access visit for Keli to see her baby in foster care. During the visit Virginia takes Polaroid pictures of Keli's baby and gives them to her, along with the baby's hospital ankle identification band, cot card and an antenatal ultrasound image.

While travelling back from the access visit, Keli tells Virginia that the baby's father, Duncan, has frozen their joint account and that she has had to see a solicitor about it.

'I just don't feel like I know Duncan anymore,' says Keli wistfully to Virginia. 'He used to tell me how wonderful I was. We did everything together. I helped him make decisions, with his budgeting and around the house. He has really changed. I hear he has a new girlfriend already, some girl named Karen.'

For the next two and a half weeks Keli makes herself scarce, continuing to keep her mobile switched off while she leaves messages on Virginia's work answering machine after hours, and sending her faxes. In one phone message Keli says she is having problems with her visa as Duncan has claimed they are no longer de facto and Keli needs to go to Canberra to sort it all out. Keli then sends Virginia a fax which claims she must leave for London within weeks. Meanwhile, Keli's baby is growing fast. The foster mother tells Virginia they have had to buy a car seat as the infant has already outgrown the car capsule and they use a stroller rather than a pram. Not that the foster mother is complaining. 'The baby is just gorgeous,' she enthuses to Virginia. 'People stop us in the street and say so.'

The foster care agreement for Keli's baby is only for a month and it's about to expire. Virginia has been in touch with the nurses about the false addresses and landline phone numbers Keli has given. The nurses tell Virginia the hospital has records of Keli being heavily pregnant several years ago. Virginia is beginning to suspect that Keli isn't being honest with her about a few things, but she is very sincere about her role in helping mothers without making moral judgments. She will help any woman regardless of how they became pregnant and why they want to put their baby up for adoption. Above all, Virginia gives the women she helps the benefit of any doubt. She wonders if the difficulty in contacting Keli and her constant delays are in fact stalling tactics on Keli's part, a reticence to move forward with her decision.

Virginia asks Keli whether she honestly wants to go ahead with the adoption. Keli says yes and agrees to meet Virginia the next day with her passport and other proof of her identification so she can sign the adoption papers. However, the next day Keli doesn't show up and her mobile is switched off again. Virginia tries the phone number of a supportive friend Keli has given her but finds it's another false number. The day after the missed meeting Keli sends a fax to Virginia claiming she had to go to Canberra to sort out her visa issues again. Virginia notices that Keli is sending her faxes from post offices and newsagencies in Sydney.

By now the foster care agreement has expired and Keli's baby is stranded with no legal status. In the eyes of the law, the baby has been abandoned, so New South Wales Department of Community Services child protection officer John Borovnik, who is based in the Blue Mountains, is assigned to the case. John sets about extending the baby's care arrangements in the Children's Court while Virginia tries for a week to contact Keli. Virginia also tells John what has happened so far. John suspects Keli is a mother who is intentionally abandoning her baby, even if she does bring presents and cry during foster care visits. He sets about ringing Ryde Hospital, the Department of Births, Deaths and Marriages and the British Consulate to verify Keli's story. A nurse from Ryde Hospital tells John she remembers something about Keli giving birth in 1996, but she will have to check the records. He also soon finds out that Keli has not travelled from London to Sydney in that year, nor in the last, and tells Virginia.

Both Virginia and John are keen to confirm whether Keli has other children – not so they can prove she is lying to them, rather so that Keli's baby can find its siblings if they want to when they are old enough to make that choice. John waits for a written reply from Ryde Hospital and thinks about other enquiries he could make. When Virginia is finally able to speak to Keli again, she asks if the child Keli is putting up for adoption is her first. 'Yes, Virginia,' Keli says. However, up in the Blue Mountains, John receives Keli's Ryde Hospital records, which confirm what the nurse told him over the phone. He leaves a phone message for Virginia saying that it's quite possible Keli has a three-year-old child and he is going to track down other records to make absolutely sure.

Virginia decides to not raise the issue again with Keli until John confirms Keli has in fact given birth before.

Five days later Virginia meets with Keli, who reports she is furious with Duncan as their joint account is still frozen. Keli claims she is due to fly to London the day before the adoption papers are due to be signed, but says she will delay the flight to sign them. She also promises to call Virginia later with Duncan's number in the UK but doesn't. Virginia begins her own search. She remembers Keli telling her that Duncan used to play rugby for Manly before they moved to London together, so Virginia contacts the Manly club. She is told that Duncan is in Sydney and playing first-grade for Manly this season. Virginia realises that Keli might be lying about Duncan, the father of her baby, being in London. Even if Keli has her reasons for not involving him, Virginia needs to obtain the father's signature so the adoption can go ahead with minimal complications.

Virginia writes a letter to Duncan via the Manly rugby club, asking him to contact her immediately 'in the matter regarding Keli Lane'. Duncan and his girlfriend Karen are living in Manly while Duncan plays in the first-grade competition. Days later, when Duncan has just finished a training session at Manly Oval, a club member walks out to the sideline and hands him the envelope. Curious as to what it's all about, Duncan rips it open. What he reads makes absolutely no sense. He takes the letter home to Karen, who is living with him, to see what she can make of it.

While Duncan spends a week deciding what to do about the letter from Virginia, the day that Keli is due to sign the adoption papers arrives. Without warning, Keli fails to show up, leaving only a message after hours on Virginia's message bank claiming she had to urgently find some work that day as she was running out of money. As usual, Keli's mobile is switched off. Virginia calls John to give him two real phone numbers for Keli that she has tracked down – one is for Rob and Sandy Lane's address, where Virginia is beginning to suspect Keli has been living all along, and the other is for Ravenswood School for Girls. She got Keli's parents' number when she called a false number Keli had given her but the woman who answered, a Manly resident, knew who Keli was and where she lived. Virginia got the Ravenswood number from the faxes Keli had started occasionally sending her from the school.

In the meantime, Duncan has another unsettling experience. A very close friend of his named Clayton wants to meet with him to talk about some strange events that have happened recently at Duncan's old place. Clayton lives at the house in Gladesville, having moved in not long after Duncan sold it to Simon in 1998. When Duncan meets him, Clayton hands Duncan an envelope with photos of a baby inside. Written on the back of these photos are the words 'Keli Lane'. Virginia had posted some photos of Keli's baby that she'd left behind after a meeting, using the address Keli had given her for where she was staying in Sydney. Clayton also tells him a woman who said she was a nurse had recently knocked on the door, asking if Keli was home.

Around this time Virginia meets with Keli and tells her she has sent a letter to Duncan via the Manly rugby club. Keli is angry that Virginia did so without telling her first. 'I don't want everyone knowing my business!' Keli yells, only calming down when Virginia reads out the letter and explains it was sent in a plain envelope. Virginia also tells Keli that she and the Ryde Hospital nurses are beginning to suspect Keli isn't staying at the Gladesville address.

'Oh, those so-called friends of mine found out I had put my baby up for adoption and they threw me out the house,' Keli replies. 'I came home one day and found my belongings on the street. I'm now staying with my other friend, Lisa.'

'I hope you aren't feeling pressured into going ahead with this adoption,' says Virginia. Keli replies that she doesn't feel pressured, confirming again that she really does want to go ahead with it. Virginia advises Keli she'll need to meet with Duncan to talk about what to do next. 'It's going to be really hard for me to meet him because Karen will probably be there,' says Keli as she reluctantly agrees.

A few days later, Duncan calls Virginia. He is barely able to believe his ears when Virginia tells him that Keli recently had a baby, names him as the father and is putting the child up for adoption. Still in shock, Duncan says that he and Keli had broken up more than a year before. Virginia asks him whether he has been living in London with Keli.

'Until a few months ago I was living overseas, but not in London with Keli,' he answers, his mind reeling. 'I thought she has always lived in Manly with her parents.'

Virginia can't tell Duncan any more about the situation because Keli wants to speak with him first. Duncan quickly calls Keli and arranges to meet her that night. Karen is very frightened and suspicious about Keli's motivations and she doesn't want Keli in their home, so the three of them meet on the street outside. Keli says things that don't make sense, leaving Duncan and Karen to stand and stare at her, open mouthed.

At first Keli says there is no baby, that she'd had an abortion a year and a half ago and that Virginia is her counsellor. Duncan tells her he has seen photos of a baby with her name written on them. 'You're not supposed to know about the baby,' Keli says, strangely, contradicting her story. Disturbed,

Duncan calls Virginia the next day to say Keli has denied there is a baby, and that even if there is one, he insists he can't be the father. 'Keli is different now to how she was when I dated her,' he adds. Virginia calls Keli to tell her what Duncan said.

'I guess you know,' Keli says very quietly. 'He isn't the father. It would have been better if I'd broken the news first. He was furious last night.'

'Do you think he has a right to be?' asks Virginia.

'Yes. But I felt that if I told the truth no one would help me,' replies Keli.

'I feel sad that you felt you had to lie to me,' says Virginia. 'You've had so many opportunities to tell me the truth. I'm just here to help. I don't care how you became pregnant.'

'I wanted to tell you the truth every time we met, but you kept asking questions about Duncan, so I felt like I had to tell you more and more,' answers Keli. 'Where do we go from here?'

'Let's have a fresh start,' says Virginia. 'Just tell me the truth.'

The next day Virginia speaks to Keli again, and notes that she doesn't seem to be embarrassed about having been caught lying or offer any real explanation as to why she lied about Duncan being the father. Concerned about the state of Keli's mental health, Virginia tells a colleague that she isn't sure Keli is capable of caring for her baby if she cancels the adoption. She also wants Keli to be psychiatrically assessed to make sure she is fit to give legally valid consent for the adoption.

Nearly a month later, after more futile attempts to contact her, Virginia meets Keli at a café just a few train stops away from Ravenswood School. She gives Keli some new pictures of her baby and tells her the adoption must happen soon as the baby is becoming very attached to its foster parents. Keli looks at the photos, complains that it's too noisy to talk in the café and asks they meet later that morning at Virginia's office. Virginia arrives only to find another message from Keli saying she can't make it as she is having difficulty obtaining a car. She calls the owner of the café where they met, one that Keli chose but told Virginia she rarely went to. The café owner said he hadn't seen 'the PE teacher' since that morning. His comment, combined with Keli sending the odd fax from Ravenswood School for Girls, leads Virginia to confirm that Keli is probably working there.

Several days later Virginia stands waiting for Keli at the gates of Ravenswood. Keli sees her and ushers her into the school chapel on the other side of a quiet road. Virginia asks her why she lied about Duncan. 'I thought it would be better for my child to know that it came from a long term relationship,' answers Keli. 'I hardly know the father and I'm embarrassed. Duncan and I were in love once. If he knew what was happening to me, he would have supported me.'

'But what if your child grows up thinking Duncan is their father and then one day finds out he isn't?'

Keli doesn't reply, but Virginia persists. 'Who is the father, Keli?'

'It's a guy who dumped me when I found out I was five months' pregnant,' answers Keli despondently. 'His name is Aaron Williams. He is a successful banker who works for Barclays in London. I hardly know him.' Keli continues on with the story that she and her parents live in London, but adds that they have cut off their support for her, so she plans to stay with a friend when she returns to London. Virginia listens to this, knowing that Keli is lying about living in London when she really lives in Manly, but she doesn't confront her about it since there are more important things she needs to ask her.

'Keli, does your baby have any brothers or sisters?'

'No,' says Keli.

'So this is your first baby?'

'Yes.'

Virginia sighs. She tells the young woman standing in front of her that she feels she is under enormous mental strain and advises Keli to have a psychological evaluation if she wants to continue with the adoption process. 'If you don't, the adoption process can still go ahead, but your baby will become a ward of the state and you won't be able to choose the parents,' Virginia explains. Keli agrees to have an evaluation done.

Another month passes, during which Keli is deemed fit to give her consent. Now that it's established that Keli is working at Ravenswood, she and Virginia meet again in the school chapel. Virginia is prepared to let Keli's lies about living in the UK go unchallenged just so long as the adoption proceeds smoothly. Keli says she wants another access visit to her baby. They travel to Penrith Plaza to meet the baby and the foster parents, whose own grandchildren are very protective of Keli's little one. Keli has bought lots of clothes and toys for her baby. She cuddles her infant and cries when it's time to say goodbye. Soon afterwards, Keli keeps her appointment at the adoption agency to choose her baby's parents from the profiles and is particularly taken with one prospective parent who says he doesn't like to keep secrets. After looking at a photo of this man and his wife, Keli bursts into tears and says they are the ones.

But that same day, John Borovnik, the DoCS child protection officer, receives a health department record of Keli giving birth to a girl three years before, the second of three confirmations he has requested about this earlier birth. He leaves Virginia a voice message with the news. A couple of days later Virginia receives another phone call from a different

DoCS officer, one who works in the adoptions branch, who tells Virginia that Keli put a child up for adoption in 1995.

However, both John Borovnik and Virginia Fung are unaware that this new information points to the existence of two previous children of Keli's. Mistakenly, they believe they are all talking about the same one.

8

CRYING IN THE CHAPEL

Ravenswood School for Girls sits in the far North Shore of Sydney, where busy freeways branch into streets lined with large homes and leafy green trees. Inside the school's gates is a world of order and prosperity. It has expanses of lawn, neatly kept gardens and networks of buildings and cottages where students practise debating, sing in choirs, play in string quartets and take their lessons. It costs parents thousands of dollars a year to send their daughters here. Besides the arts, academia and sport, it's a place where the unwritten rules of upper-class behaviour are taught.

Having attended a public school would have marked Keli as an outsider to the less friendly students and staff there, but she has mixed for long enough with the rugby union crowd to know how to fit in. Since beginning as a casual water polo coach in 1996, a month before Tegan's secret birth and disappearance, Keli put a lot of effort into being liked.

Chatty and encouraging to everyone, her hard work paid off – at the beginning of 1999 Keli was offered a full-time coaching position. Then she applied for and was given the role of coordinator for the primary school girls' physical education. Keli and her parents are extremely proud. At the age of twenty-four she's teaching at a school that prizes the very highest standards of success. She's seen as a winner.

But now, in late 1999, Keli is standing in the school chapel, sobbing. Facing her is kind-hearted Virginia. She and Virginia have met in the chapel a couple of times now, including when Keli told her the father of the baby was a man she hardly knew called Aaron Williams. The day before, Virginia had called Keli at work to say she needed to talk to her urgently. Keli insisted Virginia tell her what was so urgent over the phone, so Virginia told her that a DoCS officer had discovered she had put a baby up for adoption in 1995. After a moment of silence Keli had mumbled something inaudible, and then said, 'Yes, I have met the parents and they are lovely people,' before agreeing to meet with Virginia in the school chapel again.

Standing in muted light coloured red, blue and gold by the stained glass windows, Keli knows Virginia and DoCS have discovered her first secret baby, but she isn't sure if they have discovered Tegan. 'I was hoping this would happen,' Keli cries, adding that she's glad she's no longer weighed down by her secret.

'Why didn't you tell me?' asks Virginia.

'I didn't think anyone would help me if they knew I had made another mistake. My parents know about my first baby and they are so disappointed in me,' says Keli. 'My father used to be a policeman and he is very judgemental.'

'How are you coping?' says Virginia.

'I was so anxious about our meeting today I was sick three times this morning. I don't have much faith in myself,' says Keli.

'It isn't easy to have two children adopted out,' says Virginia soothingly. 'You might need professional help to get you through this time.'

'Sure, but I don't want to take any prescribed medication. I want to learn a drug-free way of coping,' answers Keli. 'I also don't want to rely on alcohol. I've seen what it does to people.'

As Keli and Virginia stand in the chapel, the third and final confirmation of another birth sought by John Borovnik – Auburn Hospital's actual record – arrives in his Blue Mountains office. The next day John speaks to the officer from the DoCS adoptions branch. Up until now they were under the impression that the combined records meant they had unearthed the existence of one other baby, but as they compare notes again they realise Keli has definitely had two previous children – one born in 1995 and one born in 1996. But while the one born in 1995 was adopted out, there is no record of the girl born in 1996 being adopted and Keli is pretending she never existed.

John has never met Keli Lane. He hasn't seen what a nicely dressed, respectable girl she is, never witnessed how affectionately she cuddled her babies, or how sadly she wept. All that directs John is his experience as a child protection officer, which has put him in touch with families at the very bottom of the social heap. He has learnt to recognise patterns of behaviour that spell disaster, and that is exactly what he is seeing in the black and white facts on his desk in front of him. John picks up the phone and calls Keli on the number that Virginia has said Keli will always answer, Ravenswood.

'Keli, it's John from DoCs here. Did you give birth to a child at Auburn Hospital in 1996?'

'No,' answers Keli.

'Did you give birth to a child in 1995?'

'Yes.'

'Are you sure you didn't give birth to a child in 1996?'

'Yes, I am,' answers Keli.

'Keli, I have the hospital records right in front of me,' says John. Keli is lying about a very serious matter. Not being straight about who the father of a child is may be a forgivable lie in Virginia's eyes, but the denial of the existence of a baby that has definitely been born sends loud alarm bells ringing in John's ears. 'I have no choice but to call the police,' he tells her.

'No, please don't,' says Keli, but John is firm.

While John sets about getting clearance from his supervisors to contact police, he receives a fax from Keli asking him not to contact anyone about her case, including the police, without notifying her first. A day or two later, while sitting in her office, Virginia also hears her fax machine whir into action. It is a fax from the PE office at Ravenswood. With widening eyes she reads the page-and-a-half long fax that Keli has written:

Dear Virginia,
Firstly, thank you for all of your time, your patience and your understanding, even though I have not been entirely honest with you. I'm glad now that I can stop telling half-truths and lies and perhaps move on with my life. You are the first person in a long time who has reached out to help me without me feeling like I was being judged. It must be very hard for you to understand what has been

going on and why I have done the things I've done and I'm not sure I can give you all the answers. Over all of these weeks my main concern was making sure my baby was safe and happy with a loving and secure home.

So where do I start? I'm not sure. My life for the last six years has been a nightmare and one I've had to live with mainly by myself. I have been let down so many times by people [whom] I thought loved me and who would support me but obviously I was wrong. Many people, including my family, have disowned me and looking at the situation I guess it's not hard to figure out why. There were three children. Obviously I can't lie any more as the paperwork is there. The middle child lives with a family in Perth although I have not had contact with them for a long time. They befriended me just before I had her and supported us. I am not able to give you many details as I am not sure of them myself. If my story isn't unusual enough already! I know you probably can't believe it but I know somehow that you know I am now being honest with you. I am aware that this does not have anything to do with my first or third baby's placement and is really not your issue but I feel you should know and perhaps pass these details onto John.

My family is not aware of all the details surrounding the last six years. I moved around a bit trying to settle down and find some sort of stability and security. It would kill both of them to know the full story and I don't see how letting them know would improve things. I think I would just make things worse. Perhaps in the future we could become closer again and reform the ties I broke with them so long ago, I'm not sure. I would like to see them when I go over in December but I'm not sure if they'll see me or not.

I've tried to improve things by finishing uni and working. I think I am a very good teacher, surprisingly enough. I wish I could learn as well as the students I have. I feel useful here at school and people have trust in me which feels good. I would never break that trust with them. Before all of this I was actually a very honest and trustworthy person. It makes me sick that I changed that.

Why did I? I didn't have any support any time I was in this situation. I felt very isolated and alone. People dropped off me when they realised that I was going to relinquish the babies. How could I do it? Society says that this is wrong, society says that people who do this must be mad, slutty or cruel. I just don't agree. Being able to have a beautiful, healthy child is a great gift. Being able to give someone else the opportunity when they can't is a gift as well. I don't think my behaviour itself is actually that bad, it's just the secrecy and dishonesty that comes with it.

I live with these decisions and thoughts every day. I hurt mentally, emotionally and physically every day. I have to live with this for the rest of my life. I constantly feel sick, I sleep two to three hours a night, I'm always on edge, I wish the phone would never ring again. I'm sick of bad news and I'm tired of hiding things from people. I worry constantly that people who don't know me or the situation will find out and I will lose more people. I feel terrible that I have named people who I said know the situation and really they have no knowledge of it at all. I can't even fathom what it must have been like for them – especially Duncan – to have someone call them out of nowhere and ask them questions that are so personal when they have no idea what was going on.

I think I was hoping that somehow they would help me. I was just struggling for support.

I guess I knew all along that it would all come out in the open and in some ways I'm glad it has. It has given me some sort of platform to rebuild from and obviously has taught me a huge lesson, even though I should have learnt the first time. I want to move on. I want to trust people again and I want to be trusted. I want people to see me for my positives, not all the negatives. I want to be known for my constructive efforts not my mistakes.

The future? I think it will only improve as I start to rebuild my support system. I am not trying to escape from anything – how could I? I am still going to go overseas to work and take care of myself. Each year things will improve but I will be waiting for the time when the children want to see me again. I am looking forward to this time but I know it will be hard.

This is a personal letter to you, Virginia. I feel I owe you something. However, you can pass this onto John for his information. Once again I ask for discretion when dealing with this matter as I am surrounded by people who just don't know. Could you pass on this request to John as well? I don't want to upset, alienate or hurt any more people.

As it is really difficult to talk about these issues at work I prefer you contact me by letter or on my mobile (it will be on all the time). If needed, call me on the home phone number but leave a message for me to call you as I can then get privacy. Best times are between 4 and 6 pm. Could you pass this on to John as well? I hope you are not too shocked but I figure you probably know most of these facts anyway. Thank you for listening. I will speak to you later this afternoon I guess?

The fax finishes with Keli's signature at the bottom. It appears that Keli is confident, or at least hopeful, that her lie to the Ryde Hospital nurses five months earlier that Tegan is with her in Sydney is safe from being discovered by Virginia.

Virginia passes this information to John and continues to move the adoption along, despite knowing Keli is still lying to her about living in London. She sends Keli a letter thanking her for her 'honesty' and saying it can't be easy for Keli to share her feelings about her first secret baby, her third secret baby and 'that other little girl'. They arrange other meetings but Keli doesn't turn up for them. When she does get into contact with Virginia, Keli tells her she is leaving for the UK very soon, so Virginia asks for an address that she can send the life story of her latest baby to, the document the adoptive parents will give to the child when it's old enough to want to know about Keli, its father and siblings, including 'a baby girl' born in 1996 who is believed to have been 'adopted by a family in Western Australia' but nothing else is known about.

Keli gives her an address in the UK. Virginia isn't convinced it is legitimate, but she sends a copy of the life story along with some photos to that address. Not long afterwards she receives a package from Keli containing the latest baby's hospital cot card, its ankle identification bracelet, an antenatal ultrasound and some photos Virginia took and gave Keli at one of the foster care visits. Surprised, Virginia becomes concerned that sending back these things are a sign that Keli might do herself harm. Virginia is unable to contact Keli, so she worries even more. However, weeks later Virginia hears a message left by Keli on her answering machine.

'Hi Virginia. I've received the life story and photos. I'm settling in and everything is fine. Thanks for everything.'

Virginia has no way of knowing exactly where Keli is calling from, but she sounds happy, so Virginia is relieved. She puts all the keepsakes Keli sent back to her in a filing cabinet.

'Smile Keli!' says Lisa from behind the camera as Keli poses in a London street. It's a freezing December day, but they are too excited to care. Keli has managed to extract herself from the adoption and Virginia's gentle but persistent investigation into her life in time for her and Lisa's flight from Sydney. Lisa takes the shot, completely unaware of what has happened in her friend's hidden life in the months leading up to this moment.

9

MANLY POLICE STATION DROPS THE BALL

While Keli's third baby is settling in with its new adoptive parents, and Keli is overseas on her holiday, the police at Katoomba begin to deal with the disappearance of Tegan. John Borovnik gives them the key facts he and Virginia have uncovered during the adoption of Keli's third baby, namely birth and adoption records of her first and third secret babies and the hospital records of Tegan's birth, and Keli's real address in Manly. In early November, a day or so after John approached them, the Katoomba police enter the matter into COPS, the police computer system. They also write a memorandum recommending that Keli be interviewed as soon as possible.

Even with just a fraction of her secret life pieced together, Keli is now exposed as a serial liar. There are concerns that she still may not be telling the truth. Aaron Williams, the man she told Virginia was the father of her third child after admitting she lied about Duncan being the father, cannot be found. Virginia contacted Barclays Bank in London and Sydney and neither had anyone with that name working there. The person Keli listed as her midwife while she was pregnant with Tegan, Julie Melville, is a nurse, but not a registered midwife. They transfer the matter to Manly Police Station so the investigation can get properly underway.

Matt Kehoe is a young detective at Manly Police Station when the Tegan Lane file arrives in late 1999. Despite having only been a plainclothed detective for a short while he has already distinguished himself, and this year has been an outstanding year for him. It kicked off in January with evidence he collected being used in a criminal trial that attracted international press coverage.

In 1998 Louise Sullivan, a Sydney girl, was working as a nanny in the UK when a six-month-old infant she was caring for died in suspicious circumstances. She had been alone with the baby in her employer's home when the baby suddenly had to be rushed to hospital. The infant was suffering from head injuries and died five days later. The coroner found the baby had been shaken to death.

Working under the direction of Scotland Yard, Detective Matt Kehoe set about finding and interviewing families in Sydney who had employed Louise as a nanny. What he found out was that, while she was universally regarded as a sweet young woman, she had a history of being sacked for dangerous incompetence. One mother who had fired Louise described her as 'dazed and confused'. Another sacked her after finding Louise bouncing her baby instead of rocking it to sleep. A third mother described her as being a little 'simple', and was happy to have her around until one day she found her handling her child roughly and saying 'Stop it, stop crying'. Louise was then sacked when the mother caught her violently shaking the baby. Nonetheless, several families told Detective Kehoe their children really liked her.

No one was pre-warned of Louise's ineptitude when she arrived in the UK. She found work as a live-in nanny for the family whose baby she ultimately killed in a moment of panic. The killing was not as a result of maliciousness by twenty-six-year-old Louise. Rather, it was the terrible outcome of having someone of Louise's unusually low intelligence responsible for the wellbeing of an infant. The judge gave her a suspended sentence of fifteen months and allowed her to return to Australia with her parents. Detective Kehoe's role in this sensitive and highly publicised case earned him the rare distinction of being commended for his work by Scotland Yard.

Fellow officers at Manly station don't begrudge Kehoe his success. Ever since he started his career as a foot patrol police officer reporting to Sergeant Rob Lane several years earlier he's been known as a friendly, helpful guy, and when he was promoted to Detective in his mid to late twenties he gained a reputation for being very thorough. The diligent and timely interviewing of witnesses and the collection of evidence Detective Kehoe did for the Louise Sullivan case is typical of all his work.

When Kehoe is assigned the case of Tegan Lane he knows the mother of the infant, Keli, is the daughter of Sergeant Lane. Rob Lane had retired from the force four years earlier, but Kehoe worries there is something not quite right about him working on a matter involving Rob's daughter. Kehoe asks his superiors to take him off Tegan's case, but his request falls on deaf ears.

From the beginning, Kehoe makes the mistake of not recognising that he is dealing with a missing persons case, let alone a suspected homicide. There are a number of reasons for this. For some reason Katoomba police categorised Tegan's case as an 'incident', a sort of catch-all category that doesn't attract attention like the categories of 'missing person' or 'suspected death'. While Rob Lane is no longer working in the station, Kehoe still sees him every week when he visits the newsagency on the Corso that Rob now runs. Kehoe, struggling with Keli's case, doesn't talk to Rob about his missing granddaughter. What Kehoe can see is that Keli comes from a solid family. The thought that she might have hurt Tegan seems ridiculous.

Also, there are major corruption problems within the ranks of Manly station's detectives when Tegan's case arrives, problems that mean young Detective Kehoe is working with no meaningful supervision. The corruption issues are so bad that Manly station is at the centre of a huge investigation code-named Operation Florida. The handful of Manly detectives who will ultimately be jailed for stealing money from drug dealers and other crimes don't yet realise that the New South Wales Crime Commission is quietly collecting evidence against them.

Sergeant Rob Lane never had anything to do with the illegal goings on that were to be the subject of a royal commission less than two years after the case involving his daughter Keli arrived at Manly. Rob was more interested in wielding power in the footy world than in the station, so a lot of what went on there passed him by.

Feeling awkward about possibly embarrassing Rob and his daughter over what essentially might be a private matter, Detective Kehoe treats the matter as something that will hopefully resolve itself without too much police interference.

Because of this, Detective Kehoe will not interview Keli about her missing baby for well over a year and a half, and other kinds of routine and elementary evidence gathering, such as a forensic search of Keli's car, are not carried out. He also doesn't contact Auburn or Ryde Hospital, Virginia Fung or John Borovnik to discover the different stories Keli has told about what happened to Tegan – first, that Keli and Duncan were going to live in London with Tegan; second, that Tegan was in Sydney at the time Keli gave birth to her latest baby and that Keli had breastfed Tegan for six months; and third, Keli's denial of Tegan's existence followed by Keli's fax to Virginia claiming her daughter lived with people Keli barely knew in Perth. Much to the frustration of the state's Chief Coroner and detectives investigating the case years down the track, the finely honed investigative skills of young Detective Kehoe, which have been so exalted, are not put to use in any timely fashion.

Detective Kehoe's few enquiries focus mainly on Duncan and his family. The name of Keli's supposed midwife, Julie Melville, is immediately recognised within the station. She is Duncan's mother.

Detective Kehoe calls her, and Julie is barely able to believe her ears. On top of being told that her son's former girlfriend had given birth to no less than three babies, two during the time she was dating Duncan, Julie is told that she'd been listed by Keli as the midwife of the second baby – the second baby whom police are now searching for. A stunned Julie is only able to confirm that she's known Keli through Duncan since 1994, and that while she hadn't been practising as a midwife at the time of Tegan's birth, Keli knew that Julie had been training to be one.

Detective Kehoe tracks down Duncan, who by this time has moved back to the UK with Karen, and has him interviewed by police over there on 8 February 2000. Still reeling from the knowledge that Keli had given birth to a baby the year before, Duncan is now told that Keli had another child named Tegan in 1996 and that police are having trouble finding her. Duncan appears to be unable to get his head around it. How can Keli have had a baby in 1996? They were dating then so he would have known about it, he tells the officer who interviews him.

Only two other enquiries are made by Kehoe during the whole of 2000. One is to confirm the dates of Keli's enrolment at the Australian College of Physical Education. The other is an unsuccessful attempt to learn if Medicare has any entries for medical services for Tegan. Medicare refuses to hand over that information on privacy grounds and Kehoe doesn't push the issue.

Six years later, when Chief Coroner John Abernethy hands down his finding in this case, he will say that the delay in interviewing Keli will make the task of solving the mystery of Tegan's whereabouts 'incredibly difficult'. But Abernethy will not point the finger at Detective Kehoe. He decides there are bigger questions about what was going on at Manly Police Station and, in his mind, blaming this young officer won't answer them.

In the meantime, Tegan's case quietly sits unsolved, month after month.

The moment Tegan's case lands at Manly Police also marks the beginning of change within the Lane household. A new house guest has arrived.

Peter is the son of a couple Rob and Sandy have known since the 1950s. In fact, Rob dated Peter's mother once when they were both kicking around Manly as teenagers. Peter's family had moved to Suffolk in the UK years ago, and Keli and Lisa visited him and his family during their overseas holiday, just after the adoption of Keli's third secret child. Peter had recently decided to move back to Sydney. He needed a place to stay for a few months until he could find his feet, so the Lanes invited him to stay with them.

Peter and Keli are both twenty-five years old and itching to set up their own place. There is no romance between them but they get along really well and know they can happily live under the same roof, so the idea of moving out together as house-mates naturally comes up. In mid 2000, as the case of her missing baby sits in Manly Police Station, Keli and Peter move out of the Lane's place and into one of their own. However, once they set up their household their relationship changes: overnight, Peter and Keli are living together as a couple. Things have gotten serious very quickly and they are about to get a whole lot more serious – within a few weeks of their sexual relationship beginning, Keli is pregnant.

Peter has absolutely no idea about Tegan or Keli's other children. These secrets will not be revealed to him for another three and a half years. He is also unaware that Keli is carrying his child until November 2000. Keli is four months' pregnant when she tells Peter that he is going to be a father. Peter thought Keli was on the pill; also, he is in no hurry to get married. But regardless of his thoughts or plans, Keli is keeping the baby.

As Peter adjusts to the idea of fatherhood, Detective Kehoe finally gets around to speaking to Keli, now nearly seven months' pregnant, about the disappearance of Tegan. Keli says Tegan's father is a man named Andrew Morris, who is nine or so years older than she is. Keli doesn't tell Kehoe she has never mentioned this name to Virginia Fung, nor that she told Virginia that her missing daughter is living with virtual strangers in Perth.

Keli says Andrew was living with his girlfriend, a woman named Mel, in Balmain between late 1995 and 1996 when he and Keli had a brief affair. Keli describes Morris as well built, tanned and with blond hair, who wore a suit, worked in the city as a banker and had gone to Sydney University. According to Keli, when she fell pregnant they hatched a radical plan: he and his partner Mel would raise Keli's baby as if it were their own. While recovering from the birth in Auburn Hospital, Andrew, Mel and Andrew's mother visited her in order to make arrangements for Tegan's future. When Keli discharged herself and Tegan on 14 September 1996, Andrew drove her to Duncan's house in Gladesville and then left with Tegan in his car. Keli says she saw her baby several times over the next three to four months and that the last time she saw Andrew and Mel was in January or February of 1997. She also says that none of her friends knew Andrew and that she has no way of contacting him.

On 14 February 2001, Keli is brought into the station for a formal, videotaped interview where she repeats what she and Kehoe spoke about earlier. He asks her for more details about Andrew Morris, such as his birthday. Keli says it's in July or August as in 1996 she went to drinks for his thirtieth birthday around then. In his investigations, Kehoe has discovered hospital records showing she attended Ryde Hospital a few times before arriving at Auburn Hospital to give birth.

'Do you recall what you went there for?' asks Kehoe.

'For pain in my upper ribs,' says Keli. 'They actually thought it was a gall bladder problem. I had an ultrasound and it was clear, so it was just pain from the baby moving, I guess.'

Kehoe doesn't expect any surprises and there are none – except for one. At the end of the interview, Keli reaches into her handbag. She opens her purse, pulls out her Medicare card and hands it to Detective Kehoe.

'I filled out Medicare forms for her,' she says.

Detective Kehoe looks at the card. Below Keli's name is a second name, Tegan L. Lane. Keli has been carrying around a card with her missing baby's name on it the whole time.

Despite Keli's strange story Manly Police still don't consider her to be a suspect in her baby's disappearance and they accept what she tells them as the truth. The investigation continues at a snail's pace. Nearly three months after the interview Detective Kehoe does a search of New South Wales Births, Deaths and Marriages. He can't find a birth certificate for Tegan.

'That's odd,' Kehoe thinks to himself.

Meanwhile, Keli prepares for the arrival of what Peter, her family and friends think is her first child. A baby shower is held and all Keli's friends come along. Some of her old water polo team-mates are there, including Taryn who, in the previous year, won an Olympic gold medal as part of the Australian women's water polo team.

Then the police investigation grinds to a standstill, not that anyone in the station is paying attention. For most of 2001 Manly Police Station is in turmoil since the revelation of the Operation Florida corruption sting. In December 2000 two Manly detectives were arrested on a large number of criminal charges relating to corrupt police behaviour. Public hearings on what Operation Florida found begin on 8 October 2001 and the two crooked detectives from Manly are the first cabs off the rank. Tapes are played of the two joking with another senior officer, an undercover agent for Operation Florida, after numerous raids of drug dealers' homes, describing what a good day they'd had, how a certain drug dealer's house was like Aladdin's cave for them and how stealing from criminals was what being a policeman was all about. A number of senior officers from Manly Police attend the hearings and there is a lot of laughter from the public gallery as the tapes are played, but it's no joke. Kehoe is brought in to give evidence, and it's clear that he has no knowledge and played no part in the corrupt behaviour of his superiors. The two crooked detectives had seen Kehoe as too straitlaced and headstrong to be part of their schemes, so they'd never tried to include him.

Thanks to the detail exposed by Operation Florida, it's clear that in the late 1990s Manly police station was a boys club with too many officers who weren't paying much attention to the rulebook. The inquiry found there was an unacceptable lack of proper supervision of officers, particularly of young officers, who were simply left to figure out how things worked on their own.

Not long after the corruption hearings, Manly station is closed for a few days as those officers who played a part in the old, rotten power structure are identified and told to leave. Detective Kehoe is also transferred to another station, something he has wanted for quite some time. But while Matt Kehoe gets a well-deserved fresh start, the search for Tegan doesn't. Despite all that was said about the need for proper police procedure at the corruption hearings, senior officers at Manly Police fail to notify their superiors about the case involving the daughter of their old colleague Rob Lane before they are moved out. Another eighteen months will pass between Keli's one and only formal police interview with Detective Kehoe and the next concerted effort by a police officer to find Tegan.

That officer, Detective Senior Constable Gaut, arrives at Manly Police in April 2002 as one of the new breed of officers to run the station. Six months after his arrival he is assigned Tegan's case, which had been left to languish, unsolved, all this time.

10

NO LONGER A SECRET

A few days after being assigned the case, Detective Gaut reads the transcript of Detective Kehoe's interview with Keli back in February 2001 and watches the tape. Tegan, wherever she is, is now nearly five years old. Her police file is nearly three years old. From the tone of Kehoe's questions and Keli's answers it seems that Keli's story – that she gave Tegan to a man named Andrew Morris, the baby's father – is to be believed. Tegan is still alive, even though she can't be found and there is no birth certificate for her. Her birth was just part of a sad chapter in Keli's life several years ago.

'Stranger things have happened,' Gaut thinks to himself.

A quick ask around the few remaining officers from before the corruption scandal reveals that Keli is back on track these days. She's in a stable relationship, she has an eighteen-month-old daughter and has been coaching water polo at a prestigious private girls' school for seven years. If Gaut can track down Tegan's father – and thus Tegan – Keli's failure to register her daughter's birth or organise a legal adoption can be rectified and the whole matter can be closed for good. He contacts Auburn Hospital and is told that there were four births the day Tegan was born – two boys and two girls. However, one of the girls was stillborn, leaving Tegan the only live female birth that day. He then approaches the New South Wales Births, Deaths and Marriages registry. Only one female birth at Auburn Hospital was registered that day – the stillborn child. Detective Kehoe was right when he recorded no registration of Tegan's birth.

Gaut also searches the state electoral roll for any 'Andrew Morris' living in the Balmain–Rozelle area in 1996. There are none. He also punches the name into the police computer system, COPS. Two men named Andrew Morris are listed as living in the area, but neither was born in July or August 1966. Nonetheless, Gaut goes to each address to see whether it's possible either is the man Keli described as Tegan's father. One of the men only moved to the area in the last year. A long term resident at the other address tells Gaut that no one by that name had ever lived there, so he concludes it's a case of someone giving the police a false address. A week later, on 16 October 2002, Detective Gaut speaks with Keli at the station. He doesn't think there's any need to record their conversation because he doesn't consider Keli to be a suspect. After all, as far as he can tell, no really serious crime has been committed, as long as Tegan can be found.

Gaut knows before they begin that there are some parts of Keli's story that don't add up. Keli nominated Duncan's mother Julie as her midwife for Tegan, even though Kehoe's notes record Julie flatly denying she knew anything about Keli's pregnancy back in 1996. Also, the Andrew Morris story is starting to look odd. He wonders if Keli is trying to protect Duncan.

Gaut asks Keli to sit down. Like the other new officers at the station he doesn't know Keli or her father personally, so he is looking at a stranger. Detective Gaut sees in front of him a well spoken, neatly dressed young mum. She is polite but has a slightly haughty, born-to-rule attitude about her. Keli seems to be unaccustomed to answering questions, especially from those whom she considers her social inferiors, which in the somewhat insular world of Manly means anyone outside of her social circle. She's a typical Northern Beaches girl. If not for the file in front of him, Gaut wouldn't guess in a million years that Keli had a secret past and a missing baby.

'So Keli, we need to find Tegan.'

'Yes, I gave her to her father, a man named Andrew Norris,' replies Keli.

Gaut pauses for a moment. He has been searching for a man named Morris. Gaut excuses himself for a moment and goes to another room to watch some of the video of Kehoe interviewing Keli in 2001. On it Keli clearly tells Matt Kehoe that Tegan's father's name is Morris. Gaut returns to the room where Keli sits waiting for him.

'But you told Detective Kehoe his name was Morris,' he says.

'No, I told him Norris,' insists Keli.

Perplexed, Gaut makes a note of the name change. 'OK. So two days after Tegan was born you were discharged from the hospital. You met the father, Andrew, outside, got into his car and he drove you and Tegan to Duncan's place in Gladesville –'

'No, that's not what happened,' Keli says.

Detective Gaut looks at her. Now she is denying something else she has said on tape. He shifts uncomfortably in his seat. 'Well, what did happen?'

Keli tells Gaut that Tegan's father, Andrew Norris, was furious when Keli told him she was pregnant. In fact, he called her a slut. Nonetheless, he and his girlfriend Mel wanted to raise the baby. When Keli left the hospital with Tegan two days after she was born, Andrew, Mel and Andrew's mother were waiting outside. They took the baby from Keli in the car park and left her to catch a taxi home.

Detective Gaut is stunned. Two years into this police investigation, Keli is changing the location where she handed Tegan over to her father. 'Keli, this is a very different story to what you told Detective Kehoe a year or so ago,' he says.

'Well, I lied to him because I was embarrassed about Andrew hating me,' answers Keli.

Gaut gives Keli a hard look. 'And you have absolutely no idea where Andrew or Tegan are? In fact, none of your friends have ever heard of Andrew Norris, have they?'

Detective Gaut's interrogative tone seems to surprise Keli. She pauses for a few moments before answering. 'My friend Lisa Andreatta knew him. She knew Andrew and Mel. She also knew that I had an affair with him behind Mel's back.'

Another startling new piece of information, Gaut thinks. However, at least it sounds like a lead. Gaut wants details about Lisa. Keli tells him that she'd met Lisa while studying at the Australian College of Physical Education nearly four years before.

'Does your friend know about Tegan's birth?'

'Yes.'

'Can you give me Lisa's contact details?' asks Gaut.

'Ah, no, I can't,' replies Keli. 'We lost touch over the last few years. I don't know where she is or what she's doing these days.'

Gaut's optimism drops. Keli has given him a dead end.

'Well, could you find the apartment where Andrew lived when you were seeing each other?' he asks. 'I need that address.'

Keli says she will try.

It hasn't been a formal police interview. Nothing has been video-recorded and Gaut hasn't been taking notes throughout. However, while he thought Tegan was alive before talking to Keli, now he isn't so sure. No matter how respectable and well regarded Keli is, her ever-changing story is making him suspicious. After she leaves the station, Detective Gaut sits quietly. He looks down at the thin police file in front of him and realises it's practically useless. He has a lot of work to do.

Over the next couple of months Gaut and other officers follow up every possible lead they can think of. He redoes the searches he has done for 'Morris' for 'Norris.' He also checks with Sydney University for any students named Andrew Norris enrolled in the 1980s born between 1960 and 1970. There are none. A memo is sent out to all public, Catholic and private schools in the state for them to notify Manly Police of all girls born in September 1996, particularly with the name Tegan. Gaut also asks Medicare to search its records to see if a history of medical check-ups for Tegan exists. He is persistent, and unlike when Kehoe approached the agency, this time Medicare complies. Gaut discovers that while Keli had Tegan's name added to her card, there have been no rebates for Tegan. Also, no one else has requested Tegan be put on their card and no individual card has been issued for Tegan Lane.

Gaut also looks into Keli's past. He contacts the social workers and adoption agency workers involved with the birth of Tegan and Keli's two other secret children. What they tell him leads Detective Gaut to confirm and expand on what John Borovnik, the sharp-eyed DoCS worker in the Blue Mountains, discovered three years earlier: Keli has told lie after lie to the authorities. She has lied about who fathered her children, she has lied about her family, she has lied about her life. Most worrying of all, she flatly denied the very existence of Tegan when John Borovnik called her at work at Ravenswood – even when John had hospital records of Tegan's birth in his hands – and even now has changed her story about who has her child.

It will be several years before the homicide squad discover the Ryde Hospital admission notes recording Keli's claim that Tegan was in Sydney with her in 1999 and her claim to the social worker at Auburn just after Tegan's birth that she, Duncan and Tegan planned to live together in London for a few years. For now, Gaut knows that after denying Tegan's existence, Keli claimed her daughter lives with a couple in Perth and now claims to have given her to the child's natural father, Andrew Morris/Norris, outside Auburn Hospital. Meanwhile, with the exception of having been merely registered with Medicare, there is no record of Tegan anywhere – no visits to the doctor, no birth certificate, nothing. They stop when she left the Auburn hospital maternity wing in Keli's arms.

With these facts now in front of him, the seriousness of what may have happened is undeniable. In Gaut's mind there is no reason to assume that Tegan is still alive. The days of discreet chats with Keli are over. It's time to start questioning her friends. The end of the year is approaching and Detective Gaut sees out 2002 deciding who of Keli's friends and old water polo team-mates to approach first about her secret past and missing baby.

Meanwhile, Keli is preparing for Christmas. She, Peter and their toddler are going to fly to the UK to spend some time with Peter's family. But there is someone else over there Keli is planning to visit, too. Her friend, Lisa – whom Keli told Detective Gaut knew about Tegan and was friends with Andrew Norris, but with whom she'd lost touch – is living in the UK. The truth is that she and Keli had never lost touch.

Keli has lied to police once again.

Unaware of Keli's latest deception, Detective Gaut resumes his inquiries with her friends in the new year, 2003.

He speaks with two of her old team-mates, Stacy and Taryn. They both tell Gaut that, in 1996, there were rumours around the pool that Keli was pregnant and that they looked at Keli underwater with their goggles on. However, while they both agreed that Keli looked pregnant, they didn't ask her whether she was, nor did they talk to her about it months later when it looked like she was no longer pregnant. Keli had never spoken to either of them about Tegan's birth and neither had ever met a man named Andrew Norris.

Through his investigations Gaut is able to track down Lisa's mother. She says Lisa is in the UK on a working holiday and gives him her email address. She also tells him that Keli visited Lisa when she was in the UK for Christmas. Detective Gaut sends an email to Keli's supposedly long-lost friend asking if she knew about the birth of Tegan or a man named Andrew Norris. Lisa replies she has no idea what he is talking about.

Keli's friends can't tell Detective Gaut anything new about the case, but he has caught Keli lying to him and her stories still do not make sense. In early May, after months of Keli failing to return his phone calls, he brings Keli into Manly Police Station for a formal interview. In the white walled interview room he sits her down at the end of the table facing directly into the camera, sits himself on one side, with another detective on the other, and turns the video camera on.

They start with a detailed review of the facts of Keli's short time with her missing daughter. Keli repeats the claims she made seven months earlier – that Tegan's father's name was Norris, not Morris, that she wasn't driven by him to Duncan's place in Gladesville but left to find her own way home after handing over the baby outside the hospital. Keli says Andrew visited her once in the hospital before turning up with Mel and his mother to take Tegan. She also says she has been unable to find his old apartment where they had their affair.

Keli admits she told the social worker at the hospital lies about her family living in Perth as part of her story about why she had no family or other support in Sydney at the time of Tegan's birth. Detective Gaut asks Keli why she'd lied about having no support from anyone in Sydney if she knew that Tegan's father was going to take custody of her.

'They were just coming to get Tegan. They didn't care about me,' answers Keli.

Gaut also reads out Keli's fax to Virginia where she states Tegan, 'the middle child', lives with a family in Perth. 'At the time you wrote this letter, did you believe they were in Perth?'

'I wasn't sure what Andrew was going to do,' answers Keli.

'Do you agree that you've never mentioned Andrew being in Perth to police? Can you tell us why?'

'No,' answers Keli. 'Some of the conversations I had with

Andrew indicated that perhaps he wasn't going to stay in Sydney because of the embarrassment I could cause him, I guess.'

'Did he ever say he was going to Perth?'

'Not directly. He just said something along the lines of "I don't know how I could stay in Sydney, what will everyone think, it's such an embarrassment".'

'Do you agree this letter reads like this family that has Tegan doesn't include the father of the child? That it reads like a family living in Perth that befriended you just before you had the child?'

'Was there more to the letter?' asks Keli. 'I trusted Virginia a lot. This fax comes from the end of a conversation we had when she visited me at work. It's not very detailed because we'd already had the conversation.'

'Why wouldn't you just tell her Tegan is with Andrew, her father?' insists Gaut.

'I think in one conversation I did tell her that Tegan was living with her father. Perhaps you should speak with Virginia.'

'I've spoken with Virginia,' answers Gaut, refusing to give Keli's suggestion any credit, and repeating his question. 'Don't you agree that this fax doesn't read as if Tegan is with her father? That it reads as though she is with some couple that you've met and who have befriended you?'

'I didn't just give her away to anybody! That's what you are trying to say it says and it doesn't!' Keli shoots back.

Gaut tells Keli he has done a search with Births, Deaths and Marriages and had it confirmed that no birth certificate for Tegan Lane has ever been issued. After pausing for a second with her chin cupped in her hands, Keli replies. 'So all the paperwork that the hospital gave me, that I then passed onto Andrew . . . My part has gone through but his part hasn't?'

'I don't know what part you did,' answers Gaut.

'I did all the medical things, like I've got the Medicare card . . .'

'Mmm, well, I've made inquiries with Medicare,' says Gaut. 'Yes, Tegan was enrolled on your card, but Tegan Lane hasn't had any medical services for which a Medicare benefit has been claimed.'

'Well, that's because she's never been in my care. I've never used it for her,' says Keli, either not immediately grasping Gaut's point or deliberately trying to draw attention away from the fact that there is no record of anyone ever taking Tegan to the doctor.

'But don't you agree it's very odd for a child, who would be six or seven years old now, not to have had any medical –' begins Gaut.

'Yeah, but the paperwork that the hospital gave me – I took parts that I needed to fill out and filled out the other parts and gave it to him as they left, so how come my part is done and his isn't?' Keli demands, speaking over the top of Gaut.

'I'm just saying that, to us, it shows the child hasn't been in existence for quite a few years,' says Gaut, stating to Keli for the first time his belief that Tegan is dead. 'There are also no records of Tegan being enrolled as a student with any New South Wales public, Catholic or private school.' Then, without pausing for a response from Keli, Gaut moves straight to Keli's lie about not being able to contact Lisa, her old friend. Gaut reveals to Keli he knows she stayed with Lisa in the UK over Christmas, something Keli first denies, then admits. Keli doesn't seem bothered that her lie to Gaut about having lost contact with Lisa has been exposed. Without missing a beat Keli quickly claims she didn't talk to Lisa about the police investigation.

'You didn't mention it to her?' asks Gaut. 'You didn't think it might be important that she was the one person who could verify the fact that –' But before Gaut can finish Keli interrupts again.

'But I know she doesn't know where Andrew is.'

'But you agree that you said she knew about the child and she knew who the father was,' repeats Gaut. 'Do you agree with that?'

'Yes.'

'So you didn't think that if you were to allow police to speak with her this could all be put to rest?'

'I just thought you would speak with him and it would all be fine and she wouldn't have to be involved,' says Keli stubbornly.

'Well, I've spoken with Lisa and she states she doesn't know any Andrew Norris, and she also doesn't know anything about you having a child in 1996.' Continuing in his even tone, Gaut prepares to call Keli a liar. 'Keli, it's obvious that you are not telling us the truth. Now, this matter is not going to go away.'

'I know it's not going to go away, but I don't want to hurt everyone around me.'

'Well, we have to know what the truth is. This person, Andrew Norris – he's not the father of the child, is he?'

'Yes, he is.'

'Where is the child now?'

'With him.'

'Why did you say that Lisa knew him and about the child? Did you think she might lie for you if you got the opportunity?'

'No, I just thought she knew. She would never lie.'

'If we can establish this person actually exists and your child exists, then that's the end of our inquiry. But you have been telling us lies. I've read the things you have told different social workers and they are just blatant lies. I can't understand why, if Andrew Norris existed all along, you wouldn't tell these people that.'

'Well, how do you tell people stuff like that? How do you tell people you're on your own and you've got no one?' Keli says tearfully. 'How can I say it's the second or third time? I'm not passing the blame, but how can people see me every day and not know? Not help? He was the only choice I had.'

'What do you mean the only choice you had?'

'Well, I couldn't just walk up to the doorstep and say "Hi, I had a baby yesterday." Imagine what Duncan and Dad would do . . .' says Keli, turning her mind back to the days when she and Duncan were together.

The interview rolls on. The last time Gaut spoke to Keli she had promised to look through some boxes at Duncan's old place that might contain diaries with phone numbers and names for people she knew in 1996. 'I've made enquiries of the current occupants at Duncan's old place and they say they've never had anyone attending their house wanting to look through boxes,' states Gaut.

'Well, I know I did because I went there on my way to work and I knocked on the door and I asked, "Can I please go and see if there is anything left in the garage",' Keli replies.

'Do you understand that I have spoken to each of those tenants and they all say they don't recall any female coming there asking about getting into the garage or house to look through boxes?' Gaut asks, knowing he has caught Keli lying again. Keli sits silently with no change in expression or obvious embarrassment. 'Keli, like I said before, this matter is not going to go away,' continues Gaut. 'The child is missing, so it's a matter that will have to go to the coroner's court. It's a suspected death.'

'What?' says Keli, looking up with a worried expression.

'Our investigations show you are not telling the truth, and we cannot track the child's existence or the alleged father of the child. The matter is going to the Coroner's Court. I'm going to have to do a thorough investigation. I'm going to have to start speaking with everyone, including your family. Now, I don't want to have to go to that extent, but I don't think you are being honest with us.'

'Because I don't know where Andrew is, everybody's lives are going to be destroyed?' Keli cries. 'Because I can't get in contact with someone I barely know? Because you can't find him in Sydney?'

'Because they are very suspicious circumstances in which this child has gone missing,' says Gaut. 'We've taken everything you've said on face value, we've made inquiries and we can't back up anything you've said. Now, do you want to tell me anything?'

'No.'

'Did you kill the child?'

'No! I did not! I did not do anything like that!'

'Did someone else?'

'No! No!'

'All right. So, like I said, I'm going to have to make a lot of enquiries now – '

'Please don't,' pleads Keli. 'I don't understand how . . . Can you . . . Can we stop the tape? Can I speak to you without the tape on?'

'I'd rather you speak with the tape on.'

'Nothing has happened to Tegan,' says Keli. 'Andrew said he would contact me if there was an emergency. I have not heard cooee from him or Mel, not one word. I don't have anything else to say.'

'Just before we finish, who was the father of your first child?'

'I don't want to say anything about that.'

'Can you tell me who the father was of your third child?'

'I'm not going to say anything,' insists Keli. 'I feel like I'm being backed into a corner and I feel uncomfortable.'

It's 5 November 2003. Keli and her old friend Melinda have just finished playing indoor netball, a new sport for Keli now that her gruelling water polo training is a thing of the past. They are pulling up to Melinda's place. These two friends have always been close, and their bonds are continuing into the next generation. Melinda and Brandon have had their first child, as have Keli and Peter, and the kids are growing up together.

Brandon hears Keli's car engine stop. He knows the sound of it because Keli comes over all the time. However, today he is bracing himself for an awkward conversation with the woman he and his wife have been friends with all their lives. For months now they have been receiving calls from a policeman named Detective Gaut about a missing baby named Tegan. The baby was born way back in 1996 and Keli is supposed to be the mother. He and Melinda keep telling this policeman they have no idea what he's talking about, but he keeps calling. Brandon knows Melinda has spoken to Kati, an old friend of theirs and Keli's, about these weird phone calls. In the near future Kati will start getting calls from the police about this missing baby, too.

Brandon hears the front door open. 'Hi Melinda, hi Keli.'

He, Keli and Melinda are standing in the living room. Melinda and Brandon look at each other apprehensively.

Earlier they had agreed to wait for an opportunity to speak to Keli about this together.

'Keli, we've been getting phone calls from the police about a missing baby – ' Brandon starts.

Keli looks shocked for a moment, but then begins to nod her head knowingly. 'It's something that happened a long time ago,' she says. 'It's got nothing to do with you. It's between me, Duncan, Simon and Narelle.'

When Keli was dating Duncan she would tell Brandon and Melinda about all the time she was spending with his famous brother Simon, who lived just across the road from Duncan's place in Gladesville. She'd told them about going to a New Year's Eve party at Simon's and how Simon and his wife Narelle were having real difficulties having a baby. They know she was really close to them.

'OK, OK,' Melinda says softly. 'We just wanted to let you know that the police have been calling us.'

The three friends stand together awkwardly. Dealing with her own shock that the policeman hadn't got it all terribly wrong, Melinda can sense that Keli doesn't want to talk about it much more.

'Do you think I should get in contact with the detective?' asks Melinda. 'He's been calling for ages. We had no idea what he was talking about so we didn't want to give a statement.'

'Just tell him the truth, that you don't know,' Keli replies, then pauses. 'Thanks for being friends,' she says.

Meanwhile, unbeknown to Melinda and Brandon, Detective Gaut has been talking to Simon and Narelle. Despite what Keli has told her two old friends, Duncan's brother and his wife had nothing to do with Tegan. They didn't even know she was born – that is, until Detective Gaut told them.

*

Over the following weeks Gaut again attempts to find the apartment Keli says Norris lived in with his partner Mel, and where he and Keli nonetheless carried out their affair. Gaut tells Keli he wants to drive her around Balmain until they find it. Keli agrees, but in the car she says she still can't remember the address, only that it was a five minute walk from the Town Hall Hotel in Balmain.

Gaut drives Keli to the pub and then further on. After a few minutes they find a block of flats that Keli says looks familiar. They walk inside, Keli commenting how the stairs in the foyer look familiar as well. They then walk to the first floor, where Keli picks out two apartments, numbers 10 and 11, and tells Gaut she had her affair with Andrew in one of them, but she isn't sure which. Gaut can't get entry into either apartment, but someone lets them into apartment number 2, which is directly below.

'Oh, yes, the layout is like this,' says Keli, gesturing to the combined kitchen and lounge area. 'Also, one of the bedrooms was set up as a home office.' She then walks into the bathroom. 'These tiles look familiar.'

Gaut duly organises for a number of police officers to door-knock the residents who live there and search the rental records for tenants who used to live in the building. None of them remember anyone fitting Andrew Norris's description. Rental records also fail to produce anyone who might have been the man Keli said was Tegan's father. After several months, Gaut's investigation finds itself at another dead end. Detective Gaut organises a cadaver dog to sniff for human remains at Duncan's old place in Gladesville. The dog finds nothing.

On 6 January 2004, Gaut tries to ring Keli at home. By this stage Gaut has been granted a warrant to have Keli's home phone tapped. She picks up, then says to Peter, who is near her, that she can't hear anything and hangs up. Gaut then leaves Keli a message to call him, careful not to reveal what he is calling about just in case Peter hears it. Keli doesn't return Gaut's call. Instead, Keli calls the caterers about her wedding to Peter, which is the following month. Peter asked her to marry him not long after they had come back from spending Christmas 2002 in the UK. On 7 January 2004, after trying to call her again, Gaut and another detective go to Keli's apartment and knock on her door.

'Hello Keli,' says Gaut as she opens the door. 'I tried to ring you yesterday and today. Is Peter home?'

'No,' says Keli. 'Can you come in?'

'No, I would prefer to speak to you down at the police station. Are you free today or tomorrow?'

Keli insists they come inside so no one can overhear them. Keli and Peter's apartment, which is a few blocks away from Keli's parents' place and close to the heart of Manly, is perfectly positioned to have a view of Sydney Harbour. However, the building doesn't make the most of this, with only the kitchen window opening out to the view of the water. The walls of the apartment are painted a cheerful aqua green.

Keli leads the detectives to the living room where her toddler, Macy, is playing. 'I haven't heard from you for months,' says Keli. 'I was wondering why you didn't contact me. This has been on my mind every day. I don't just sit at home when you don't call me and not think about it.'

Gaut explains again he had tried to call her a couple of times and tells her he has been following up Keli's claim of where Andrew Norris lived when she had her affair with him.

'Well, I'm not trying to point the finger or anything, but you spoke to my friends and they are all talking behind my back,' Keli says angrily. 'I've got no friends now. No one calls me anymore.'

'I don't believe you have no friends, Keli,' replies Gaut coolly. 'I suggested to everyone I spoke to that this was a sensitive matter and asked them to be discreet.'

'One of them called me out of the blue yesterday,' says Keli. 'It was Alison. I haven't seen her for three years. I don't understand why you have to speak to people who don't know anything about it. What did she tell you?'

'I'm not going to do an interview with you in your lounge room, Keli.'

'You don't know what it's like,' cries Keli. 'I'm going to lose everything. I'm supposed to be getting married next month, but I'm going to lose Peter, our daughter, my job, my parents – everything! – when people learn I gave Tegan away. There is no way a private school will employ someone who has given away a child.'

'There is no reason why you would lose your child,' says Gaut, looking down at Macy.

'Yes, I will. You don't know my dad like I do.'

'No, I don't know your dad.'

'Don't you?' asks Keli, clearly expecting Gaut to say he did. 'What about you?' she asks the other detective, who answers he doesn't know Keli's father either.

It's 8 January, 2004. Keli is back in the police station, ready for a second videotaped interview with Detective Gaut. She says she is panicking about what will happen if Tegan's case goes to the Coroner's Court. 'It's going to become a massive

issue, isn't it? Everyone is going to know. Mum, Dad, Peter
– they are not going to want to be near me. After they hear
everything you have been looking into, who is going to let
me stay with my daughter?'

Gaut tells Keli that no one is going to take her daughter
away and begins the interview. Keli tells him there is no
way Duncan could be Tegan's father as while they were
sharing a bed, they weren't sexually intimate around the
time of Tegan's conception. Gaut listens, but by now he is
firm in his belief that Andrew Norris is one of Keli's lies.
Gaut asks Keli at what gestational stage did she find out she
was pregnant with Tegan, to which she answers, 'Twelve to
fourteen weeks.'

'So that'd be about March or April 1996. At what stage did
you tell Norris that you were pregnant?' asks Gaut.

'Two to three weeks after that I'd say.'

'That would be about May. What was his reaction?'

'He was very rude and aggressive and not pleased,' answers
Keli sadly. 'He said that I had trapped him and that I was a
slut.'

'How was your relationship with Andrew after that?' asks
Gaut. Keli answers that there wasn't any contact between her
and Andrew after she told him she was pregnant. Gaut asks
Keli when they made the arrangement for Andrew and Mel
to take custody of the child. Keli says she called him from
hospital the day after she had Tegan.

'Did you at any stage insist he take the child?'

'I didn't beg him to take her. I just thought I had nothing
and they had each other.'

'What about Mel? What was her view on – '

'She hated me,' interrupts Keli.

'Was she happy to take the child?'

'I think so.'

'Do you find that odd?'

Keli nods in agreement.

Gaut asks Keli about Andrew's thirtieth birthday; that she told Detective Kehoe she went to the Town Hall Hotel for drinks in July or August 1996. Keli confirms that is correct. Gaut then points out that Keli has just told him that she and Andrew had a terrible relationship with next to no contact after she told him she was pregnant in May, a month or so before the supposed birthday drinks.

'Can you tell me why you were celebrating Andrew's birthday if you had no social contact with him?' asks Gaut.

'I wasn't really with him,' answers Keli quickly. 'Like, there were big groups of people that used to all go up there. I wasn't in his group of people.'

'So you're saying that you weren't actually with him; you just saw him there?'

'How do you want me to explain it?' says Keli with an exasperated tone. 'Like they were there and we were kind of here,' she says, gesturing with one hand, 'and he knew I was there,' she says, gesturing with the other, 'I knew he was there. I couldn't very well go up and make a show when all these people didn't even know who I was.'

'I was under the impression from your answers in your interview with Detective Kehoe that you were with him celebrating his birthday,' persists Gaut.

'I was there. I was at the same place.'

'But you weren't talking.'

Keli casts her eyes down to the table and makes no reply.

Gaut makes Keli admit she lied about Duncan's mother Julie being her homebirth midwife. He also asks her why she put Duncan down as Tegan's father and her main contact person on hospital documents if he wasn't the father and didn't know about Tegan's birth.

'I wanted Duncan to be there if something was going to happen to me, if I was going to die or something,' Keli says dramatically.

'Were you expecting to die?' asks Gaut deadpan.

'I almost did!' exclaims Keli, her eyes wide.

'Were there complications?' asks Gaut, unmoved. 'When you say you almost died – '

'They said I was very sick,' insists Keli.

'Nothing I've been told indicates you almost died giving birth,' Gaut says flatly. 'I don't understand why you used Duncan's name.'

'Just being foolish,' Keli replies, her chin cupped in her hands again and her eyes cast down.

'I don't understand why you would give hospital staff the names of people like Duncan, Julie and your friend Kati, who you say had no knowledge of the baby, along with wrong numbers for all of them,' says Gaut.

'It was a long time ago,' answers Keli vaguely.

Gaut now moves on to the lie Keli told her friends Melinda and Brandon about police inquiries into Tegan's whereabouts being a matter between Keli, Duncan, Narelle and Simon.

'Why did you say what you said to Melinda and Brandon?' asks Gaut.

'Probably just to calm them. I didn't want them involved. I didn't want them to worry or to ask me any more questions.'

'So you are saying you just picked those names out basically to put Melinda and Brandon off the track?' says Gaut.

'No, not to put them off the track, just to make them feel they don't need to be involved. It's got nothing to do with them, you know. They probably don't even know Simon and Narelle that well.'

'I'm just asking why – '

'I've just said why,' interrupts Keli.

'Just hear me out. Did you say those three names so that people wouldn't be talking about you behind your back, saying "What's Keli done to the baby?" That instead they would be saying "Maybe Keli has given the baby to Narelle and Simon?"' asks Gaut.

'Is that what they think?' demands Keli.

'No, I'm thinking it is a possible explanation for why you said that. Was it something to squash the rumours?'

'No, because I thought you'd only spoken to them. I didn't realise you had spoken to everybody. I didn't realise it was common knowledge. I just said Duncan, Simon and Narelle because Melinda and Brandon are aware of who they are . . . and that wouldn't involve . . . Like, just, don't ask me any more, don't get involved. I didn't want them to go through this.'

'Melinda and Brandon are obviously concerned about you so they wanted to speak to you about it,' says Gaut. 'I didn't ask them to speak to you.'

'I just wanted to keep them out of it,' repeats Keli.

'Do you understand the way we're looking at this inquiry?' says Gaut firmly. 'We've got a child who's missing, who we're presuming is not alive now. If it's simply a matter that you've given the child to the natural father there's absolutely no problem, but we've yet to establish that. This is the reason we've had to go and speak to your friends, and why we will have to speak to your parents.'

Keli seems to be listening to Gaut, but she also seems to be more concerned about who Gaut has spoken to than the possibility that Tegan is dead. 'I don't understand why you would ring Alison, a girl I was barely friends with, who I have not spoken to in years and years, who then rings me about this,' Keli says angrily. 'If she knows, then everybody bloody knows. I understand what your job is, but why did you speak to Alison?'

'Because Alison was apparently a friend of yours around that time.'

'No, she wasn't,' lies Keli. Alison had moved out of Manly and the whole social scene several years ago, but back in the early-to-mid 1990s she was in Keli's group.

'There are good reasons why I speak to these people,' Gaut says. 'I'm not doing it so I can broadcast your personal life all over Manly. Now, I've been told that when you were discharged from Auburn Hospital – '

'From where, sorry?' interrupts Keli.

'Auburn Hospital,' repeats Gaut. 'After giving birth to Tegan you were given a blue book and had all the vaccinations yet to be given to Tegan explained and when they were due. Do you recall all of that?'

'Yes. I gave all that to Andrew, and a social security and birth certificate form.'

'And what about the ongoing medical care for Tegan?'

'That was up to Andrew.'

'I've been told you cancelled the routine post-birth home visit by a hospital nurse two days after leaving the hospital. You refused the service, saying that your homebirth midwife would take care of Tegan's needs. Do you remember that?'

'I remember saying I didn't need a home visit . . .' Keli begins slowly.

'Right,' says Gaut, urging her to continue.

'. . . because I . . .'

'Because . . . ?' Gaut prompts again.

'. . . I didn't . . .' Keli says vaguely, before falling silent.

'You also told the hospital that your homebirth midwife would do the heel prick blood test, the Guthrie test. So that was never to happen?'

'I don't remember saying that,' says Keli. She simply does not have an explanation as to why she told the hospital her imaginary midwife was going to take care of Tegan's health needs when she had apparently already given the child away.

'Are you prepared to give a written consent for police to access Tegan's Guthrie test if it exists?' asks Gaut. 'It will allow us to compare Tegan's DNA with, say, for instance, Duncan's, to see if he is the father. Duncan has already said he is happy to give us his DNA if we need it.'

'I think I should speak to someone. I'm not sure,' says Keli with a concerned look in her eyes.

'Are you talking about a solicitor?'

'I guess so.'

Keli was told at the start of the interview that she is free to leave any time she wants, but despite having said she wants to speak to a solicitor, she remains in her seat. Gaut talks to her about how she might go about finding a solicitor and then continues his questioning.

'You told Virginia from Anglicare that your parents were aware of your first secret child and they disowned you. Did you tell her that?'

Keli stays silent for a few seconds before admitting she did.

'All right, *were* your parents aware of your first child?'

'No.'

'*Did* they disown you? Obviously not.'

'They would have,' Keli says with her eyes full of tears. 'That is exactly what would have happened.'

'Can you remember why you told Virginia your parents had disowned you?'

'Because I wanted her to help me.'

Gaut then asks Keli about the car she owned in 1996. 'Do you still have the car Duncan gave you?'

'I still own it. It's parked on a street in Mosman.'

'Is it registered?'

'No.'

'Were you driving any other cars in 1996?'

'I used to drive Duncan's Ford truck thing occasionally.'

'Are you prepared to let us forensically examine the car Duncan gave you?'

After a couple of moments of silence Keli says yes.

'Keli, I think you should see a counsellor,' Gaut says. 'I think you need help.'

As the interview draws to a close, the other detective in the room makes a few comments about Keli's claim she called Andrew Norris from hospital after giving birth to Tegan. 'You say you had no conversations with him to establish the fact he is going to take Tegan, so I want to understand how you came to the conclusion he was going to take her.'

'We had the discussion when I told him, you know, and he said "What are you going to do? Are you going to get rid of it?" says Keli. 'I said "No, it's too late. I can't keep it. Can you take it?" He wasn't really happy about it.'

'So just to clarify, the first time that you told Andrew you were pregnant you discussed the option of him taking the child. And the next time that you spoke about it was when you rang him yourself from the hospital and he has turned up with Mel and his mother to collect the child. You haven't had any conversations in between. He hasn't called you and said he is or isn't taking the child, he just turns up on the day.'

'Yeah, pretty much,' answers Keli.

The day after her police interview, phone taps record Keli's call to her friend Kati. 'I've had to speak to Richard again,' Keli says to her old friend, referring to Detective Gaut. 'And . . . um . . . I have to speak to Peter tomorrow. It's been playing on my mind for the last three days.'

Kati knows that Keli is talking about the police search for Tegan. 'Does Peter know?' she asks.

'No,' replies Keli. 'I tried to explain to Richard that none of my friends know anything. He won't even really tell me who he's spoken to,' complains Keli.

'Well, I don't know exactly who he's spoken to, but I've had some weird phone calls from people who haven't said that they know but ask me how you are, and I think "Why would you ask me that?"' says Kati.

'Like who are you talking about – who?' asks Keli.

'Oh, just people like Alison, and she has spoken to people like Kimberley.'

'It's funny – well, not funny – but I made one comment to Brandon and Melinda that was very . . . um . . . didn't have anything in it,' says Keli vaguely. 'Like it was just a comment, but they quoted me on it to Richard. That's fair enough, that's what you have to do, but it's really strange,' says Keli, fishing for information from Kati as to what she has heard.

'He was asking me a lot of questions about what you looked like when you were pregnant, he's asking for my phone numbers and my whereabouts, and I'm like "What do you want me to say, mate? I don't know anything",' says Kati, clearly not picking up on what Keli was saying about Brandon and Melinda.

Keli then tells Kati how scared she is about telling her fiancé Peter about Tegan and the police search for her. 'I just don't want to see the hurt in his face. People have different judgements. Like, you are a good person. You're like Lisa,' says Keli, referring to her college buddy Lisa Andreatta. 'You look at it and say, "The past is the past, you've moved on." I am such a different person now.'

'But I think all of your friends would think that,' says Kati kindly.

'I don't,' replies Keli.

'I do. I think your closest friends – like, I don't know the extent of who knows – but the few people that do know who know – '

'Like?' Keli interrupts.

'Melinda and Brandon. I just think that is how they think,' says Kati, gently.

'Like who else knows besides them?' insists Keli, ignoring Kati's kindness.

'Pardon?' says Kati, a little surprised at Keli's intensity.

'Like who else?'

'Look, I honestly – '

'Who else do you know definitely knows besides them?' insists Keli.

'I think Luke knows,' says Kati, racking her brain for people in their wider group of friends.

'Is that why Emma's been ignoring me?' asks Keli, refering to Luke's partner.

'No. Emma has been sick all week. She isn't seeing anyone.'

'I know I'm being paranoid, but I'm frightened. I don't want to lose Macy,' sniffs Keli.

'You're not going to lose Macy, mate. And you're not going to lose your friends. You're not going to lose me,' says Kati stoutly.

'Gaut says to me "This is my job" and I say "This is my fucking life",' sobs Keli. She then tells Kati that she put her name down as a contact person while she was in hospital giving birth to Tegan. 'I knew you would help me,' says Keli. 'I know I've made some foolish decisions, but it was so long ago.'

'It was a lifetime ago, Keli,' say Kati gently. 'You say Brandon and Melinda might have said something, but they were so concerned about you. They would never do anything to hurt you. They're behind you a hundred million per cent. I don't know what that Richard Gaut wants,' says Kati, exasperated. 'No one knows anything except you and Duncan,' she adds, still under the impression that Duncan is Tegan's father. Keli hasn't mentioned the name Andrew Norris to her friends yet.

'It's going to hit the papers,' says Keli, sidestepping Kati's misunderstanding about Duncan. 'My parents are going to be so embarrassed. It's going to be a disaster,' wails Keli. 'If Richard is so gung-ho about wanting something to happen, why the fuck didn't he do it three or four years ago before I was with Peter and had Macy? Like, I'm not trying to flick the blame back to him . . .'

'Your family is very strong, OK. Your parents love you,' insists Kati.

'But I don't think they will after this,' says Keli.

'Oh, don't be silly. They love you and your brother more than anything. They'll be hurt and shocked, but they'll support you.'

'There won't be a wedding, Kati, you know,' says Keli quietly.

'There will be a wedding. It will be fine,' says Kati reassuringly.

'There won't!' cries Keli. 'You know, I went grocery shopping the other day and bought all of these things just in case I am not here to look after Peter and Macy.'

'Please don't think like that, OK?' says Kati. 'You're thinking the absolute worst-case scenario times one million, and it's not going to happen, OK? You need to speak to Peter and speak to your parents. Where the fuck is Duncan?'

'He's overseas.'

'Well, is Duncan going through any of this?'

'I don't know, but I don't know that he has to,' says Keli with false graciousness. 'But thank you. I spoke to Lisa briefly this afternoon and at least I know that my good friends won't neglect Peter or Macy.'

'Don't be so silly. I've told you a thousand times . . .'

'I used to worry so much about wanting to be a sports star and achieving all these wonderful things, but the only thing I'm really good at is being a mum,' says Keli, crying. 'I spent so much time worrying about all that other shit and it doesn't matter. It doesn't matter.'

Kati tells Keli it will be better once she tells Peter. 'It'll bring it out in the open,' she says soothingly.

'It will be better once I tell him but that's not going to be the end of it,' says Keli ruefully. 'That Richard is going to dig and dig and dig until he gets whatever he wants . . .'

In the days following her conversation with Kati, Keli tells Peter about Tegan. Peter and Keli have been engaged for a year. Peter loves Keli and their daughter to bits, so it's only natural to make Keli his wife. The big day is in February, the following month. To say Peter is in shock when Keli tells him she gave birth to three other babies before their own – and that police are investigating the disappearance of one of them – is an understatement. With his mind racing to comprehend what his fiancée is saying, Peter calls Detective Gaut who comes to their house that day and confirms what Keli has told him.

Police taps of their home phone reveal Peter to be a particularly loving and forgiving man. On 13 January he calls Keli from work. After asking her how she is feeling, and Keli telling him that she is going to have a wedding dress fitting that afternoon, he raises the topic of Tegan.

'I hate to talk about it, but I just looked in the White Pages for how many Norrises there are in New South Wales,' he says.

'Yeah?' replies Keli unenthusiastically.

'There's a total of 130 A. Norrises. Like, you just go through and phone . . .'

'Phone?' says Keli flatly.

'. . . phone them all, yeah.'

'Mmm,' replies Keli.

Seven days later Peter calls Keli from work again. Keli had planned to tell her parents about the police investigation that day but she still hasn't worked up the nerve.

'I don't even know how to put into words . . . You know, like, it's just going to be so hard to hurt someone again,' says Keli. 'Like, I've already hurt you and that's just ripped my guts out all week. I felt sick all week.'

'Well, don't, because I'm all right,' says Peter.

'I just feel like I'm going through all of it all again and I'm sick of talking about it,' says Keli, crying. 'But I have no choice. You know? I have no choice and that's how I felt ten years ago. That's how I feel now. Do you know what I mean?'

Peter talks about how Keli should be easy on herself. 'Don't think you've got to go home after telling your parents and look after Macy. If you're struggling, go and see that bloody woman,' he says, referring to a counsellor Keli saw on Gaut's recommendation. 'Or go and see Melinda. Maybe go for a walk. You don't have to be superwoman.'

'But I am on my own,' cries Keli. 'That's what I feel like.'

'You're not on your own,' says Peter. 'I'm with you. I love you.'

Peter calls Keli again the next day. 'We will get through it,' he says to his soon-to-be wife.

'I don't know that we will,' says Keli.

'Why not?' asks Peter.

'I don't know,' she replies.

Keli's friends have always thought the relationship between Keli and her mother is a funny mixture of love and cool distance. It was pretty clear to them that Keli was Daddy's girl, while Sandy was known to be close to Keli's brother. However, Keli decides to tell her mother about Tegan first, when they are alone in her parents' kitchen discussing her parents' upcoming weekend away. She isn't exactly sure when she's going to tell her dad.

The next day a nervous sounding Keli calls her mother.

'Hello?' says Sandy answering the phone.

'Hi Mum, it's me,' says Keli.

'Hi,' says Sandy, flatly.

'Hi. How are you?' asks Keli nervously.

'All right.'

'That's good,' says Keli.

'Would you come up and feed the cats tonight, please?' Sandy asks her daughter dispassionately. 'Because we're going today. We're going in an hour.'

'Um, yep sure,' says Keli, her voice relaxing slightly.

'And turn the dishwasher off,' continues Sandy. 'It's on at the moment and I don't want to leave it on all weekend.'

Keli and her mother then have a brief and tense discussion about when Rob and Sandy will be arriving home that weekend before Sandy cuts to the chase.

'And the other thing is I don't want Macy around when you tell Dad. I don't know if you are going to tell him on Sunday or Monday.'

'Probably on Monday,' says Keli, her voice tight.

'You've got to be telling the absolute truth, because he'll know how to find out things that you wouldn't believe.'

'Yeah,' says Keli in absolute agreement.

'I mean, you told me that this young guy has taken the baby to raise it, which is really unusual, you must admit,' Sandy says slowly and deliberately.

'Yeah.'

'Was his family behind him on this?' Sandy asks.

'Yep,' says Keli.

'Well, how come they're not badgering them as to where the child and he is?' asks Sandy, referring to the police investigation and their questioning of Keli. 'He's disappeared too, has he?'

'They can't find them,' Keli tells her mother.

'He's gone too?' Sandy asks again. 'And the family know nothing?'

'But I don't know the family,' replies Keli.

'I'm not saying you know the family. What's this copper told you? Where did this policeman interview you?'

'Down at Manly station.'

'And was there anybody else with him at the time?'

'Yeah.'

'I hope you gave a coherent statement,' Sandy says in a reprehensive tone. 'How long ago did this happen?'

'The last time was about two weeks ago.'

'And this counsellor, how did you get onto this counsellor? Did you ask for counselling?'

'Um . . . He said I should speak to someone and he rang . . . um . . . the health clinic down at Queenscliff. And she's the manager down there.'

'Who, the policeman?' Sandy asks sharply.

'Yeah.'

'Right.'

'And um . . . you know, she's been very good. She thinks that Richard has manipulated me and put me into a corner.'

'Who, the policeman?' asks Sandy again.

'Yeah.'

'Well, what about the father and the child? I mean why isn't information given to you about what their family has got to say about all of this?'

'Because they don't know where they are, Mum, that's what I've told you.'

'Yes, I understand that. Don't get cranky with me, because you know that all these questions are going to be asked.'

'Yeah,' says Keli quietly.

'I mean, I am trying to support you and my trust has been violated, do you understand that?'

'Yeah, I totally understand that.'

'Right, well, I'm trying very, very hard to keep myself together,' says Sandy who, on top of learning of Keli's secret missing child, is dealing with the death of her own mother a few weeks before. 'I told your brother yesterday. When he came in yesterday morning I was distraught. He said "You've got to tell me what's wrong, Mum," and I did.'

'Yeah,' says Keli.

'I just hope to God this doesn't become a court case. This will hurt your brother's career.'

'Oh, Mum, this has nothing to do with him!'

'So was the child still alive up until three years ago?' asks Sandy. 'You said the police first contacted you three years ago.'

'I'm under the assumption she is still alive now,' Keli stutters.

'And that he's just disappeared with the child?'

'Yeah.'

'Well, I just hope to God he's gone interstate or something. How did this crop up?' asks Sandy about how the police found out about this missing baby. 'I asked you that before but I can't remember what you said.'

'Yeah, I'm not sure,' says Keli. It's a lie, of course – she still hasn't told her mother about her two other secret children and how Tegan's existence came to light during the adoption of the third.

'He should have told you why they are now asking you about this, you know?' continues Sandy. 'But anyway, as I said, I've got to act dumb on Monday. Otherwise your father will never trust me again.'

'Yeah, that's understandable,' agrees Keli.

'As I said, I'd rather Macy not be around because – I know and you know – there is going to be a severe reaction. So I'd rather Macy not witness that.'

'He's not going to hurt me or anything?' asks Keli dramatically.

'No, he's not going to hurt you but he is going to blow up,' says Sandy firmly. 'You know that, don't you?'

'Yeah.'

'Obviously, I was too stunned to say anything the other day, but I've been trying to reason things out. It's really unusual,' says Sandy. 'So, when you left the hospital he took the child home with him?'

'On that day, yes,' confirms Keli.

'To his family, I assume?'

'Yep.'

'It's just so unlike a young bloke to want to raise a child. That's the thing I can't get a grip on. But obviously that's what you agreed.' Then there is a small pause. 'Isn't it?' asks Sandy.

'Yeah, well, I didn't really have too many options, you know,' Keli retorts.

'You could have put the child up for adoption,' answers Sandy curtly.

'Mum, I don't want to talk about it all right now. Just leave it to Monday.'

'OK, dear. Well, you know I love you.'

'Yeah, I love you.'

'OK. All right.'

'OK,' says Keli, crying.

'Well, see you on Monday,' says Sandy with a sigh.

'Yeah, see you Monday,' says Keli.

As agreed, Keli visits Rob and Sandy at home to break the news about Tegan. Peter offers to accompany her, but she chooses to go alone. After Keli has spoken to them, Detective Gaut visits Rob and Sandy. They confirm that Keli has told them about Tegan, her missing baby, but when Gaut begins to hint that Keli has given birth to two other secret babies, Rob and Sandra clearly have no idea what he is talking about. They only know about Tegan. Gaut tells Rob and Sandy about their two other grandchildren. Sandy bursts into tears, while Rob paces back and forth muttering 'We will get to the bottom of this.'

Keli's desperate struggle to keep three of her babies secret is over. Everyone in her life now knows. However, regardless of how shocked Peter and her family are, they show remarkable determination to recover very quickly. A few weeks after learning about the police investigation to find Tegan and his fiancée's two other secret children, Peter marries Keli in the beachside ceremony she has always dreamed of. Keli's friends and family, some having been questioned by police about Tegan, attend. They celebrate the newly married couple as if nothing is wrong. It seems clear that Keli's family and inner circle believe Keli's claim that Tegan is still alive.

11

RELEASE THE HOUNDS

Keli and Peter go on living in their apartment with Macy. Keli's friends are still coming to terms with her history of secret babies, but they stand by their old friend, telling her the worst of her ordeal is over now that they and her family know. Keli's parents are rock solid in their love for Keli. They would never abandon her or her brother, come what may. Yes, what Keli has done is a shock, but they believe Tegan is safe and well just like the other two children. Once she is found, this whole drama can be relegated to the past where it belongs.

Despite the Lanes' determination to act as if everything will soon return to normal, big wheels are now in motion. In a matter of months Keli's secret will go beyond their Manly circle of friends and Keli's old water polo team-mates to the front pages of the national news. On 18 March 2004, four and a half years after police were first notified about the disappearance of Tegan, Detective Gaut refers Tegan's case to the Coroner's Court as a possible death.

For now, the media have not been told of this case. Gaut continues his determined but unpublicised search for Tegan and the man Keli claims to have given her to. He searches for records of any social security payments made in relation to a female born on 12 September 1996 by a man named Andrew Norris and finds none. He approaches the Births, Deaths and Marriages registry in every state and territory for any female born in 1996 with a father named Andrew Norris and finds none. He approaches the Department of Immigration for records of any child born on 12 September 1996 with the last name of Norris who has either left or entered the country. Again, he finds none. He also begins a nationwide search for any men named Andrew Norris, but instead of using the date of birth suggested by Keli – July or August 1966 – Gaut extends the age range to men born between 1960 and 1976.

He also requests searches of all the nation's electoral rolls, road traffic authorities for drivers' licence records, Births, Deaths and Marriages registries and police forces for records ranging from those convicted of crimes through to law abiding men who might have made complaints about noisy neighbours. As well, he approaches the Australian Taxation Office, electricity companies for billing histories of men of that name, and the Department of Immigration again, this time for men named Andrew Norris born between 1960 and 1976 moving in or out of Australia between October 1995 to February 1997, to cover the time between when Tegan was conceived to six months after she was born.

In Fairlight, the gloves are off. Keli now refuses to speak to police. Rob and Sandy have retained a solicitor and a QC to represent Keli, and they refuse to give police formal written statements. Meanwhile, despite Gaut's ongoing search, there is no sign of Tegan. Homicide investigation specialists are preparing to join Gaut's investigation later this year should the child not be found in time for the coronial hearing. Throughout 2004, time after time Keli is asked to tell police more about Tegan's disappearance. However, she is advised by her legal team to stay silent.

In late 2004 the hearings into the possible death of Tegan Lane begin. Gaut is now being assisted by the New South Wales Police's missing person's unit in his search for the man Keli says she gave Tegan to. Besides helping him carry out all the searches with different agencies and companies Australia-wide, they approach Australia Post for any records of mail registration or redirection for men named Andrew Morris or Norris in the Balmain area. They also approach the Department of Fair Trading to search for any rental bonds paid for in the area by men of those names during 1995 and 1996.

Up until now the Coroner's Court and the police have kept Keli's case quiet. Besides not notifying the media of the case, the court has also issued a non-publication order, meaning that if a journalist happens to walk into the Coroner's Court and hears the details of the case in question, they can't write about it or broadcast details about it on TV. The authorities are doing everything they can to give Keli the benefit of the doubt and to respect her privacy, but they also have a duty to do everything they reasonably can to find Tegan, dead or alive.

In August 2004, just as the hearings begin, the police get a warrant to have a listening device planted in Keli and Peter's living room. The beginning of preliminary hearings also mark the beginning of the 2004 Olympics, which are blaring from Keli and Peter's TV as they discuss the case.

'Darling, don't sit there and get yourself worked up, all right? Please,' says Peter.

'Honey, our whole lives are going to be fucked,' cries Keli.

'Mummy?' says little Macy.

'Mummy's OK, Mummy's OK,' says Peter to his daughter.

'There's nothing, they've made no real effort,' complains Keli about the police search.

'All they've done is electoral roll and electricity checks. That's all they have done to find this person,' agrees Peter about the search for Tegan's father. 'They're determining whether there are any other areas of investigation they can do or they'll allocate a hearing date.'

'You've just stepped into this mess. I let you step into it,' cries Keli. 'All this for something I did so long ago. How do we get on with our everyday lives with people looking at us? This whole mess is because I didn't have a thick skin, because I couldn't ask anyone for help, because I couldn't stand the embarrassment. I can't handle the pressure.'

'It's all right. You can't sit there and dwell on it,' says Peter.

'This isn't a case against me, is it?' asks Keli. Macy can be heard in the background asking for pizza.

'Not at the moment,' Peter answers Keli as one of them hands Macy her dinner. 'Basically they're saying you did some harm to the girl. So at the hearing the barrister will just go through it. You know, what happened to Tegan Lane.'

'I know exactly that's what they're trying to infer,' says Keli angrily. 'I know it's going to cost us a hell of a lot of money, but what choice do I have? I don't have any more choices.'

'Yeah, well that's right. So money is no object,' says Peter, who has spent the first few months of his marriage pulling together loans from Keli's family and funds from other sources to pay her legal bills. Keli is crying as he speaks.

'Don't cry, Mummy,' says little Macy.

'I'm trying to think about what I can do now,' says Keli, weeping. 'It seems to all be out of my hands, like I really don't have any choices. I didn't have any choices then, I've got no choices now.'

'You had choices then, Keli,' says Peter the irritation and confusion audible in his tone. 'Fuck, what's an abortion then? What are they? Then they come and fucking hit you up in 2000 . . .' he says, referring to the early police investigation when, as it is now known by Peter, Keli didn't say anything about Tegan and Andrew Norris, or whoever supposedly has her, being in Perth.

'Why I didn't say anything in 2000, Peter, was because I thought that they would find where he'd gone or I would be able to,' says Keli defensively. 'I didn't realise the severity of it. It didn't start off like that. Do you understand that? Now, if you don't believe me that's a different story altogether. You don't have to stay. Do you know what I am trying to say, baby? Like if you think I'm that fucked, that's it's gone that far and I'm totalled, I prefer you take Macy somewhere safe.'

'Don't say that, please,' says Peter, crying.

'Daddy, give me a cuddle then,' says little Macy.

'I'm not going to get backed into that corner again,' says Keli, defiantly. 'Yeah, I did make stupid choices. I can't tell you what sort of person I was then and who surrounded me. People just didn't even notice or care enough to ask.'

A couple of days later Keli's conversations with her husband are recorded again.

'He has put me in a very unusual situation,' says Keli about Detective Gaut. 'The case is very unusual. I just thought he would do more, considering not all avenues have been exhausted. Andrew could be living in Parramatta. The solicitor says he could be living in England. If I were him I wouldn't want to be found. He knew the risk we were taking, by not signing anything when I handed Tegan over. Maybe Andrew died, or got married and now has a family. I don't know anything about his situation.' Then Keli makes a strange comment. 'Why isn't the same pressure being applied to Tegan? Yeah, like why is all the pressure on us? Why isn't Andrew under the same pressure? After a pause she asks, 'Do they have what they think would be the best way I am supposed to have . . . killed this kid?' Peter has no reply. After a few moments Keli continues. 'It's really hard, it really is a heavy burden. It's so sad.'

'Do you love her or not?' asks Peter, trying to steer the conversation away from these dark ponderings.

'No, fuck her!' exclaims Keli, hysterically.

In the background are sounds of Peter trying to calm Keli and the TV announcer talking excitedly about an Australian who is just about to win a gold medal.

'Having a baby . . . Giving it away . . . I never thought I would have to explain it all,' continues Keli now that she is calmer. 'That's why I couldn't really care about the details because I wanted the problem to go away. Someone was saying "I'll take the problem", and that's why I gave it to him. I spend the whole time not wanting the problem to come back. I've already lost so much. I don't know why they are going to fucking bother with the next couple of months because it's so obvious they've already made up their minds. I feel like I'm being hunted. What about my fucking good points? I actually have a few of them.'

The secret police recordings of Keli, Peter and Keli's friends are not going to be played in the coronial hearing. The police interviews will be, but the listening device recordings, phone taps and other evidence is being kept aside for any future criminal proceedings that might happen later. Right now, the police and the Coroner's Court are still trying to see if Tegan can be found alive. The Deputy State Coroner tells Keli's lawyers that if she continues to refuse to be more helpful they will have no choice but to alert the media as a way of reaching out to the general public to see if Tegan can be found. The decision to go down this path isn't one that is made lightly. The police and the court know full well the mayhem that will be unleashed on the Lanes if the media gets involved. In October 2004 they decide to show Keli and her family what awaits them if she maintains her silence by inviting reporters to turn up to court, their cameras and notebooks in hand, every one of them waiting for permission to report on Keli's big secret.

'At this point the non-publication order, in terms of what is happening inside of my courtroom, is still present,' Deputy Coroner Milovanovich tells the assembled reporters. Keli is sitting in the courtroom behind her barrister, in view of the reporters, staring straight ahead.

Then, turning to Keli's lawyers, Milovanovich demands to know whether he is going to be forced to allow the media circus to begin. 'I made it very clear that on this day, today, that if there wasn't that information forthcoming I would be lifting the non-publication order,' he says.

Keli and her lawyers are sent away for ten minutes or so to see if she wants to take this opportunity. When they walk back into the courtroom, Keli's lawyer approaches the bar.

'Your Honour,' he says, 'all I can put on the record is that, as your Honour is aware, Miss Lane has assisted the police in their investigations and has provided three records of interview. There is nothing further she can add at this point in time. It is the case, though, that both she and her family are very keen to find the child Tegan, to find her safe and well.'

Keli is going to stay silent. It's time to release the hounds.

The Deputy Coroner turns to the public gallery where the journalists sit and tells them all about Keli Lane and her missing baby. Reporters furiously write page after page as the basic facts of her bizarre story are outlined. They hear that Keli has given birth to four children, one who lives with her now, and three others who were kept a secret from all of Keli's friends and family. One of those babies, named Tegan, has disappeared and is now feared dead. They learn that Keli was living with her parents throughout all three pregnancies and that authorities stumbled upon the existence of the missing second child when the adoption of her third child was being arranged. They are also told that Keli was an elite water polo player throughout the years of her secret pregnancies and that she had a long-term boyfriend, and that when they were told that Tegan had disappeared and was the subject of a police investigation, Keli's family and her ex-boyfriend claimed to never have known the baby girl or the two other children existed.

The journalists walk out of the courtroom with a spring in their step. This story is going to be huge.

The start of the public hearing rolls closer. In June 2005 the matter is handed to Chief Coroner John Abernethy. Coroner Abernethy is to be assisted by Sergeant Rebbecca Becroft, a policewoman whose softly-spoken manner contrasts with his own abrupt, occasionally gruff, tone. Both he and Becroft have been landed with this case with relatively short notice and they face a huge dilemma.

Controlling the damage the media inflicts is always a challenge. Coroner Abernethy fully expects poor behaviour from the cameramen who push and shove anyone in pursuit of a story and the producers and journalists who will happily go into the gritty details of peoples' sex lives and other salacious, but ultimately trivial, matters. Abernethy openly hates tabloid TV journalists with a passion. But this isn't the problem. The dilemma he faces is how to deal with the shoddy-looking early police work carried out by Manly Police now the case is going to be a media circus.

He and Sergeant Becroft go over the evidence in his chambers. There are huge questions to be answered here. Why on earth didn't senior officers at Manly police station notify their superiors in New South Wales Police about the obvious conflict of interest in investigating a case involving the daughter of an ex-sergeant at that station? And why was so little real investigative work done in the first three years? He could put Detective Matt Kehoe and other Manly station officers on the stand and demand they answer these questions, but as important as these questions are, making them a prominent part of this inquiry could be disastrous.

As Abernethy will write once the inquiry is over, coroners often hear cases involving so-called 'missing persons'. They are, however, almost always missing adults or teenagers who can walk, talk, form friendships, get involved in poor relationships and get themselves into trouble. The case of an infant who has been missing for nearly nine years is almost unheard of. Tegan Lane couldn't do the sort of things a normal missing person can do, so finding her alive or working out what happened in her final hours is going to take all the help the media's reach into the wider public can give. The last thing Coroner Abernethy needs is journalists being distracted by a story of a new police scandal at Manly Police, particularly one that can be beaten up to accusations of a police cover-up. Coroner Abernethy could tell reporters that this is a coronial inquiry and not a police integrity hearing until he is blue in the face, but the media is a wild and untamed beast that runs whichever angle takes its fancy. The bottom line is that Abernethy doesn't trust the media to help him carry out his duty to find Tegan.

The coroner's fears are not helped by what happened during another inquiry he'd presided over just twelve months earlier. The case involved a seventeen-year-old Aboriginal boy, T.J. Hickey, who died in February 2004 after racing away from police on his bicycle, falling off at high speed and impaling himself on a metal fence. It had all the ingredients of a major scandal and the media were all over it from day one. The angry accusations of T.J.'s grieving relatives against police and anyone else who could add to the uproar were broadcast and debated. A riot broke out where T.J. died, resulting in almost forty police being injured.

By the time Abernethy heard the case in the middle of the year the story was white hot. To his horror, some TV camera crews were chasing witnesses down the street after they appeared in his courtroom, stopping at nothing to keep the tension-filled story going. On one occasion camera crews surrounded a house where a witness had taken shelter. In the end, Abernethy was forced to delay handing down his decision for several months so the media would lose interest and the fires of racism and rage could cool down. As imperfect as police evidence was, Coroner Abernethy decided the police officers weren't to blame for the boy's death – but both he and the media knew there was a real possibility of another riot if he'd made his decision public at the height of the frenzy.

Coroner Abernethy decides he can't take the risk. His job is to do everything he can to accurately decide whether Tegan is alive or dead, and he needs the media to stick to that question. Abernethy won't put Detective Kehoe or any other Manly officers involved at that time on the stand; Detective Senior Constable Gaut will alone face questions about why early police investigations were so poor, even though he had nothing to do with them.

Meanwhile, Detective Senior Constable Gaut and the officers helping him have found thirty-seven men across Australia named Andrew Norris or Morris born between 1960 and 1976 and are in the process of interviewing all of them. The schools search is extended to all schools and Department of Education registers of home schooled children Australia-wide for details of girls born on 12 September 1996. Girls with fathers named Andrew Morris or Norris or without any fathers listed on school records are investigated and hospital records for each one obtained. On 9 June some information is received from a school in Queensland about a girl named Teagan. The fact that a little girl with the same birth date and a very similar name had been found is reported in the press. Detective Gaut flies up to Queensland to speak to the girl's grandparents. He obtains DNA samples and her medical records, but the little girl is not Keli's missing daughter.

The woman who gave birth to a stillborn child in Auburn Hospital while Keli was giving birth to Tegan is also questioned, just in case the bereaved woman took Tegan in a moment of mad grief. She hadn't. The police statement didn't record how this woman felt learning that, while her baby was born dead, another was apparently being given away in the hospital car park.

Despite all the problems of dealing with the media, going public has already led to new information for police. An anonymous tip alerted them to Keli and Duncan's attendance at a wedding in Manly only hours after Keli left Auburn Hospital with Tegan in her arms. Gaut approached the bride and groom and was given a video of the wedding. Sure enough, in the footage, there was Keli, finding her seat and sliding her sunglasses up over her hair as if nothing out of the ordinary had happened that day.

As Keli sits in the courtroom wiping away occasional tears, witnesses begin to give their evidence. On 20 June 2005 Detective Gaut is first on the stand. Sergeant Becroft reads out the dates and times of Keli's stay at Auburn Hospital. Journalists, still wrapping their minds around this strange case, jot down every detail about where the missing baby was last seen.

Keli's barrister, Peter Hamill SC, begins to cross-examine Detective Gaut. 'Do you agree that the New South Wales police's investigation into this case has been tardy in the extreme?' he begins.

'Yes, I agree with that,' replies Detective Gaut.

Keli's barrister's then bombards Gaut with questions that infer the poor quality police work done by Manly Police is why Tegan can't be found. 'The truth of the matter is that Miss Lane was not interviewed until the year 2001. The whole of the year 2000 went past without a police officer crossing her doorstep or giving her a call. That is true, is it not?'

'I don't know if there was contact made in that meantime, I don't know,' answers Gaut.

'Have you got any information to suggest that contact was made?' Keli's barrister asks.

'No, I don't,' replies the detective.

'Have you asked?'

'No.'

'And I think you said in your statement – I think it is at paragraph nineteen – that the investigation was suspended?'

'That's correct.'

'What does that mean?'

'That means that it was, I suppose, ceased to be worked on.'

'Do you know why that was so?'

'No, I don't.'

The journalists note everything that Keli's barrister is saying, but their real interest lies in what has been said about Tegan's birth and the day she disappeared, not the failure of Manly Police to search for Tegan properly. The camera crews crowd around Keli and her father as they leave the court. This case is only just heating up. Tomorrow they will learn more about this innocent looking young mum and her outlandish story about her missing secret baby.

In time, they will also learn another incredible fact, one that has only come to light nineteen days earlier. Besides travelling to Australia to give evidence, Duncan has complied with the police directive to do a paternity test for Keli's first child, who was conceived when they were dating. The results have surprised everyone. Duncan isn't the father. Keli's secret double life is more mysterious than ever before.

The following day, Coroner Abernethy is angry. As he suspected, lifting the non-publication order has resulted in some poor behaviour from the television crews assembled outside the court.

'I think in one sense my client was probably subject to a technical assault as she attempted to get away from the court,'

Keli's barrister says, referring to Keli and her father being jostled by the media pack as they attempted to leave the courtroom the day before.

Today the big media outlets have sent their lawyers to see if they can get their hands on Keli's police interview tapes and the wedding video. Coroner Abernethy knows he will have to hand them over but he is going to make his feelings known. 'Yes, I have to say some of the media acted disgracefully in front of this courtroom and I can't for the life of me understand why.'

Turning to the media's lawyers he continues to vent. 'I do not feel like granting your application. I really do not. Those cameramen and photographers are like what the Europeans call the paparazzi. I would like to think they have just a little bit of decency about it, you know, perhaps it is just a little too much to expect. The press is a necessary evil sometimes, like in these proceedings. I'm not talking about the print media, they are little angels, as we all know, until the matters get to the sub-editor, and then the truth becomes stranger than fiction.'

Having finished his lecture, Coroner Abernethy grants the media access to the tapes and gets on with the hearing. It's now time to begin the procession of social workers, doctors, nurses and adoption agency staff who dealt with Keli's secret children over the years.

The first on the stand is John Borovnik, the Department of Community Services officer who discovered Tegan's existence when he was processing Keli's third child's adoption. He outlines in precise, impressive detail the way Tegan's existence and Keli's lies were exposed. Borovnik is followed, one by one, by the nurses who presented Keli with a birthday cake just after the birth of her first secret child and the social workers who arranged the first adoption. And following them is every doctor and nurse who dealt with any aspect of Tegan's birth. Their exhaustive records of everything they do means they are able to account for every one of their actions, hour in, hour out, that day nine years ago, and for a birth that seemed sad, but didn't attract any special attention or suspicion.

Also giving evidence is Virginia Fung, the social worker who spoke to Keli while she sobbed inside Ravenswood's chapel almost six years earlier. Having worked closely with Keli during the adoption of her third baby, Fung remains impressed with what she saw of Keli's mothering skills at that time.

'She was very competent. She was very caring and loving when she held her baby,' Fung tells the court. 'It wasn't an easy time, so there were lots of tears in terms of her agonising over her decision. She was always very happy to actually see her baby, to see how much the baby had grown and how well the baby was doing.'

'Is it the case you formed a very positive impression of Keli Lane as a person?' asks Becroft.

'Yes.'

'And even this morning, when you arrived, you asked if I could pass on to her your support?'

'Yes,' confirms Virginia, adding, after a pause, that she doesn't think Keli is capable of harming a baby.

12

MURKY WATERS

Keli's life is turned upside down by the news reports about the search for Tegan. Just as she predicted when talking to Gaut, Ravenswood are keen to distance themselves from scandal and she loses her treasured coaching job. People look at her strangely on the street. She is becoming infamous. However, she still has her friends. They all go out to lunch with her at a Manly restaurant as a public show of support.

Back at the coronial hearing the press have seen enough of the dutiful doctors, nurses and social workers. They want to hear from the people in Keli's life, the friends and family who say they had no idea about the secret children born right under their noses. Keli's old friend Kati is one of the first to give evidence.

'Look, to be honest, I can't recall 1996 specifically,' she tells the court. 'I didn't play water polo with Keli at that time, so there were a lot of periods when we didn't socialise.

I've probably been out in Balmain once or twice in my life, so the socialising that I would have done with her and Duncan was through the Manly rugby club.'

Becroft asks Kati to turn her mind back to the rumours the surf club boys spread about Keli being pregnant all those years ago.

'Did you say to her "This is what the boys are saying"?' asks Becroft.

'No, I never would have,' Kati replies. 'Seriously, you don't know what that culture is like until you've been in it. You could put on one kilo or wear a baggy t-shirt and they would say something like that.'

But even though Kati and her friends were part of the Manly scene, they never played by the surf boys' rules. All the girls in their group wore t-shirts, shorts and whatever else they felt comfortable in, regardless of what the boys thought. 'We never got around in hipsters and boob tubes,' she says. 'None of us in my particular group of friends wore that stuff.'

'So what you are saying is that if Keli was pregnant, due to the clothing she wore you might not be able to tell?'

'No. Well, I never suspected she was pregnant,' Kati says, adding that when Keli was around five months' pregnant in very early 2001 with Peter's baby, she didn't have a big, obvious pregnant shape. 'Before then I thought everyone who was pregnant was massive.' Then Kati clarifies this point, saying that her own pregnancy and those of her other friends opened her eyes as to how different it is for each woman. 'I wore this shirt when I was nine months' pregnant,' Kati says to press her remark home, gesturing at the clothes she is wearing that day.

'When did you become aware of the fact that Keli had been pregnant in 1996?'

'After the police had questioned a friend of mine.'

'Which friend was that?'

'Melinda,' answers Kati, referring to the enquries made by Detective Gaut which Melinda and Brandon confronted Keli about in their living room.

'So Melinda spoke with you and said, "Look, the police officers have come around and told me this information?"' Becroft continues.

'She didn't tell me anything specific. She rang me to see if I'd been approached by the police. We didn't discuss details. She just rang and asked me. At that stage I hadn't been approached,' Kati answers.

'Did she say anything about the fact that the inquiry related to a secret pregnancy or pregnancies that Keli had been through?'

'Yeah. She said that they were making inquiries about a missing child.'

'Did you subsequently make any contact with Keli?'

'Not about that, no.'

'And you maintained contact with her generally?'

'Yes.'

'And then on 11 November 2003 – is that the date you made the statement?'

'Yes.'

'Was that at the Manly police station?'

'It was at my house.'

'After that, did you speak with Keli? Not about the details of your statement, but about the fact that you had made a statement?'

'Yes, yes.'

'Has she at any time attempted to influence anything you would say in evidence in this court?'

'No.'

'You've maintained, I think you said, that you'll always be friends, that friendships ebb and flow but she will always be a friend. Is that still your position?'

'Yes, definitely.'

'Have you an opinion of her as a person?'

'When it comes to this case I don't want to form an opinion either way. I think, as a friend, all I can do is believe that what she is saying is the truth, and I do believe her. She's a fantastic mother. She comes from a fantastic home. If I needed anything, she would help me and she would be there for me, and I hope that she knows I will be there for her, and her child and her parents and her husband.'

Looking slightly upset, Kati continues. 'I try not to think about it. I don't want this to influence our friendship. Of course, it does – it influences, unfortunately, everyone around us at this time. It's taken over from a lot of things, but we haven't discussed the case at all. Keli said she doesn't want to discuss it and, to be honest, I don't particularly want to discuss it either. I don't want to put myself or herself in a position of – or any kind of position where . . . I don't know how to put it . . . I don't want to be in a position where I might say something that I don't believe is true or I haven't . . . I've lost my train of thought.'

'I think we understand,' says Becroft.

'I think we do,' says Coroner Abernethy from the bench. Turning to Kati, he addresses her directly. 'We do not want to be in this forum discussing and dissecting Keli Lane's private life, much less the lives of all her friends, but we have an obligation to try to find out what happened to this baby, and that is why you have been brought here and asked to cooperate, and you have. I have only one question – and I think you have probably answered it in saying that Keli did not want to discuss this matter – but is there anything, any more you can tell me from talking to your friends, from talking to Keli, from talking to anyone or anything you have learnt that might assist this inquest in finding out the details of the whereabouts of the baby or her father?'

'In all honesty, no one I know or have spoken to knows anything.'

Kati's evidence would set the tone for much of the evidence given by Keli's friends through the rest of the trial. They had heard the rumours about Keli being pregnant back in 1995 and 1996 but they didn't suspect they were true and they never spoke to Keli about them. They considered Keli to be a good friend and had kept in contact with her throughout the police investigation, but they never discussed it with her in any meaningful detail. By now they had also heard Keli's claim she gave Tegan to a man named Andrew Norris. None of them, with the exception of Lisa Andreatta – who will claim she may have a vague recollection of the man Keli has described when she takes the stand – has ever met or heard of Andrew Norris.

The next witness from Keli's world to take the stand is her husband, Peter. It's clear that he wasn't in the country when Tegan was born and had nothing to do with her disappearance, but simply by being Keli's husband he has found himself at the centre of the storm. Sergeant Becroft runs over the facts of his relationship with Keli. Peter confirms that their parents have known each other since the late 1970s, that he lived with the Lanes in early 2000 when he returned from living overseas and that Keli and he quickly became lovers – and parents – after they moved out together as housemates. He says Keli didn't look pregnant for much of her pregnancy with their child; that when she was due to give birth she looked wide rather than round at the front. Becroft then questions him about the day Keli told him about the police investigation into Tegan.

'Did she tell you about all of the pregnancies, or only about Tegan?'

'No, she told me about all of the pregnancies.'

'How did you react?'

'Obviously my initial reaction was, you know, a state of shock, I guess.'

'So you were shocked. Did you ask her any questions about the pregnancies?'

'Not really . . .' Peter goes on to say that her confession was a lot to take in. He says Keli explained that there was an investigation in regards to the second child and that if he had any questions he could speak to Detective Gaut.

'So you found out about three pregnancies. No doubt you asked her about each pregnancy?' Becroft asks.

'Yes, but not in great detail, no.'

'Did you ask her why? Why, in the case of baby number one, that she gave the baby up for adoption?'

'No, I haven't actually gone into those kinds of details. It's not something I really need to know personally. I'm comfortable with our relationship so it's not something that I think I will benefit from, and I certainly don't think it will benefit us as a couple for me to delve into those sort of details, I guess.'

Four times Peter is questioned on the stand about how he felt when Keli told him about Tegan and the two other secret babies. Four times he tells the court that he was shocked, but that he never felt the need to ask her about what happened to Tegan.

'Did you go with Keli when she told her parents about the three children?' Becroft asks.

'I didn't, no.'

'So she went there by herself?'

'I believe so, yes.'

'Did you discuss her parents' reactions with Keli after she came home?'

'No, we didn't.'

Peter tells the court that he believes his wife's claim that she handed Tegan over to a man named Andrew Norris, Tegan's supposed father, two days after her birth, even though he has never met or heard of this man, that he knows police had been unable to find him and that Keli had a history of lying to authorities about who fathered her secret children.

'In your own personal opinion, do you think that Keli has done anything to harm Tegan Lane after she left Auburn Hospital?' Becroft asks finally.

'No, never.'

'Why would you say that?'

'Why would I say that?'

'Yes, what do you base that on?'

'Well, from our relationship together. She's been a fantastic wife, a wonderful mother, you know, and I love her dearly. There's really no way in the world that she would ever do anything to harm a child.'

The evidence of Kati and Peter is typical of the silences and unquestioning loyalty towards Keli in the witness testimony yet to come. If Coroner Abernethy and Sergeant Becroft are becoming frustrated they are not letting it show. Instead, they prepare to turn their attention to the next witness due to take the stand – Keli's father, Robert Lane.

13

ROBERT LANE TAKES
THE STAND

Rob Lane has a steady gaze. His conservatively cut, dark suit hangs well on his ageing but tall and erect body. His ruddy face is topped with short white hair that stands on end. All eyes are on him as Becroft begins her questions.

'You've been sitting through the proceedings over the last four days, so you've heard a number of witnesses give evidence?'

'I have,' replies Rob with his typical disdain for chatter or elaboration.

'And heard certain things that they've said?'

'Yes.'

'And in relation to Keli, she had three pregnancies?'

'Yes.'

'. . . Babies in 1995, 1996 and 1999. And it was the case up until January of 2004 that you were not aware of those pregnancies?'

'No,' Rob answers by way of agreement with Becroft's statement.

'Is there any time at all during any of those pregnancies that you may have suspected that Keli was pregnant?'

'No.'

'OK. And why do you think that is the case, that you never suspected that she was pregnant?'

'Well, I had no reason to feel that she was pregnant. In hindsight I feel a bit foolish that I didn't notice anything, but I had no reason to believe she was pregnant at all.'

'Did you notice any change in her body shape at all?'

'Well, that varied at times due to water polo training and physical exercise; if she was doing one sport as compared to another sport. I might have mentally thought, "Oh well, Keli's put on a bit of weight", but she was a strong girl and I didn't give it any more thought than that.'

'OK. And it's the case that Keli spent some nights a week at your house?'

'Yes.'

'And at the time she was seeing Duncan and spent some time at his house, is that correct?'

'That's the case.'

'So for her to be absent from your house for a period of two, three or four days, that wouldn't have caused you any concern?'

'No, because we always knew what – well, we believed we knew what she was doing. Her training was at Balmain or at Homebush or at Liverpool, and it was her lifestyle at the time.'

'And it's the case that, when you were initially told by Keli about these pregnancies, Keli only told you about Tegan?'

'Yes.'

'She didn't tell you about the first baby or the third baby?'

'No.'

'Do you know of any reason why she didn't tell you of those other two?'

'I think that, right till the end, she wanted to hide it from our family.'

'Why do you think she would have wanted to do that?'

'Ah, because she didn't want to disappoint the family. She was held in very, very high esteem in the family, and still is. She was very, very well known in the community. I believe she was trying to hide this episode in her life from everyone because of those pressures.'

'And do you feel that if she had disclosed the fact that she was pregnant with any one of those children, you would have disowned her?'

'Certainly not.'

'What makes you think that she was put into the position where she felt that she had to hide them?' asks Becroft.

'Well, I don't know for sure, but I'd say it was a multitude of circumstances at the time. It was the first time in her life that she had a lot of freedom. Not that she was held back, but she was constantly in our care and doing her training and sport. We had a very close-knit family, and then these pregnancies happened, together with other stresses she had while she was trying to achieve things. I think that it became overbearing and then the thing multiplied and multiplied and multiplied.'

'OK. When you were told about Tegan I believe that, when Detective Senior Constable Gaut inadvertently mentioned baby number one and baby number three, you were quite shocked?'

'I was. He didn't inadvertently say it, but he delicately told us, you know, that did we know that she had had two other children, and that floored us.'

'Because Keli hadn't been honest with you?'

'Well, yes. No, not that she'd . . . It was just the shock of knowing that there are additional children that had been adopted out.'

'So you were told of Tegan, and then Detective Gaut mentioned the other two children, so three children. Did you question Keli about the circumstances of those three children?'

'Not at any great length.'

So Keli's father, just like her husband and her friend Kati, was apparently deeply shocked to learn that she had had three secret children, but never felt the need to ask her why. It's a strange phenomenon, something Rob seems to be aware of as Becroft's questions continue.

'Did you ask her any questions?'

'Yes. Basically: why didn't she come to us? She knew that we loved her – we were a close-knit family – that there'd be no difficulties that I knew of, or that my wife knew of, and that we wished she'd come to us. She would have got support from the very start and this thing wouldn't have blossomed or ballooned into the serious thing it is today.'

'Did you ever ask her why she never terminated the pregnancies?'

'She said she couldn't hurt a baby,' answers Rob. Whether having a termination and hurting a baby are the same thing is something people hold strong and different views on. Most dads are unaware of their daughters' teenaged abortions, and it seems that Rob is no exception.

'And they were her exact words? "She couldn't hurt a baby"?'

'Well, ah, they may not have been her exact words, but she said, "I couldn't do it, Dad. You know I couldn't hurt a baby or hurt children", or something to that effect.'

'Is your family religious?' asks Becroft.

'Ah, we don't go to church regularly, but I think we've got certain beliefs, yes.'

'Do you think that religion may have influenced Keli in relation to her decisions?'

'No, no,' Lane answers quickly.

'I'm only asking your opinion.'

'No, not at all. I did ask her why . . . The easy way out would have been to terminate the children and she said, "Dad, I couldn't do it".'

'And you believe that?'

'I certainly do.'

Becroft then outlines the latest explanation Keli gave police as to who fathered Tegan, asking Rob to clarify whether it matches with his understanding. 'That version is that she had a brief affair with an Andrew Norris?'

'Yes . . .'

'And that during the course of that brief affair she fell pregnant?'

'Yes.'

'Then she contacted him, told him about the pregnancy and he'd basically called her a slut?'

'Yes.'

'And then shortly – '

'Ah, yes, yes, yeah,' Robert cuts in.

'OK,' says Becroft as she tries to continue her questions. 'And that they had no social contact after that point?'

'Yes.'

'OK, and then just prior to her going into hospital to give birth to Tegan she contacts Andrew Norris?'

'That's listening to . . .'

'Yes?' asks Becroft, giving Rob time to recognise which

story she's talking about. After all, Keli has given several
different versions about how and where Tegan was handed
over that day.

'Yeah, yes,' answers Rob.

'That's the version – ' resumes Becroft.

'Yes, yes.'

' – when then at the hospital, the final plans are finalised for
Andrew Norris to take custody of Tegan.'

'Yes.'

'And that his girlfriend at the time, Melanie, or Mel, also – '

'Yes.'

' – had also come to the hospital?'

'Yes.'

'OK, do you believe that version?'

'Yes.'

'Does it seem believable to you?'

'Yes.'

'OK. Andrew Norris is in a relationship, and this Mel
person has agreed to take this child into her home and raise
this child – you don't find that unusual?' asks Becroft.

'Oh, well, of course it's unusual,' answers Lane. 'This is
a most unusual matter.' Changing the subject slightly, he
continues. 'I don't necessarily believe that Andrew Norris or
Morris was his correct name, because that's probably not the
normal thing for guys to do when they have affairs.'

Becroft turns the questioning to Robert's reaction to Keli's
2004 confession to him and Sandy that police were investigating the disappearance of Tegan.

'Did you become angry with her?'

'No. I was shocked. My wife and I were shocked.'

'What did Keli tell you had happened?'

'Well, I can't remember having much of a conversation

about it,' Lane answers. 'We didn't know the seriousness of the matter, and we became detached to some extent because her wedding was coming up and that was the main objective at the time.'

After repeating how he and his wife didn't understand the seriousness of what Keli was telling them, Robert continues. 'It was obviously distressing to my daughter, and because I didn't know the extent of the investigation I didn't want to create any more trauma for her. I didn't want to stop myself and my wife from giving her the support that she obviously needed at that time, together with her husband and particularly our grandchild.'

'Is it the case that, after you'd spoken with police, you wanted to get to the bottom of what this was all about, like why this all had happened, why she has kept all these pregnancies a secret?'

'No.'

'You never wanted to get to the bottom of it?'

'No, basically not. Why? Because we were detached from it and we didn't know the seriousness of it at the time.'

Lane isn't going to be questioned about how his old colleagues behaved during the initial investigation undertaken by Manly Police because of Coroner Abernethy's decision not to let his coronial hearing be sidetracked by issues that belong in a different courtroom. But despite the fact there is no spotlight on Robert's long career at Manly police station, his claim that he, an ex-police officer, did not understand the seriousness of the police investigation into the disappearance of a baby is extraordinary. However, his claim is made earnestly. Lane is a witness who never gets angry, flustered or embarrassed.

'And have you asked Keli whether she has harmed Tegan, if anything had happened to Tegan?' asks Becroft.

'No. Oh, I've just said to her, you know, "I believe what you've said to me" and she said, "Yes Dad".'

'Because you were a serving member of the New South Wales Police – '

'Yes.'

' – so you're fairly familiar with laws in relation to homicide, manslaughter, infanticide and all those sorts of offences?' Becroft asks.

'Well, I wasn't a working-class policeman as such. I wasn't in those roles, but I'd have a working knowledge of it, of course, yeah.'

'And you still believe that Keli didn't harm Tegan?'

'Of course.'

'And that Tegan is still alive?'

'I do.'

Robert Lane looks composed. Coroner Abernethy decides to question him. 'Mr Lane, did it occur to you as odd that Keli would have babies one and three adopted out with success – '

'Yes.'

' – but go in a completely different direction with Tegan?'

'It did.'

'Did you question her about it?'

'No, because I accepted her version of what happened with the second one.'

'But I don't think she's told anyone why she took a course of action with number two that's so different from numbers one and three, unless I've missed it,' observes Abernethy.

'Well, the only thing I can think of would be that she knew who the father was – so Keli may have thought that to give her to the actual father might be a bit more beneficial than an adoption, in that particular instance,' replies Lane.

'The fact that, according to her version, the father, his mother and his partner rock up to Auburn Hospital and simply take a child – that didn't seem to you to be hard to believe?' asks Abernethy.

'Well, it's most unusual, but I don't know the relationship that he would have been in with Mel or what the situation was. I just took it for what was said to me.'

'So you basically accepted Keli's story about that adoption, about the way it happened, despite all the lies she's told professionals during that process and other birth processes – you know that now.'

'Yes.'

'A litany of them, to health professionals and police?'

'Yes.'

'Do you still accept her version as it stands?'

'Yes.'

'Unequivocally?'

'Yes.'

'Because she is your daughter?'

'Yes.'

'And you love her?'

'Yes.'

'It's surreal, isn't it?'

'It is surreal,' agrees Lane.

'It's bizarre?' continues Coroner Abernethy.

'I cannot . . . Yes . . . it's just most bizarre.'

Keli's barrister then lets Rob explain how he timed the car ride from Auburn Hospital to the Lane's family home. It was the trip Keli would have made one way or the other the day Tegan disappeared so that she could get ready in time to go to her friends' wedding with Duncan that afternoon.

'Do you remember that day?' asks Keli's barrister.

'No, I don't,' Robert replies.

Robert Lane's time on the stand now comes to an end. The words he has used have spelled out the fact that he is an ex-senior policeman who doesn't ask too many questions about his missing granddaughter. But the impression he leaves is that of a bewildered father who can't explain what has happened in his daughter's life but who is standing by her.

Coroner Abernethy shifts irritably in his chair. He is no closer to finding Tegan.

14

DUNCAN AND HIS FAMILY
TAKE THE STAND

Keli's and Duncan's families march separately through the
throng of TV camera crews waiting outside the courtroom. The image of Keli and Duncan at a wedding together
a couple of hours after Tegan disappeared has been on the
TV news and in the papers. Duncan is now recognised as
the co-star of this drama. Duncan, his wife, his brothers and
his mother are in one camp; Keli, her father and just about
everyone else Keli knew in those days are in the other. Today
the media are waiting to hear from the man who shared Keli's
bed, but first there are others to hear from, including another
of Keli's friends.

Lisa Andreatta is the friend Keli spent Christmas 2002
with in the UK after she had lied to police that they had lost
touch. After admitting she knew Keli had lied to police before
visiting her, Lisa claims Keli didn't talk to her about the police
investigation while she was overseas. Lisa had only become

friends with Keli at college in 1996, but she'd spent enough time with Keli and her friends to form a strong opinion of Duncan.

'How would you describe that relationship?' asks Becroft.

'I don't know. I didn't really think very highly of Duncan myself but they were in a relationship and they seemed to love each other, so that's their personal choice.'

'Now you say in your statement that "I have a very close relationship with Keli now. In 1996 we were good friends but not as close as we are now",' states Becroft.

'Yep,' answers Lisa.

'How often do you see her?'

'Depends; sometimes once a week, sometimes once every couple of weeks.'

'What has she said to you about this matter?'

'Just clearing up, like, stuff that's in the media, stuff that I just couldn't quite piece together, so she's cleared up a few matters.'

'Such as?'

'That she did have an affair.'

'Yes?'

'That she did have those children.'

'Yes?'

'That I may have met Andrew Norris one time in Balmain,' says Lisa, now contradicting her original flat denial to Detective Gaut about ever hearing of a man named Andrew Norris.

'Whereabouts?' asks Becroft.

'I don't remember the places we went to . . .'

'She didn't say?'

'No, I didn't ask,' answers Lisa, adding herself to the growing number of close friends and family members who never ask Keli probing questions.

Duncan's brother Simon now takes the stand. The house he lived in with his wife back in 1996 was diagonally opposite Duncan's house, so they saw a lot of each other during that year. Simon tells the court that the relationship his brother Duncan had with Keli reminded him of the kind of relationship he had with his own wife before they were married. He says the possibility of Duncan and Keli tying the knot was talked about.

'They'd been going out for a long time. I think it's something that you just generally discuss, you know.'

Simon comments that while Keli was 'a lady who could put weight on and take weight off in varying degrees', he never suspected she was pregnant and Duncan never said anything about her being pregnant to him.

'I'm just going to run a scenario by you and I just would like you to comment on it at the end,' says Becroft. 'On 5 November 2003, Brandon and Melinda Ward, who are friends of Keli Lane, spoke with Keli at their home about the police inquiries in relation to Tegan Lane. During that conversation Keli stated to both Melinda and Brandon, "It has nothing to do with you guys. It's between me, Duncan, Simon and Narelle." Do you have any opinion in relation to that particular comment that Keli has made?'

'My wife and I know absolutely nothing about what Keli has done or hasn't done,' says Simon. 'For her to say something like that, I think, is dishonest. She's trying to avoid people asking her questions by saying something like that.'

This will not be the last time Simon will sit in a courtroom and be asked about that statement. In five years' time he will publicly reveal one of the most painful experiences in his life to try and explain why Keli would possibly say such a thing. By then, years of dedicated police work will reveal the incredible extent of Keli's lies. But here in the stand, all

Simon can think of is how shocked he is. He's at a total loss to explain anything.

Simon and Duncan's mother, Julie Melville, is next. Julie had trained as a midwife late in her nursing career and by 1996 she had spent two and a half years working as a nurse in a maternity ward while finishing her training.

'And even though you are experienced as a nurse you did not suspect at any time that Keli was pregnant during 1996?' Becroft asks the woman with steely eyes in the stand.

'No,' answers Julie, adding that she didn't suspect Keli was pregnant the year before, either. And just as she did when police first told her she was nominated by Keli as her midwife for Tegan's birth, Julie denies it outright. She also says that the mobile number Keli gave the hospital was a fake – Julie didn't own a mobile back then.

'Has Keli ever asked you for any advice in relation to having a child, giving birth?'

'Not that I remember.'

'Did you have any conversations with her about home-births?'

'I don't agree with homebirths, so no. But if she had, it would have been a very short conversation.'

Julie also recounts the time in 1999 when she saw Keli at the Manly Surf Lifesaving Club. Julie felt awkward because Duncan's new girlfriend, now wife, was there. Nonetheless, she'd said hello and Keli had told her about her full-time job coaching at Ravenswood. 'She looked terrible,' says Julie of Keli that night, adding that Keli wore a short skirt despite having put on weight since the last time Julie had seen her. 'I felt sorry for her.'

Julie finishes and Duncan enters the witness box. Naturally enough, every reporter is curious to see what Keli's ex looks like. Duncan, like his brother Simon, is still a good–looking, athletic guy now that he's in his thirties. He has a confident, somewhat defiant air about him as he takes the stand.

The fact that a DNA test proves Duncan is not the father of Keli's first child, despite being her boyfriend at the time, is revealed. 'So it's obvious then that, some time during your relationship with Keli in 1994 and 1995, another man fathered Keli's child?' asks Becroft.

'Yes.'

'Did you ever suspect that she was having an affair?'

'Most certainly not.'

'Now, thinking back, do you now have any suspicions about who that father might be, might have been?

'No, none whatsoever,' answers Duncan.

'In relation to baby number two, Tegan Lane, the subject of the inquest today, are you aware of any person who may have fathered that child besides yourself?'

'No.'

'At the end of 1995 were you aware if Keli was having an affair?' asks Becroft.

'Just to clear this matter up, if I was in any way aware that Keli was having an affair I would have ceased the relationship,' states Duncan firmly, unaware that the double standard he imposed on their own relationship would soon be revealed in the court.

Duncan goes on to claim he didn't see much of Keli when she was pregnant with Tegan due to their respective training schedules, stating that in 1996 he would have 'been lucky to see her on weekends'. Keli's water polo commitments meant that Duncan's place would have been a much more convenient place to sleep than her parents' place in Manly, a fact that is not lost on the court.

'What about during the week, with Keli's connection to the Balmain water polo club and its proximity to Gladesville?' asks Coroner Abernethy.

'She would drop in. She'd beep the horn outside,' says Duncan. 'I can see what you are saying. Geographically my place was a great location there but it just wasn't working as easily as . . .' says Duncan, trailing off vaguely.

'I don't want to put words into your mouth,' says Coroner Abernethy. 'You don't believe there were that many sleepovers in 1996?'

'Looking back on the evidence of where I was and what I was doing, I would have to say there were certainly far less than the previous two years or even in 1997,' Duncan replies.

'You've indicated in your statement that you were in a sexual relationship with Keli, basically from the time that you first met. You've also indicated in your record of interview that at the very beginning of your relationship, you and Keli had sex on a daily basis.'

'Yes.'

'You've indicated that you believed that Keli was on the pill because you saw it in her bag.'

'That's correct,' says Duncan, adding that he saw her taking the pill frequently.

'Now it's obviously the case that Keli was pregnant while she was in a sexual relationship with you.'

'I understand how it looks,' says Duncan, aware that most reporters in the courtroom have now dragged their eyes from their notepads to look at him. 'I had no comprehension whatsoever that she had two babies while I was sleeping with her during the four years we were going out.'

'Did you ever see Keli naked without her clothes on?' asks Becroft, resuming her questions.

'Yes, I did see Keli naked without her clothes on, but at no time did I assume she could have been pregnant.'

'Did you form the view that her physical body shape had changed, in that she may have put on weight?'

'I'm sure I did.'

'I know these questions may be difficult, but you've indicated in your record of interview that at times, when you had sex with Keli, you had sex in the spoon position?'

'That's correct,' says Duncan, as every journalist in the room takes furious notes.

'When you say spoon position, what exactly are you referring to?' continues Becroft.

'Would you like a demonstration or . . . ?' Duncan jokes.

'No, thank you. OK,' replies Becroft.

Despite Duncan's bravado, it's clear he's deeply uncomfortable. For a split second, his confident, brash mask slips. His mouth drops slightly open, his smile falls into the shape of an anguished silent moan and his eyes look heavenward under closed lids. It's a look of pure pain. After all his hard work and his dreams of fame as a footballer, it has come to this.

Quickly collecting himself, Duncan answers the question. 'I mean we are lying down; sex is from behind. It's not the missionary position, it's not any other position, we're lying down, I'm cuddling into Keli's back.'

'On your side?' asks Coroner Abernethy.

'Yes,' Duncan replies flatly.

'So you're on your side and you've also indicated that, at times, you have attempted to put your hand around the front of her and that she would push your hand away saying "No, I'm putting on weight",' says Becroft.

'Yes.'

'Did that raise any suspicion for you?'

'No,' says Duncan. 'She put on weight, she lost weight. Keli wasn't the first girlfriend I'd had and I'm fairly certain all of them were rather careful about their weight.'

'And did Keli try to prevent you from seeing her naked? Do you recall her ever doing that?'

'I don't recall her ever doing that, no.'

'So at no time did she – after say, when she got up in the morning – quickly get dressed so that you couldn't see her?' asks Becroft.

'I wasn't living with the predetermined spy attitude where I would catch her; you have to imagine I never thought any of this was happening, so at no stage was I trying to put the pieces together,' says Duncan, his hands open and facing upwards. 'She could quite easily have jumped out of bed, whipped on her tracksuit and said "I've got to go home". She could have done that for six months even if she hadn't been pregnant, and it wouldn't have made a difference if she did it when she was . . . Do you know what I mean? I wasn't looking for anything.'

'Did you and Keli often speak about becoming married?'

'I wouldn't say we spoke about it often. I know at the start of the relationship, in first few months, we did talk about how in love we were and that it was amazing that we could be thinking of marriage so quickly.'

'You never proposed to her at all during the course of your relationship?'

'No.'

'Do you believe that at any time you conveyed those thoughts to Keli?' queries Becroft.

'In the world I was living in, the relationship I was having with Keli, the two of us were madly in love. Now we know there was something else going on but, take it as you will,

I didn't know it was going on. I'm in this relationship where I'm madly in love. We enjoyed each other immensely. We always had a great time together, fought rarely and, yes, of course I'm sure that if we had fallen pregnant outside of wedlock I would have jumped at the chance.'

'Would you have put any pressure on Keli to terminate the pregnancy?'

'Never.'

Becroft now turns the questioning to what Duncan thought of Keli's family. 'Is it the case that she held her mum and dad in high regard?'

'Certainly, yes.'

'Did she ever indicate to you that at times there may have been pressure put on her to perform in relation to school or sport?'

'I don't think Keli ever indicated to me that there was pressure, but it's there, it's always there,' answers Duncan. 'She was a semi-professional sports person, as was I. There is pressure to perform, but in no way would I say the idea that sport was the be all and end all was the message sent to Keli by her family.'

'During your record of interview you were asked whether you'd had any sex with any women while you were with Keli, and you quite honestly admitted that you had.'

'Yes.'

'That was after a surf club party and Keli found out. How did she find out?'

'I told her.'

'How did she react?'

'She was quite upset.'

'And . . .?'

'The words she used that afternoon in her backyard were "You're not getting away from me that easily."'

'What did you imply from that?'

'That she had forgiven me.'

'And that she didn't want to let you go?'

'That's right.'

'Who was the woman you had sex with?'

'Well?' asks Coroner Abernethy as Duncan fails to answer.

'It was Keli's best friend,' Becroft answers, reading from the police report while Duncan remains silent.

'How did Keli react when she found out?' asks Abernethy

'I don't think she was overly surprised,' answers Duncan defensively.

'What made you think that?'

'To be quite honest, Keli had warned me before that this girl had attached herself to other girls' boyfriends. I swore it wouldn't be a problem with me, that I'd be awake to her friend's little game, but unfortunately on this specific night I wasn't,' Duncan says unchivalrously.

'Were there anyone else you cheated with?'

'No,' says Duncan, omitting to mention the woman who is now his wife.

'How would you describe the term "player"?' asks Becroft.

'In which context are you referring?' asks Duncan.

'In the context that you were a player.'

'How would I describe it? As an upstanding, intelligent, good-looking member of the community,' Duncan replies, attempting to make a joke of the question. Realising that no one thinks he is being funny, Duncan answers again. 'There are different types of players and I know the context you're using it in. There are people who play over people, there are people who play some sort of role . . . Flamboyancy and that sort of thing.'

'A witness who gave evidence, and I believe it was your

old housemate Juan, described you as a player, and as someone who drank a lot. How would you interpret what he says?'

'If he's using the connotation of "player" in a sexual reference, of me having several partners, I've no idea why he would say that,' answers Duncan. Then, deciding to make light of the reference to his drinking back then, he adds he used to do a bit of beer brewing at home.

'Some people have described you as a player but you deny that, instead saying you were faithful to Keli except for that one time?' persists Becroft.

'That's correct.'

'Obviously, now it's the case that she must have cheated on you, but you're not aware of who that could have been?'

'No.'

'Do you remember, in the winter of 1996, Keli being associated with a man then, about thirty years old, tall, blond-haired, a suit in the city, who may have gone to Sydney Uni, good-looking? Can you think of anyone who generally fits that description and was either a friend of yours or Keli's?' asks Coroner Abernethy.

'There are thirty or forty people I know who fit that description,' answers Duncan. 'If I had an inclination that something was going on I would have acted on it. To answer your question, do I specially remember anyone along those lines? No.'

Becroft then starts to question Duncan about spending time with Keli on the day Tegan disappeared.

'I don't recall 100 per cent going to the wedding with Keli,' says Duncan. 'I've tried to recollect it. I'm fairly certain I drove my F100 truck but as to whether or not I was meeting Keli there, or picked her up from her house, or if she got changed at my house, or any of that, I'm not sure.'

'This is a big ask, but do you remember what happened after the wedding, after the reception? Just keep in mind that Keli's just had a baby and just come out of hospital that day,' asks Coroner Abernethy.

'I don't remember. My guess would have been me returning to the Lane's house in Fairlight.'

'Do you have any recollection of the wedding itself, at the reception?' asks Becroft.

'Not specifically. I think it was the third wedding I had been to at the Pier Restaurant in Manly by that stage. As one can imagine, they blur into each other.'

'There was nothing about that wedding, about Keli's actions or her behaviour, on that particular day that stood out?'

'No.'

Chief Coroner Abernethy considers Duncan for a few seconds. 'Since you became aware of all this, it must have been a hell of a shock,' he says.

'A hell of a shock is a bit of an understatement,' Duncan replies.

'Very carefully and under oath, you still can't think of anything more than you're telling us?'

Pausing for a second, Duncan collects his thoughts. Then he says, 'Looking back, I can see how she managed to achieve it. I can see how, when she was coming towards full-term, she probably wouldn't come into the house; she might beep the horn outside my place and I would see her out the window, run out and give her a kiss. She'd say, "I've got to go to training, I've got to go here, I've got to go there." And there was a comment by Rob Lane, Keli's father, at one stage in the house where he mentioned, "You're looking beautiful, Keli, don't put all that weight on again", and Keli got really flustered. But you have to understand this is all in hindsight.'

'Yes, of course,' says Coroner Abernethy.

'And of course she's going to be temperamental about her weight. It is a feminine gift. But looking back now I can see that her father's comment meant something else to her.'

'But hindsight is a very clear window and at the time it meant nothing?'

'That's right. Just to add to that, I dealt with the police for four years believing Keli could not possibly have had a baby in 1996; from when I was first notified by the police until I came over to Australia for the interview in late 2004.'

'You thought it all ended with that letter about the adoption being resolved?'

'Yeah, I was under the impression for such a long time that it was just virtually impossible, as I'm sure we're all thinking, for me to be in this relationship and not notice that she was pregnant. I had a four-year battle with accepting Keli had been pregnant . . .'

'Yes, I understand,' says Coroner Abernethy, ending his questions so Becroft can resume.

'During the course of the inquest and the investigation into Tegan Lane, it's become apparent that Keli's told a number of lies during the birth and adoption process of baby number one, two and three. And in all three of those births Keli has nominated you as being the father – ' she begins.

'All three of them?' interrupts Duncan, clearly surprised.

'That's correct. Your mother has been noted on Tegan Lane's medical records as being the homebirth midwife that Keli utilised during her pregnancy. That, of course, is also a lie. As indicated, there's also a number of other lies in relation to the adoption of the third secret baby where Keli has indicated to the adoption workers that you were unwilling to sign consent forms and that you didn't want any involvement with this baby,' Becroft outlines, adding that these consent forms had been sent to a post office in Harbord where Keli later signed for them and picked them up. 'Is there any reason why, in your own opinion, Keli has lied and concealed all three of these pregnancies?'

'Objection!' shouts Keli's barrister, not wanting someone who is no longer a friend of Keli's to give his opinion of her actions.

'Have a go?' says Coroner Abernethy to Duncan, allowing Becroft's question.

'I would prefer not to, your Honour, if that's all right,' Duncan replies.

'Just going back to the conception of Tegan,' says Becroft, taking another line of questioning. 'Obviously it's hard to estimate, but it's possible that it happened some time at the end of November 1995, any time in December and perhaps during the first couple of days of January 1996. Do you recall what you were doing at that particular point?'

'I have a fairly good idea of what I was doing the whole time. I was out there just living life and having a great time and taking every opportunity that came towards me. I wasn't skulking around in the dark to see if the woman I loved was having babies out the back door,' says a despondent Duncan.

Duncan is finally allowed to step down from the witness box. His performance hasn't exactly painted him in the colours of a nice guy. Despite all of his claims of love for Keli when they were dating, Duncan had a reputation as a player and cheated on her at least once. The truth is, he cheated on her a second time when he met Karen, who is now his wife, in 1998. He even tried to infer that Keli's best friend, the one he says he cheated with in 1995, was mainly to blame for his infidelity. And he also claimed he would have jumped at the chance to marry Keli back then, but never proposed to his clearly smitten girlfriend. Neither did he ever ask her to move into his house, despite the fact that living there would have been very convenient for Keli's heavy training schedule.

But while Duncan certainly wasn't the most attentive of boyfriends for most of the time he and Keli were together, there's a big difference between being a selfish young footballer and someone involved in the disappearance of a two-day-old baby. Despite Keli's supporters' clear dislike for Duncan, those on the outside looking in, including the police now handling the case, are convinced that Duncan had nothing to do with Tegan's disappearance.

15

KELI'S FRIENDS KEEP
THE FAITH

Duncan's face is on the news. 'Is it possible that he really didn't know?' viewers ask themselves. It seems incredible. So, too, is the ongoing lack of engagement by Keli's friends and family with the whereabouts of Tegan, as Coroner Abernethy and Sergeant Becroft are rapidly finding out.

'So it's the case that you have known Keli all of your life?' Becroft asks Brandon, Keli's childhood friend.

'That's correct, yes.'

'And you were never aware of – '

'Not until Detective Gaut came to us, and came to us, and came to us, and came to us again about the investigation. We gave him the same answer every single time,' interrupts Brandon, barely concealing his annoyance at being in the witness box.

'Did you notice anything about Keli, a change in her physical appearance?'

'As I said in the statement, in 1995 a few of the boys were saying "Jeez, Keli has put on a bit of weight", which is just typical boy banter. It's not really mentioned to the girls because girls are fairly touchy about their weight, but it was nothing more than typical banter. If a bloke goes overseas, puts on weight and comes back, the boys would say "Jeez, you look like you've swallowed a sheep". It's the same sort of thing. But apart from that there was nothing.'

'Your wife Melinda played water polo with Keli back then, and you've indicated in your statement that there were whispers in the team about Keli being pregnant in 1995.'

'No, it wasn't really Keli's team-mates saying that. It was more the boys on the sideline.'

'OK, so it wasn't so much actually – '

'It was the boys being boys, actually,' Brandon says, interrupting Becroft again.

Becroft then asks Brandon about where he socialised with Keli in the mid 1990s. Brandon lists three or four Balmain pubs that sponsored Keli's and Melinda's water polo club at different times, adding that he and Melinda would go with the team, have a drink and then head back to Manly.

'Would you say that Keli became drunk on occasions?' asks Becroft.

'Possibly. I think we all did . . .' Brandon begins. Then he snaps, 'Your best bet is to ask Keli that.' Now he stares down his nose at Becroft.

'I'm only asking you – ' she starts, but Coroner Abernethy has had enough and steps in.

'Well, court cases don't work like that,' he shoots back at Brandon. 'Just bear with us, please.'

Slightly subdued, Brandon answers more of Becroft's questions, but when he's asked to recall when Keli confessed to giving birth to Tegan to him and Melinda in their living room, he gets short-tempered again. 'The detective has rung us time and time and time again to the point where it's like, "God, what more can we tell you!" He told us "Look, if you make a statement then that'll probably be the end of it", so Melinda and I said "Well, OK, if that's the end of it we will make a statement." Then all of a sudden we're here.'

'That's right, because a child is missing – ' begins Coroner Abernethy.

'I understand that, but – '

' – and you have an obligation like all of us to – ' continues Coroner Abernethy.

'Yeah, but I am saying – '

' – play your little role in helping us try to find her,' Abernethy finishes.

'You can only say so many times you don't know anything. We've done as much as we can,' Brandon continues to complain, refusing to back down.

'I don't doubt that, but you've become very impatient about the whole process,' says Coroner Abernethy firmly. 'I'm afraid we've got to subvert our own impatience about these matters for the greater good. We're just trying to find out what happened to the child. You understand that, surely?'

'I do understand it but, you know, there is a point where it does start affecting our family,' he whines.

'Yes, yes, no doubt it does,' says Coroner Abernethy with the patience that only decades of practice dealing with stubborn witnesses can provide. 'There is also a point where witnesses have to be tested about what they have said. That's what courtrooms are for, and that's what magistrates and judges and coroners are for, and – '

'Fair enough. I understand where you're coming from, but you can't see where we are coming from,' says Brandon.

'I do, I do,' says the Chief Coroner, managing to remain polite. 'As a matter of fact you are probably one of the few who have been really resentful about the whole process. Most people were very cooperative, but you and your wife weren't.'

Keli's barrister sets about putting Brandon in a better light by suggesting that, despite Brandon's annoyance about having to help police and be here today, he takes the search for Tegan seriously.

'I take it very seriously,' emphasises Brandon. 'I'd love this thing to be sorted so we can all get on and have everything work out really well.'

'And you'd like them to find Tegan?' adds Keli's barrister.

'Definitely,' replies Brandon in an upbeat tone. 'I had my fingers crossed when that thing in the paper came up the other day,' he says, referring to the little girl whom police thought may have been Keli's missing child. 'Melinda and I were so happy and thought, finally, everything has been resolved. Unfortunately it didn't work out that way. We just hope that this works it out.'

'Is it the case that you and your wife are quite protective of Keli?'

'We're very protective of Keli. She's one of our closest friends, but in saying that I know the truth does have to come out. We've told you everything we possibly know.'

Brandon goes onto confirm that he and his wife have two children, a three-year-old and an eleven-month-old. Keli babysits them now that Melinda is back at work. 'Keli is sensational with them,' he says, his voice warm with feeling. 'She's caring, she's generous, she's an awesome person. Just, you know, a good friend.'

His wife Melinda gives similar evidence, claiming that, while there were rumours around the pool that Keli was pregnant, no one said anything to her. When asked about the time she and Brandon confronted Keli about the phone calls they'd been receiving from police about Tegan, Melinda says, 'I think she was quite shocked that we had been informed. She didn't want to pursue the conversation or add to the conversation. So we just left it and I haven't spoken to her about it since.'

'And obviously you remain friends with her to this day?'

'Yes.'

'And she will continue to look after your kids?'

'For sure, yeah.'

'And what do you say as to her character, her personality?'

'She's a loving, caring person who would stick by you, a really good friend. She's been my friend since I can remember. She's always been there for me. She's a great girl.'

The next witness, Alison, has moved out of the Manly social scene in recent years. She speaks about how the pregnancy rumours going around Manly in 1995 and 1996 didn't make her suspect anything because of Manly's often 'toxic' culture. Nasty rumours like those were common.

'You said that you heard a rumour about Keli being pregnant and going away north?' asks Becroft. 'Can you be any more specific with the time that you heard this rumour?'

'No, I can't, because at that time I was in a career where I wasn't around a lot. As I said, I think it could have been at Manly Skiff Club. Normally there were about twenty people who got together there. Someone said "You know that she went north with her mother" and I just didn't think that would be true. I dismissed it.'

'Because your view is that Keli and her mother's relation-ship — '

'I mean, Keli loves her parents, but I just thought it was silly that that would happen,' answers Alison, declining to shed any light on what she thought of Keli's relationship with her mother.

'You never said to Keli when you saw her, "Look, this is what I heard, this is a rumour, can you tell me, like, is it true?"'

'No. Keli and I had a nice friendship when we were growing up,' says Alison, unaware that, in one of the interviews with Detective Gaut, Keli had denied they had been friends. 'I suppose because I didn't believe it, I just didn't want to enter into any of that type of gossip. I wasn't going to go and say "Look, Keli, you know, I've heard this about you" because I didn't believe it.'

Alison then recalled socialising with Keli around Manly. 'Keli wasn't into the guys as such. She was a social butterfly who would chat to everybody in our group. Yeah, she would talk to the men but they were our friends. Keli never really went off into any dark corners to chat up men or anything like that. She was always a happy-go-lucky, very enthusiastic person who really took life on with a lot of gusto. My sister did water polo with her and absolutely adored her.' Keli smiles and nods tearfully at Alison from her seat.

The day ends just like the others. Tegan is still missing and there are no new clues. Coroner Abernethy asks the journalists to spread his message.

'Again, I simply ask the public to turn their minds to it. It must be odd if one considers a two-day-old child is handed over, presumably in a hospital car park or somewhere in the grounds of a hospital, to a couple who are hitherto childless. If you knew them, if you are family and friends close to the persons to whom the child is alleged to have been handed over to, you'd notice that all of a sudden they have a child. It's the sort of thing that I would have thought would stand out. We'd like to see them. If they come forward, I think the solicitor for Keli Lane has made it very clear that the Lane family would support them.'

16

SANDRA LANE TAKES
THE STAND

While Keli's father has been by Keli's side every day of the hearing, Keli's mother, Sandy, has not turned up once. However, today Sandy Lane is here because she is to give evidence, and she isn't happy about it.

As the court staff set up for the day, Sandy makes her displeasure known. She demands that she be allowed to have a cigarette in the enclosed staff area at the back of the building. She argues with staff, who tell her repeatedly that the area is out of bounds for anyone but staff and that she will have to smoke at the front of the building. Sandy angrily retorts that she can't smoke where all the TV cameramen are milling around. Her agitation is not helped by the way the day's proceedings are kicked off.

'Is the journalist from the *Tele* here?' asks Coroner Abernethy just before Sandy takes the stand. A small, pale, determined young woman with dark hair swept back into a plain ponytail stands up from her seat in the public gallery, one eyebrow arched.

'Front page story yesterday – very nice, but no mention of my appeal for someone to come forward. Did it get caught in the sub-editing as usual?' says Coroner Abernethy.

The journalist relaxes slightly. This sort of dressing down is nothing compared to what is dished out by the editors at the paper.

'Can you tell your sub-editor the coroner made you stand up in front of a courtroom full of people to ask why not?' Now Abernethy looks for someone else. 'Is the journo from the *Herald* here? Well, they did it yesterday, so thank you very much.'

As the journalist from the *Daily Telegraph* resumes her seat, Keli's barrister refers to the revelation in her front page story that Keli had posted messages on an internet message board looking for Andrew Norris. The coroner accepts Keli's barrister's request this be tendered as evidence of Keli's small but ongoing search for the man she says she gave Tegan to and asks for the first witness. Sandy Lane steps into the witness box, clearly aware of the presence of all the journalists.

'Could you to explain what your relationship with Keli is like?' asks Becroft.

'I think my relationship with Keli is very good,' answers Sandy, her voice strained and nervous.

'Is it an open relationship?'

'I think so.'

'Is she honest with you?'

'I think so.'

'It's the case you have a close family?'

'I think so, yes.'

'Would you describe Keli's upbringing as being strict?'

'Not particularly. I thought it was very normal.'

'Was she given leeway to go and do teenage things as she wanted to?'

'She had a very busy time because she was involved in sport,' answers Sandy.

'Were you also involved in Keli's sport?'

'To a certain extent, yes.'

'In relation to Keli becoming pregnant before being married, what were your views?'

'I didn't have any particular view. When it happened, it happened,' answers Sandy in relation to her grandchild Macy, Keli's fourth baby, who lives with Keli and her husband Peter.

'So you didn't hold any views that a person should become married before they have children?'

'Not particularly, not in this day and age.'

'If Keli was to have come home in 1995, 1996 and 1999 and said "Mum, I'm pregnant", how would you have reacted to that?'

'I would've supported her.'

'Do you think she would have been aware of that, that you would have supported her?'

'Not necessarily, no.'

Slightly surprised by this answer, Becroft probes Keli's mother further. 'It's not something that you spoke about?'

'No, we didn't.'

'You never spoke with Keli about if she did become pregnant, what she should do and what she shouldn't do?' repeats Becroft.

'Well, we obviously had the usual talks when she was younger about sex education, but I would've thought that since she is an adult, she had her views and she'd make up her own mind.'

'Were you aware if Keli was using any contraception in '95 or '96?'

'I thought she was, yes.'

'What made you think that?'

'Because I bought them sometimes.'

'You filled the script for her – took it to the pharmacy and – '

'I gave her money for it.'

'She asked for the money for the script?'

'Yeah.'

'So she didn't conceal the fact that she was having sexual relationships then?'

'No,' says Sandy defensively.

'She felt comfortable to ask you for money for the pill?'

'Yes.'

'What is your personal view in relation to termination of pregnancies?'

'I don't particularly believe in it.'

'Would Keli have been aware of your views in relation to terminations of pregnancies?'

'Quite possibly,' answers Sandy vaguely.

'Do you recall if you spoke to her about it?'

'We didn't have any specific conversation about it that I can recall,' says Sandy, looking more uncomfortable with every minute that is passing by.

Sandy then confirms that Keli lived at home until 2000, when she moved out with Peter. Sandy also confirms that when Keli was in a relationship with Duncan she wasn't at home every night of the week as she regularly stayed over at his place.

'While she was living with you did you ever form any opinions that Keli may have been pregnant?'

'No, definitely not.'

'No changes in her breasts or anything like that?'

'No.'

'What sort of clothing did Keli wear?'

'Well, she lived in tracksuits most of the time because she was involved in sport and that's what they wore,' Sandy says, adding that the tracksuits were not tight.

'In summer, did she wear loose fitting clothing or . . . ?'

'Loose t-shirts, shorts, whatever,' answers Sandy abruptly.

'So at no stage while Keli was pregnant with any of the three children were you aware of those pregnancies?'

'No, I wasn't.'

'If Keli came home and told you that she was pregnant you would have been supportive of her?'

'Definitely.'

'Do you know of any reason, and I'm only asking for your opinion, why Keli could not disclose to you that she was, in fact, pregnant three times?'

'I don't know.'

'Haven't you asked her?' asks Coroner Abernethy in a loud voice.

'I beg your pardon?' answers Sandy, slightly startled.

'Haven't you asked her?' repeats Coroner Abernethy, looking straight at her.

'No, I haven't,' she answers, still startled.

'Why ever not?'

'Because it's been very distressing,' Sandy says weakly.

'I'm sure it has,' says the coroner, his gaze unswerving. 'But she is your daughter; you can ask her why she didn't tell you about her pregnancies.'

'I've had a very distressing year with several different things that have happened. When I tried to approach it, I'd get very upset. I felt it wasn't appropriate to go into an in-depth conversation about it,' Sandy replies defensively.

Unimpressed, Abernethy allows Becroft to resume the questioning.

'I know this question may be difficult, but why do you get upset when you think about the whole case? What makes you so upset?' asks Becroft.

'Because Keli was so distressed when she told us about what had happened,' answers Sandy shakily.

'You haven't enquired with her why she adopted out her first and third babies?'

'Not directly. I assumed that she did that because she wanted them to go to a good home and be looked after well.'

'Have you broached the subject of why she didn't adopt out Tegan in the same way?'

'She wanted the child to go to its natural father.'

'I see, but wouldn't that have been possible through adoption?'

Sandy doesn't know what to say in reply.

Becroft moves on, querying Sandy's unquestioning belief that what Keli said happened to her missing granddaughter is true. 'Have you ever questioned Keli as to why she didn't tell you of the pregnancies?'

'No, I haven't.'

'Have you ever stated to her that she may have denied you having contact with your natural grandchildren?'

'No.'

'Do you feel that you've been denied that opportunity?'

'I haven't particularly thought about it,' Sandy answers coldly.

'Is it the case that you haven't spoken to Keli about this particular case at all?'

'We've had some conversations about it but not in great depth,' answers Sandy dismissively. 'When she told me that this had happened, it was about a month after my mother had died, and I just sort of tried to work things out from there,' she adds by way of informing Becroft of how preoccupied she was at the time.

'Did you ask Keli why she didn't tell you about the three pregnancies? Why she only told you about Tegan?'

'Not at that time.'

'Have you asked her since?'

'Yes.'

'What did she say to you?'

'She said that she didn't want to upset me more by telling me about the others.'

'So the reason was she just didn't want to upset you?' asks Becroft by way of clarification.

'Yeah. I was . . . It was very distressing.'

'How did you react when she told you?'

'I told her that I loved her and I would support her in anything.'

'And yet she still couldn't tell you about the other two children?'

'It's not that . . . I don't know.'

Becroft then turns her questions to Keli's latest version of what happened the day Tegan disappeared. 'Do you believe that your daughter gave Tegan to her natural father, this Andrew Norris?'

'Yes, I do.'

'Why do you say that?'

'Because I feel that, if he said he wanted to look after the child, she would believe him and she thought that was the best thing to do.'

'You don't find it odd that Andrew Norris and his girlfriend would accept a child that was born out of an affair?'

'Well, it is unusual.'

'But you believe it is the case that happened?'

'Yes, I do.'

'How would you describe Keli, in your own words?'

'She's a beautiful, loving girl.'

'This question may be difficult for you to answer, but would you believe that Keli could harm a child?'

'No, I do not.'

'Do you believe that she could have harmed Tegan Lane?'

'Definitely not.'

Becroft now starts to question the still shaky but increasingly defiant Sandy about the wedding Keli and Duncan attended in Manly, just hours after Tegan disappeared.

'You have some memory of that?' Coroner Abernethy asks from the bench.

'I do have some memory of it.'

'How do you remember it so particularly?' he asks.

'Well, we were talking about this at a later stage and Keli said she went to a wedding that day and it came to me. I said, "Oh, that was Wally's wedding."'

'He was a friend of the family for many years?'

'He was.'

'And do you recall Keli coming into the house that day or not?'

'Yes, I do.'

'What time did she get in?'

'I can't give an exact time.'

'Well, a rough one?'

'It would have been some time after 3 pm.'

'How did she get home?'

'I just assumed she drove.'

'In her own vehicle?' asks the coroner, firing questions at Sandy at a steady rate.

'Well, I didn't actually see her pull up in the car, she just came through the gate and – '

'Where did you first see her that day?'

'That afternoon.'

'I'm asking you where.'

'At home.'

'In the house, at the front door, through, inside the house, at the back door or at the gate?' asks the coroner, his gaze not leaving Sandy for a second.

'At the back. At the gate, at the back.'

'Did she have a motor vehicle at that stage?'

'She did,' answers Sandy, referring to the car Duncan had organised for Keli.

'Do you remember seeing it parked there after she arrived?'

'No, I don't.'

'Where did she usually park it?'

'Just out in the street, or on the footpath outside our place. In the driveway if there was room.'

'So you're pretty definite that she came in that day at something like 3 pm to get dressed for the wedding?'

'That's right.'

'How did she seem that day?'

'She seemed OK.'

'Not upset?'

'No.'

'Just OK, you say. What does that mean?'

'Oh, just normal.'

'Normal,' says Coroner Abernethy, staring at Sandy. 'You know, of course, that an hour or so earlier she's given her child, on her own version of events, to someone else?'

'I do know that now.'

'Yet she seemed normal?' repeats Coroner Abernethy.

'Well, just rushed a little, I guess.'

'Looking forward to the wedding?' asks Abernethy with a deadpan expression.

'Was I looking forward . . . ?' Sandra asks with some confusion.

'No, was she?' says the coroner, carefully controlling his impatience.

'I don't recall that.'

'Where did she go? Did she go to her room and get dressed?'

'Yes, she went in and showered and – '

'Do you remember the outfit she put on? Wasn't it a suit?'

Up until this moment, for the entire time she has been in the witness box, Sandy has looked unsure of herself as she tried to meet the gaze of whoever was questioning her. However, now, when she is asked to recall what Keli wore to the wedding that afternoon, Sandy straightens herself up and answers in a clear voice.

'It was a creamy coloured Country Road suit.'

'What happened next?' continues the coroner.

'I just drove them down to Manly.'

'Who is "them"?'

'Duncan and Keli.'

'When did you see Duncan for the first time that day?'

'Well, he'd come in not long before.'

'So he was there at your house, waiting for Keli?'

'Yes.'

'He seemed normal?'

'He seemed normal.'

'So Duncan's there, having a cup of coffee or something, waiting, and then Keli came home,' confirms the coroner. 'You're not sure how she got there but it certainly wasn't with Duncan.'

'No, they arrived separately.'

'Did Duncan have his ute or pick-up truck, whatever he drove in those days?'

'Truck, Ford truck,' says Sandy.

'Truck, yes. She got changed. Was Duncan ready for the wedding, was he already dressed up?'

'No, he was getting ready.'

'So they both got dressed.'

'That's right.'

'And then at some time before four o'clock they hurtled down the hill to the church?'

'That's right, but I drove them in our car.'

'You drove them, right, OK. And was that the last you saw of them that day?'

'That's right.'

'They didn't come home after the wedding?'

'Oh, they stayed the night.'

'They stayed the night but you'd probably gone to bed?'

'Yes.'

'And Keli just seemed normal to you? Nothing stood out?'

'Nothing stood out.'

'Pretty cool, don't you think?' says the coroner, giving Sandy a hard look.

'Well, I don't know . . .' begins Sandy, her newly acquired confidence beginning to falter.

'Put yourself in her position. Imagine having a baby secretly, giving it to someone who you hardly know and coming home, getting dressed and going with your boyfriend – and the baby is not his, by the way, or we don't think it is, and . . . Well, it might be – and going to a wedding,' says the coroner.

'Well, there was a bit of a rush on to get ready,' explains Sandy weakly.

Coroner Abernethy sits still, silently staring into space for a moment. Then he indicates to Keli's barrister that he can go ahead and examine her.

'Very briefly, just on the questions that the coroner was asking you about whether you remembered anything about Keli that day – whether she was upset or whether she was cool – did you have any reason to be thinking about that back in 1996 when it first happened?' asks Keli's barrister.

'No, definitely not,' answers Sandy.

'When did you first turn your mind to the day of Wally's wedding?'

'About six months or so ago.'

'So quite recently.'

'Yes.'

'That's when it became clear that the day that Keli was released from hospital with Tegan was the same day as that wedding.'

'Yes.'

'So would it be fair to say that Keli may have been quite distressed but that you didn't really pay her any mind?'

'Well, that's right,' says Sandy, leaving some observers with the impression that her relationship with Keli was, at times, distant.

'It's obviously been a long time between that day and when you started thinking about it.'

'Yes.'

'Are you clear in your memory that Duncan and Keli came separately to your house before the wedding?'

'Yes.'

'You're clear that you drove them down to the wedding?'

'Yes, I am.'

'Are you also clear in your memory that they came back and stayed the night, or are you guessing a little for that?'

'Possibly a guess, but I can't imagine they'd have gone anywhere else when the wedding was in Manly.'

'You told me they stayed the night. Which is it? If you don't know, say so. You're under oath.'

'I don't know for a fact.'

'Finally, when Keli arrived home that day she didn't have a newborn baby with her?'

'No, she didn't,' answers Sandy, adding that she has never set eyes on any of her three secret grandchildren.

With her testimony at an end, Keli's mother steps out of the witness box. Her son, Keli's brother, gives his brief testimony next. As soon as he finishes, Sandy walks arm in arm with him out of the courtroom, through the crowd of photographers and into a waiting car. She will not sit next to Keli in court or show any other public demonstration of support until years later when, during Keli's murder trial, she will sit in the courtroom and shower her daughter with tears and kisses. Only then will it be apparent that behind Sandy's tough and cold exterior there is love, confusion and fear.

17

UNCERTAIN CONCLUSIONS

More witnesses who were close to Keli during the years of her secret births take the stand. The court hears from Stacy, the water polo player from Queensland who shared Keli's room when she was pregnant with her first secret baby, who admits she looked at Keli underwater with her goggles on in 1996. Also taking the stand is the footballer from the Manly rugby club whom Keli dated just before she started seeing Duncan, and the Ravenswood physical education teacher Keli talked to about her break-up with Duncan. None of them were able to tell the court anything.

The time for Keli to enter the witness box is getting closer. Before then, Coroner Abernethy wants to hear from Taryn and her father, Keli's old coach, David. Both Taryn and her father do not want to be involved in this hearing. Taryn is far away, playing water polo in Italy. She and her father have refused to give statements to police. Their obvious reluctance to be involved is of small consequence to Coroner Abernethy. The hearing is postponed for eight months as Taryn makes her way back home.

The coroner wants to make sure those eight months aren't just spent waiting for Taryn and her father. He orders the New South Wales Births, Deaths and Marriages registry undertake a cross-check between all birth certificates and midwife certificates for female babies born between September 1996 and September 1997 and for all schools across the country to keep checking their records for children born on or around the day Tegan was born. Keli's barrister asks for any closed circuit TV tapes Auburn Hospital might have of September 1996 and that the car she drove that year be found and forensically examined.

'We might be able to track it down, we might not,' the coroner says wearily when the requests are made. Both he and Keli's barrister know full well that the chances of her car or the closed circuit TV tapes being found or yielding any helpful evidence this many years later is practically zero.

The Births, Deaths and Marriages registry sets about doing what the coroner ordered them to do. There were 86,430 female babies born in NSW between September 1996 and September 1997. A new computer system is installed and more staff members are employed to undertake the task of cross-referencing all the registered births with the raw hospital and midwife records held by the Department of Health. The computer system finds 12,083 seemingly unregistered births, which are manually cross-checked by staff over a number of months. Once things like spelling mistakes and typos for dates are accounted for, 729 births are left. To make sure none of them are Tegan, staff make hundreds upon hundreds of phone calls to hospitals and midwives to track down all birth records, a process that takes several more months. At the end of this huge exercise there are eight female babies other than Tegan who have not been registered by their parents. The details of these eight girls are passed onto police. In time they will track down each of those eight children. None of them are Tegan.

Registering a child's birth is not a matter of picking up an application form from a newsagency or post office. Hospitals and midwives who attend homebirths are the only source of these application forms, which are stamped to show which hospital or midwife issued it. There is a legal requirement for parents to register their children with Births, Deaths and Marriages within a month of the birth, but by and large the system relies on parents doing the right thing. A failure to register means parents usually run into problems when they try to enrol their children into a school or obtain a passport, so almost all children are registered at some stage. Despite these problems, every year some people neglect to register their child's birth, often out of sheer laziness. When parents find they need a birth certificate for their child, they have to go back to the hospital where their son or daughter was born to get an application form. However, once someone has a birth registration form it's possible for parents to provide false names and dates of the birth. Much will be made of this by Keli's barrister during her trial for Tegan's murder. But while it's possible to hide a child's true identity this way, not a single fraudulent birth certificate is found during this mammoth cross-check. Not one of the 86,430 girls checked could be Tegan registered under a false name or date of birth.

By the time court resumes one morning in early February 2006, no closed circuit tapes have been found and Keli's old car holds no traces of its use ten years earlier. Every journalist present knows Keli is unlikely to say anything interesting today, but they all want to hear from her anyway. Keli will be the last witness to take the stand, but before she finally speaks it is Taryn's turn. She had been overseas for most of 1996, but she had heard the rumours about Keli being pregnant and, with Stacy, had looked at Keli through her goggles underwater to see for herself.

'Did you say anything to Keli?' Becroft asks Taryn.

'No.'

'Why wouldn't you have told her about these rumours or ask her if she was pregnant?'

'I guess it's hard to say. Weight gain at a young age is a very delicate issue and certainly, while her weight gain may have suggested she might have been pregnant, she was still playing water polo, so I assumed that it probably wasn't the case.'

Coroner Abernethy sits back and listens to Taryn answer the questions that all of Keli's other friends have been asked. About halfway through her testimony he leans forward to ask her about something that had happened in Manly not long after Tegan's disappearance had become front page news.

'When was that lunch you had with Keli in Manly?' he asks.

'April last year.'

'So this case had already started.'

'Yes.'

'And you say that there was no discussion at all about the case or about Tegan Lane?'

'No.'

'Not a word?'

'None, other than that I had been called.'

'And you weren't interested to find out a bit about it?'

'Well, it wasn't just the two of us at lunch,' replies Taryn. 'It was a big group of people.'

Given the circumstances, this lunch now looks almost defiant, a perception Keli's barrister is keen to dispel. 'I take it you have been aware of the publicity surrounding this coronial inquest?' he asks Taryn.

'Yes.'

'Were you aware of that last year when you had lunch with a group of people, including Keli?'

'Yes.'

'At any stage at that time, or at any subsequent time, had Keli made any attempt to influence what you might have said to the police of to the court?'

'No.'

Taryn's father and Keli's old coach, David, is unable to shed any further light on the matter, confirming that he didn't talk to Keli about the change in her physical shape. Next, Detective Gaut gives an update on the continuing searches for Tegan and for Andrew Norris. The Assistant Registrar of Registration Services at the New South Wales registry of Births, Deaths and Marriages gives evidence about the cross-checking of records ordered by the coroner, which has found no trace of Tegan. Then Senior Constable Epstein from Glebe morgue gives her evidence about how the records of unidentified dead children have been searched, but nothing found.

Coroner Abernethy and Sergeant Becroft exchange glances.

'One final witness to call,' says Becroft. It's time for Keli. Coroner Abernethy wants Keli to consider saying something that will actually help police find her missing baby when she enters the witness box. Perhaps if she sleeps on it she might decide to do just that.

'Tomorrow morning. I'll give you overnight to make a final decision about your client,' he says to Keli's barrister.

'Well, we've made that final decision,' Keli's barrister answers.

'You have?' says the coroner, his final hope dashed.

'I can indicate what that is to your Honour now if it pleases the court.'

'All right,' Coroner Abernethy responds flatly.

'It's self evident, your Honour, given the evidence of Detective Gaut and his investigations and some of the opinions that he stated in his various statements in interviews with other witnesses and in the courtroom that Ms Lane, my client, is a suspect in what is likely to be an ongoing search for a missing person and an ongoing police investigation. This means, as your Honour would be well familiar, she enjoys a right to silence. She has, as the court has heard, voluntarily participated in lengthy records of interview in 2001, 2003 and 2004. She has, through her solicitor, continued to cooperate with the investigation by the provision of banking records, medical records, information about her medical history and photographs which assisted the police in making a public appeal for information. I have great concerns that any evidence she gives in these proceedings could be used against her in future proceedings, and that fear, in my respectful submission, your Honour, would accept to be a real – '

'So you have advised her not to answer any questions,' interrupts Coroner Abernethy, cutting to the chase.

'I have.'

'On the basis that any answers she gives may incriminate her.'

'That's been my advice.'

'You feel that any question has the potential to do that. Is that your advice to her?'

Keli's barrister says that is right.

'All right, let's get it over with,' says a thoroughly annoyed Coroner Abernethy. What he has heard in the inquest has led him to believe that Tegan is dead, but there isn't enough evidence for criminal charges to be laid against anyone.

Keli enters the witness box.

'For the record, could you please state your full name,' asks Becroft.

'Keli Lane.'

'You and Tegan Lane were discharged from Auburn Hospital around 2 pm on 14 September 1996. Can you tell this court what happened to Tegan Lane around 2 pm on 14 September 1996 when you left the hospital with her?'

Then, as he is obliged to do, Coroner Abernethy reminds Keli of her right to say nothing if she believes that by answering she might incriminate herself. Having done that, he sits back to hear her reply.

'I do not wish to answer the question, sir,' says Keli in a polite voice. Becroft confirms that, in that case, she has no further questions and Keli steps down from the witness box. She is free to go. The media pack is in a full feeding frenzy as Keli and her father fight their way to their car outside shortly afterwards.

The next day, 15 February 2006, Coroner Abernethy hands down his written finding. 'There are factors going to the proposition that Tegan Lane is alive,' it states. Abernethy lists them: the child's body has never been found; there is no forensic evidence of death such as suspicious blood splatters; and Keli put her first and third secret children up for adoption. He also lists the possibility that Keli did hand over Tegan to her natural father in the hospital car park and that the people caring for Tegan are for some reason refusing to come forward and identify themselves, although he thinks the likelihood of either of these things being true is remote.

What Abernethy finds convincing are the reasons why Tegan is dead. His finding states:

These include the fact that Tegan Lane has not been seen since she was in Auburn District Hospital just after birth; the multiplicity of versions and untruths given to a range of persons [i.e. Keli's lies]; the initial denial [by Keli] of giving birth to the child at all; the fact that there has been a very careful search at least in this state of birth records and no sign of the birth being registered; the publicity surrounding 'Andrew Norris and Mel' and the efforts police have made to locate him [Norris]; the school inquiries; [and] the intense media coverage of this matter from the time Keli Lane was teaching at Ravenswood.

Of course, there is also Keli's startling behaviour on the day her baby disappeared. Abernethy writes, 'Within hours of handing Tegan Lane over, on Keli Lane's version, she was enjoying a wedding in Manly.' This, combined with Keli's many lies to nurses, police and other authorities, leads the coroner to simply not believe Keli's final version about what happened that day, namely that she handed Tegan over to the infant's natural father in the hospital car park. Abernethy's finding continues:

Keli Lane has continued to tell a series of untruths in relation to this version. Why? To police at one stage she said that Norris saw her in hospital, and that Norris, Mel and Norris's mother were all present when Tegan was handed over. If she was intending to hand the child over at the hospital, why lie to a social worker about having no support persons in Sydney? She was, after all, handing the child over to its natural father. She gave no direct or logical answer to this question.

Coroner Abernethy's finding also states that even if he were to believe Keli's story that Norris was 'prepared unconditionally to take the child, thus saving Keli Lane from the bothersome adoption process where she might have to lie again', there were still huge questions left unanswered. He elaborates:

Of course she told a similar litany of untruths to both [John] Borovnik and [Virginia] Fung, originally denying the existence of the baby. Why? She had given it to its natural father. If she did indeed hand the child over to Norris, why not simply tell Fung?

I have to say that I find it inherently unlikely that a man with whom she was having an affair, who already had a partner, who initially at least was incredibly angry on learning she was pregnant, nevertheless was happy to take the child. This is all the more unlikely because that man's cuckolded partner also agreed.

Finally, Keli Lane added Tegan Lane's name to her own Medicare card while at the hospital. No arrangement was ever made to alter that so that Norris could take care of claiming Medicare benefits later on.

The coroner's finding also accuses Keli of wasting a great deal of police time by taking them to a block of units in Balmain where she claimed Andrew Norris lived when they were having their affair, observing that:

. . . detailed police enquiries confirmed that there had never been an Andrew Norris at those premises. Further, it is highly unlikely that any tenant there might be the father of the child.

In relation to Keli's final interview with police in January 2004, Abernethy states:

> In my view, the contradictions in what she has said to police are obvious and the answers become increasingly vague. On a reasonable review of this particular interview it is fair to say that Keli Lane appears to realise just how incredible her story is.

He goes on to outline that there isn't enough evidence to charge anyone with Tegan's murder or any other offence relating to the baby's disappearance. He also points out that the unusually slow investigation into Tegan's disappearance by Manly Police has made matters worse:

> I am far from satisfied that any senior officer at Manly had any input at all into the matter, or took any meaningful responsibility for ensuring that there was a timely and efficient investigation into it.

However, Abernethy adds that he doesn't blame Detective Gaut or Detective Kehoe for the series of extraordinary delays in the investigation that have made ongoing efforts to find her 'incredibly difficult'. About the wall of silence Keli's friends and family have built around her Abernethy states: 'Not one of them can give any meaningful evidence in relation to Keli's pregnancies or the father of Tegan Lane. I find this most surprising.'

But while Keli's family and friends might believe Tegan is still alive, Coroner Abernethy doesn't. 'I am comfortably satisfied that Tegan Lane is, in fact, deceased,' he concludes. However, he is forced to hand down an open finding, meaning the case is not closed yet. Abernethy outlines his intentions:

> Because of the nature of this particular investigation and the inadequacies of the initial investigation, I am ordering that the brief of evidence and transcript of these proceedings be forwarded to the New South Wales Homicide Squad for assessment and, if necessary, a re-investigation or further investigation. I ask that any assessment done be carried out by a senior criminal investigator, or former criminal investigator with homicide experience.

The case, which is now well and truly cold, is handed to the homicide squad immediately after the coroner's finding is handed down in February 2006. The Lanes and their circle of friends return to their lives in Manly, clear in the knowledge that the police think Tegan is dead and that the search for her killer is far from over.

18

PIECE BY PIECE

Keli sits behind a desk, looking at an appointments book. She misses standing poolside at Ravenswood, coaching the girls. There is no way they will ever have her back, not after all the headlines about Tegan. So, here she is. Being a receptionist at a Northern Beaches physio isn't a dream job, but Rob had to pull strings for Keli to get it.

The odd photographer has followed Keli from time to time in the months since the inquest, snapping photos of her taking Macy to kindergarten. Every now and then Keli gets a stare and hears whispers as she walks past people on the street. Rob still has a lot of friends, but he no longer drinks at the Steyne Hotel with the rest of the locals as much as he used to. Things between Keli and her mother are pretty much as they always were, a touch cool and distant. Rob and Sandy had to sell their investment property to pay for Keli's lawyers. They still have their Fairlight home, but a huge part of their life savings is gone. Rob and Sandy can only hope that one day Tegan will be found and their daughter's notoriety will fade.

Naturally, there is plenty of gossip and speculation about Keli's secret babies. As Duncan isn't the father of the first baby, rumours as to who is, and who fathered Tegan and the third baby, are rife. Did Keli have anonymous sex with men her friends weren't aware of? That would explain why no one had heard of Andrew Norris, Morris, or whatever his name is. Rampant promiscuity is the most popular theory for Keli's behaviour, but some guess at a much darker explanation. Was Keli the victim of sexual abuse, something so horrific that she was in denial about being pregnant all those times? Did she even welcome being pregnant as a way of repulsing her tormentor? If sexual abuse was the reason behind her extraordinary behaviour, it may also explain why Keli might have felt that concealing her babies was easier than dealing with whoever kept getting her pregnant. Keli might be a big strong girl, but abuse is rarely a problem fixed by being able to push the abuser off. What if her tormentor had a deep emotional hold over her, one that she couldn't break without her whole life falling apart?

Whatever the truth is, after all the sound and fury of the coronial hearing, there is still no sign of Tegan. The search for her is now in the hands of the homicide squad. In late 2006 they form a taskforce, headed by two detectives with around fifteen other detectives, police officers and intelligence analysts involved. The task force decide to redo the schools search undertaken by Detective Gaut and begin to search all primary schools Australia-wide for girls born in September 1996 to see if Tegan who, by now, is ten years old if she is alive, turns up. However, the gigantic size of this task quickly becomes apparent. There are over 9000 primary schools in Australia, ranging from ones in the Northern Beaches to those in remote Western Australian Aboriginal communities. The police plan to rely on the birth certificates schools are normally required to have copies of for each student to check if any of the girls might be Tegan, but what the search uncovers is that tens of thousands of students born in September 1996 attend school without their parents or guardians having produced a copy of their birth certificate. The schools either never asked for one or only asked carers to show the birth certificate without taking a copy for their school's records.

Faced with the prospect of having to send police out to interview each one of these tens of thousands of students, half of whom will be male, just to get basic information as to the circumstances of each child's birth, isn't practical. Police decide they need to change their search criteria. Instead, they look for girls born on 12 September 1996, or whose name is Tegan Lane, or whose father is Andrew Norris or Morris. It isn't perfect, but the squad reason a meaningful search of the nation's schools for Tegan needs to be completed within a couple of years with the resources available.

On top of the schools search is a number of other searches for Tegan. Having had the New South Wales Births, Deaths and Marriages registries go over their own records with a fine toothcomb the year before, the police now track down, interview and eliminate the possibility of the eight children it found without birth registrations being Tegan. Police then approach every Birth, Deaths and Marriages registry in Australia, all adoption agencies throughout Australia and Medicare Australia for records of female children born in September 1996, or girls around ten years of age whose first name is Tegan, Teegan, Teagan, Teaghan or Teigan, or whose mother's name is Mel, Melinda, Melissa, Melanie or Melek, or whose father's name is Andrew Norris or Morris. They also approach Medicare for all records of girls of Tegan's age who have received their Rubella shots to see if any girls can be found who might possibly be her.

The combined searches result in the birth records of 86,000 children being checked. Out of those, 1037 girls are identified as requiring further investigation before they can be ruled out. Over the next couple of years the police will set about obtaining birth certificates, birth records from hospitals, statements from parents, and in several instances, DNA samples for most of the 1037 children. None of them are Tegan. Some of these children are excluded as being Tegan purely on ethnic grounds – for example if the child is a black South African and both parents are black South Africans. The New South Wales Births, Deaths and Marriages registry search also closes off one other possibility. There were no foundlings, the term used by the Department of Health for babies left anonymously at hospitals, churches, police stations or on the street in New South Wales in 1996. Keli didn't leave Tegan alive anywhere with the hope that she would be found.

The searches for Tegan are carried out in tandem with searches for Andrew Morris/Norris. For the sake of completeness, the task force decides to redo Detective Gaut's search of government agencies, as well as searching a number of additional electricity and phone companies for billing records that might unearth the man Keli insists has her baby. Like Gaut, the task force find thirty-seven such men. They also find a further four men with the middle name of Andrew and the last name of Morris or Norris, or men who have used the name Andrew Morris or Norris as an alibi to police. The police check immigration records to discover whom among them was in the country at the time of Tegan's conception and around the time of her disappearance. Police then take statements from each one of the men who were. These men, who range from professionals in suits to a trucker nicknamed 'Cauliflower' with tattoos and false teeth, are asked if they ever lived in Balmain and if they have children. Then they are shown a photo of Keli and asked whether they know her, have ever had a relationship with her and whether they took a newborn girl from her in 1996. None of them have. Photos of each of the men are also gathered by police, either from driver's licences, passports or simply happy snaps. There is no trace of Keli's well-built, tanned banker.

Keli's family and very close friends are still standing by Keli, but cracks are beginning to show. Despite marrying Keli only a month after learning about her secret children, the strain of the mystery of Tegan's whereabouts and the shock of learning their child was Keli's fourth, not her first, is too much for Peter. Within a year of the end of the inquest, he and Keli separate. Macy lives with Keli, but Peter stays close and remains very involved with his beloved little girl.

Meanwhile, the media's coverage of the inquest keeps yielding new information for police. The receptionist of the Queensland abortion clinic that turned Keli away when she was six and a half months' pregnant in 1999 calls the homicide detectives after watching the news. People who work in abortion clinics are usually the last to be judgemental about women and girls who terminate pregnancies, but there was something about Keli that stuck in her mind and she was happy to help police. There are also over fifty possible leads that have been phoned in from all over the country via the police hotline Crime Stoppers, mainly about little girls whom callers think might be Tegan. All the leads are investigated but find nothing.

Other evidence is gathered and checked. Virginia Fung's extensive notes, combined with the detectives' growing familiarity with the people in Keli's life, leads to the realisation of a small but startling fact. The UK address Keli gave Virginia right at the end of the adoption process and the one to which Virginia sent the life story of Keli's third baby was Peter's family's home. Peter's parents had unknowingly taken delivery of a document describing all three of Keli's secret children and photos of her third around the same time that Keli was visiting them. Either they handed it unopened to her in their home or forwarded it to the Lane's home in Sydney. Either way, Keli was able to leave a message on Virginia's answering machine that she had received it and everything was fine. Within a year Keli was pregnant with Peter's child.

Police also check the records of every taxi company in Sydney. Not a single taxi picked up a passenger from Auburn Hospital the day Tegan disappeared. By 2008 the answer as to whom fathered Keli's first and third babies is found. Having compiled a list of Keli's ex-boyfriends, police have taken DNA samples from them. The father of her first baby is the Manly footy player Keli was seeing just before she started dating Duncan. He had reconciled with his long-term girlfriend after seeing Keli and now, having had two kids of his own, he is devastated to learn he is the father of another child. The father of Keli's third child is a friend of her brother's whom she saw casually after breaking up with Duncan. He is several years younger than Keli, and she was one of his first sexual partners. He, too, is totally shocked. For police, it means there is no obvious suggestion of horrible sexual abuse in Keli's life. Keli's secret babies were simply a result of her falling pregnant to whomever was her boyfriend at the time.

Police also find what they think is a pattern in Keli's hidden life. By searching Keli's medical history, police uncover not only the abortion she had when she was seventeen, but also a second abortion she told no one about in 1994, a few months before she fell pregnant with her first secret child. This second abortion was when she was five months' pregnant. While the practice is completely legal, given her string of unwanted children in the following years and her failed attempt to have an abortion at six and a half months' pregnant in 1999, a theory now develops that when Keli realised she was pregnant early enough, she had the pregnancy terminated. When she realised it too late, she was forced to give birth.

Police keep this information, along with everything else they uncover about Keli's sex life, to themselves, but word of who the two fathers are spreads throughout Keli's close–knit circle as the fathers themselves tell their friends of their shock. Aside from the weirdness of having had so many children, Keli's love life is shown to be the open book they always thought it was, populated by the boyfriends they all knew about. But rather than reassuring them, the knowledge makes them increasingly uneasy. Melinda, Brandon and Kati find it hard to believe that Keli had a fling with a man while she was dating Duncan, the man she was so desperate to hang onto. The fact that the police still can't find him makes it even harder to take. Keli's inner circle also realise that the father of her first secret baby was at the wedding she went to the day Tegan disappeared. Not only was Keli as cool as a cucumber despite having just given away her newborn, she was also keeping secret the fact that she'd put a baby up for adoption the year before. The strangeness of Keli's behaviour is becoming overwhelming in the eyes of Melinda, Brandon and Kati. They begin to distance themselves from her and tell people she is no longer their friend.

In 2008, a woman who used to date Keli's younger brother helps Keli obtain a job in the logistics office for Woolworths.

For the first two months Keli's hair is dyed dark brown; many of her new workmates don't recognise her. However, when she dyes it blonde again, someone recognises her and the fact that she is the infamous Keli Lane spreads like wildfire.

Any hopes the Lanes had of her infamy fading is dealt a huge blow in August 2008. Acting on a tip-off, police begin a large scale dig under Duncan's old place in Gladesville for Tegan's remains. The media is notified about this seemingly sensational development in the case and there is a press conference at the Gladesville police station.

'The Gladesville property was the home of one of Keli Lane's former boyfriends and she may have attended this location briefly on the day she was discharged from hospital,' says Homicide Squad Commander, Detective Superintendent Geoff Beresford. 'As a result of further inquiries over almost two years, we have uncovered information which suggests Tegan's remains may be at this location.' While the police don't actually say so, journalists immediately know it is the house Duncan owned and lived in when he was still dating Keli. Photographers descend on the house, which is now surrounded by police vans and plastic blue and white tape, marking out the forensic dig now in full swing. Reporters also knock on the Lane's door in Fairlight. An angry Rob Lane orders reporters off his property. Keli's new workmates gossip furiously about her. Some complain to management about having Keli in their workplace.

That night and the next morning it's all over the news. One newspaper reports the dig on the front page, a place usually reserved for court verdicts rather than investigations yet to find anything. New South Wales's biggest circulation newspaper, the *Daily Telegraph*, is a little more reserved, printing the story on page seven. Under a huge picture of police searching under the weatherboard house, and next to a picture of Keli, is a picture of Duncan. The media can now only wait to see if the police find anything. A fortnight passes and then, without fanfare, police issue a short statement saying some bones have been found under the house and are undergoing forensic analysis. Then there is silence. Finally, an announcement: the bones are not human. The police have only found the remains of a long-lost pet. But while the story disappears from the daily news cycle, the notoriety of the case is as strong as ever.

Duncan and his family are distraught. He is living overseas when the police undertake their highly publicised dig in his old backyard. As he isn't the father of Keli's first secret child, the idea that Keli's hidden life is so mysterious that even he wasn't aware of Keli's pregnancies seems plausible, and since the end of the coronial hearing the media have left him alone. But while the police dig under the house in Gladesville hasn't found anything, it drags Duncan into the centre of the scandal once again. His picture in the news is enough to link his name with Tegan's disappearance in the minds of many Sydneysiders.

By now Duncan's family has had time to reflect on Keli's lie to Brandon and Melinda that Tegan's birth was something between her, Duncan, Simon and his wife, Narelle. Together, they work out that Keli used her knowledge of a tragedy in their family to falsely insinuate there was a surrogacy arrangement. Just before Keli and Duncan broke up in 1998, after many years of trying Simon's wife finally fell pregnant, but heartbreakingly, her baby was stillborn. Keli was among the well-wishers who had come to the hospital expecting to find Simon and Narelle celebrating their much longed-for baby, but instead Simon caught Keli in the hospital hallway to tell her the awful news. It seems that Keli, having told her friends about the stillbirth to make sure they knew how close she was to Duncan's family, used it again to hint her missing baby was promised to, or even with, Simon and Narelle. Brandon and Melinda didn't have any direct contact with Simon and Narelle, so they didn't have any way of knowing if they were still childless or now raising Keli's daughter. It was just another story that Keli dragged Duncan's family into so that people would stop asking her questions about her missing baby.

A couple of weeks after the dig, police record Keli talking to one of her friends about Andrew Norris. Natalie, at whose twenty-first Keli gave a speech and who has been overseas for a few years, comes back to Sydney in August to visit her gravely ill father. On 26 August, police interview her. Immediately afterwards, Keli calls Natalie. 'Everyone is totally sick of this investigation,' Keli complains. After asking how her father is, Keli asks Natalie if she has just given a statement to police and whether she told detectives that she remembers meeting Andrew Norris back in the mid 1990s.

Natalie is keen to please Keli, gushing that she felt it was 'an honour' to be considered a friend whom Keli would talk to about such personal matters. Natalie lies, saying she did tell the police about meeting Norris once, when in fact she said no such thing. Police listening to the conversation interpret it as Keli trying to manipulate Natalie into saying she may have met Andrew Norris. Police think Keli attempted to manipulate Lisa Andreatta in a similar way before the coronial inquest, resulting in Lisa telling the court she may have once met Norris after originally denying any knowledge of such a man when Detective Gaut first contacted her.

The police also gather some not-so-helpful evidence. One

of the ex-tenants of the apartment building where Keli claims
Andrew Norris lived approaches police after seeing news of
the dig in Gladesville. During 1995 and 1996 this man and his
brother lived in one of the apartments. During the inquest,
both brothers gave evidence that they, and not Andrew
Norris, lived in that apartment. Like all the other tenants at
that time, the man said he hadn't seen anyone like the male
Keli described or any evidence of anyone like that being
elsewhere in the building. Now, years later, this ex-tenant
contacts police saying he remembers seeing letters addressed
to Andrew Norris scattered around a letterbox. Detectives ask
him why he didn't say so during the inquest. He replies that
having heard the evidence of the real estate agent, who told
the coroner that no Andrew Norris or Morris appears on the
rental records, he thought he must have been mistaken. This
seems somewhat plausible until, oddly, he also says he was
afraid of being sued by the Lanes if he mentioned seeing these
letters. Detectives have serious doubts about the credibility of
what this man is claiming, but they add his statement to the
investigation files.

The inquiry into the disappearance of Tegan Lane was
one of the last cases Chief Coroner Abernethy heard before
stepping down from the bench. Now retired, a month after
the police dig he gives an interview for a TV program about
cold cases.

'Tegan Lane was arguably the most frustrating case I did,' he
tells the reporter. 'It was a case that I simply could not solve.'

As usual, the presenter outlines the strange facts surrounding
Tegan's birth and disappearance, but there is another side to
this report than just the bizarreness of it. The reporter points
out that Manly Police at first failed to recognise they were
dealing with a possible homicide, a theme Abernethy has

some strong words about. 'It was left at Manly police station for far too long without being properly looked at,' he says. 'And, that, sadly, has made a bit of a difference to that case in my view.' Abernethy goes on to add that coronial inquests can be the last throw of the dice in terms of solving mysterious cases, and for the next twelve months it seems that this is it for the Tegan Lane case.

But the homicide squad do not give up. The scale of the search for Tegan and the man Keli claims to have given her to is so large that it takes a couple of years to complete the bulk of it. Finally, in late 2009, after four years of investigation, the police make their move. They haven't found Tegan's body, so the enormous search for her and for Andrew Morris/Norris is going to be part of their proof that Tegan is dead. Keli's behaviour the day her daughter disappeared, her behaviour during their inquiries and her unconvincing stories make her the suspect.

Keli is charged with Tegan's murder.

19

THE MURDER TRIAL BEGINS

It's 9.30 am, 4 December 2009. In half an hour, Keli and a number of other people accused of murder, manslaughter or high-level drug dealing will plead either guilty or not guilty to their charges. The small courtroom on the thirteenth floor of the Queen's Square Supreme Court building on Phillip Street is quickly filling with solicitors and barristers. With camera crews waiting downstairs, the media enter early so they can get a seat. The TV journalists wear immaculate but heavy make-up. One flips open her compact to touch up her face while she waits.

'All rise,' calls out the clerk. Justice Howie enters the courtroom dressed in a red robe, white cravat and horsehair wig. 'Right, the matter of Dennison,' says the judge once he takes his seat at the bench.

A bearded young man in a sloppy green prison tracksuit is lead through another door from the cells into the dock by several policemen. He is Brendan Dennison, a homeless man who, in late 2008, slipped into a high-rise apartment building and forced his way into a unit where two young students lived. Armed with a knife, he subjected the pair to a prolonged sex attack that was so horrific that both jumped off their balcony in an attempt to escape. The eighteen-year-old woman died when she hit the concrete 25 metres below, while her nineteen-year-old boyfriend broke both of his legs and shattered his pelvis and his back.

With a small sigh, the judge reads out the two pages of charges relating to that orgy of depraved violence. The police sit behind Dennison with expressions of indifference while the journalists and everyone else in the public gallery feel shock at being in the presence of this deranged man. Dennison answers each charge with a quiet 'guilty'. Once finished, he stands and turns so he can be led back to the cells, exposing the fat on his back which hangs slightly over the top of his pants.

The next accused is an obese young woman wearing jeans, a long-sleeved brown cotton top and a soft smile on her face. Unlike Dennison, she has not been abandoned by her family, who stand quietly in the courtroom as a show of support. She is charged with the murder and manslaughter of her younger sister. With the eager expression of someone at a job interview, she pleads guilty to the manslaughter of her teenaged sister, whom she stabbed in the neck following an argument over a hair straightener, but not to murder. The accused suffers psychiatric problems, something her loving family have dealt with privately all their lives until that tragic day. She, too, is led to the cells.

Now there is a procession of anonymous accused. One enormously strong-looking, fit and fashionably dressed young man is charged with supplying commercial quantities of drugs.

Another equally strong-looking, fit young man in a well-cut suit is charged with murder. Both have the calm, hard look of underworld soldiers who expect to do prison time. Far greater in number are the seedy-looking riff raff. There is a man with a huge beak of a nose jutting out from under his bowl-cut hairdo. He stares at the assembled crowd of journalists and solicitors, barely listening to the judge speaking about his upcoming trial. Two or three thin, shabbily dressed alcoholics and addicts, their cheap suits hanging awkwardly, try to muster an air of respectability as they enter their pleas before being led through the door and back to the cells. Then there are two greasy-haired co-accused, one charged with murdering a man, the other of hiding his mate from the police once the deed was done, who exchange glances while they sit in the dock together. Once these men are gone, the judge pauses and looks up.

'OK, go and get her.'

The judge and his staff know that Keli is the one the TV cameras are waiting for. Unusually for someone facing murder charges, she is not waiting in the cells below. Keli and her father have been waiting quietly outside the courtroom. She strides in, dressed in a crisp, long-sleeved white blouse, a navy skirt and shiny black high-heeled shoes. Keli is tanned and her brushed blonde hair hangs to her shoulders. She walks past the seated solicitors and journalists to the small gap between the public gallery and the dock. Once there, Keli stands still, unsure of where to go.

'In the dock please,' the judge instructs her.

Keli steps into the dock and takes a seat, gingerly perching herself on the chair where one of the two greasy-haired mates had been sitting just minutes earlier. She is now clearly an accused, just like the people in the prison greens in the cells below.

'Right, Miss Lane, please stand up. You are charged with the murder of Tegan Lane on the fourteenth of September 1996. How do you plead?'

'Not guilty,' Keli replies.

'Miss Lane, you are also charged with two counts of perjury in this court on the third of April 1995 during proceedings relating to the adoption of your first child, namely that you were living with a man named Duncan Gillies when the child was conceived and that Duncan Gillies is the father of that child. How do you plead?'

'Not guilty.'

Keli remains standing as the possibility of bail is discussed.

'In cases of alleged murder bail is only granted in exceptional circumstances,' the judge says. Keli's face is alert but expressionless as she looks at him, her hands clasped together. The judge is about to decide whether she spends her time waiting for her trial in jail or at home.

'But these are exceptional circumstances. Miss Lane has been at liberty since the offence is alleged to have happened. Also, the Crown does not oppose bail, so I will grant it.' Keli's face remains expressionless at the news. 'Right, conditions of bail. She will have to surrender her passport. Does she have a passport?'

'She has an expired passport,' Keli's barrister answers.

'All right. Bail will be set at $30,000 and guaranteed by Robert Lane. She will also have to report to Dee Why police station each day.'

During Keli's arraignment, her father Robert has been standing near the dock. His once erect posture has become slightly stooped and his complexion is more ruddy than it was at the coronial inquest. The defiance he showed walking arm in arm with his daughter back then has gone. Robert

Lane walks out of the courtroom behind his daughter with the gait of an old man. Sandra Lane is nowhere to be seen.

The journalists leave the courtroom. As they walk towards the lifts they turn their heads to observe Keli standing in a corner, brightly illuminated by the massive windows looking over Phillip Street. She is dabbing her eyes with a folded white tissue, her father standing close by. The journalists know better than to approach Keli and her father inside the building, so they head straight outside to wait with the camera crews manning each exit, peering through the windows to check when Keli is about to make her exit.

'Is that Robert?' one journalist asks, gesturing to the first floor balcony that overlooks the security doors in the foyer. By now, the media have been waiting for over an hour and a half for Keli to appear. Robert Lane is standing with Keli's frizzy-haired solicitor. But no matter how long they make the media wait, the cameras will not go away. Finally, Keli and her father decide to leave the court building. Cameramen and journalists waiting at the other exits run over to catch them. Keli and her father are separated. The media swarm around Keli as she walks towards a waiting taxi, her father ignored in the rush to catch Keli. 'Don't touch me,' she snaps as microphones and cameras meet her face at every turn.

As Keli's taxi drives off, her solicitor reads out a prepared statement to the media. 'Keli maintains her innocence and will continue as she has done in the past to assist with the search for Tegan, whom she believes to be alive, well and happy. Keli asks for anyone with any information about Tegan to contact police.'

Unlike every other accused that day, Keli goes home.

*

It has been twenty years since the height of Keli's parents' rule over the Manly rugby scene. Despite the passing decades and Keli's infamy, the Lanes still have social clout. There are people who report who said what about Keli's upcoming trial to Rob and Sandy. While Keli gets the occasional stare, she still carries on her life as usual. Kati, Melinda and Brandon may no longer be friends with Keli, but others are as keen as ever to please the Lanes.

Any misgivings locals have about Keli are kept quiet. Outsiders asking questions about her missing baby are met with hostile silence. Even questions from people who grew up knowing the Lanes are met with mumbled refusals to say anything. But no matter how much influence the Lanes have in their insular world, Keli's upcoming criminal trial is thrusting them into a place where their usual ability to control events does not exist.

The Department of Public Prosecutions assigns the state's senior prosecutor, Mark Tedeschi QC, to Keli's murder trial. Tedeschi is famous for putting many of the state's worst criminals behind bars, including Ivan Milat, who murdered several young backpackers; the gangster who murdered renowned heart transplant surgeon Victor Chang; kidnapper and killer Bruce Burrell, whose two victims' bodies have never been found; pedophile Robert 'Dolly' Dunn; and Sef Gonzales, a young man who was jailed for life for the stabbing murders of his parents and sister. Intrigued by the unique human drama of her case, Tedeschi asked to be the one to prosecute Keli.

Having paid for solicitors and a silk to represent Keli during the coronial inquest four years earlier, the Lanes must now set about defending her from Tedeschi. The financial strain of the immense legal fees is beginning to show. The legal team that represented Keli at the inquest has cost Sandy and Rob Lane most of their life savings and has been disbanded. Keli's defence is now to be paid for by Legal Aid, the state legal defence fund for those unable to pay legal fees themselves. Despite this, Keli's case is attracting a lot of attention from potential counsel as it is obviously going to be high profile. She is represented for a short while by a barrister who offers her services for free while the Lanes decide whom to approach to defend Keli in the murder trial.

It's widely believed among barristers that the Lanes want Winston Terracini SC, whose famous client list includes ex-judge Marcus Einfeld, media heavyweight John Laws and underworld figure Arthur 'Neddy' Smith. The gossip is that Terracini has turned down the Lanes as he is going to be overseas when Keli's trial is due to be held, but they are still chasing him. The court isn't sympathetic to the family's continued requests to delay the trial as they try to secure their preferred counsel. One judge tells Keli's lawyer that there are plenty of defence barristers to choose from.

No matter how hard the Lanes try to put it off, Keli's trial is set to begin in late July 2010. In late June, Keith Chapple SC, an experienced defence counsel, receives Keli's brief. Meanwhile there are pre-trial hearings to sort out what evidence can be put in front of the jury. Such pre-trial matters can be dull and media rarely attend as they can't report anything that happens at this time until after the trial. However, a group of keen court watchers who go from courtroom to courtroom to watch dramas unfold and see the baddies sent to jail, sit through it all.

'Some people like really gruesome murder and rapes trials, but not me,' says one keen Tedeschi fan with blonde hair, settling onto the hard wooden court bench in the old fashioned courthouse adjacent to the modern high-rise where Keli was arraigned more than six months earlier. 'I like the mysteries and ones that explore the psychology of murders, and that is the sort of trial Mark does.'

The court watchers' dedication is rewarded by some tastes of what is to come once the trial gets properly underway. Keli's old friend Natalie is heavily pregnant and has to give her evidence early as she lives overseas and will not be able to fly once the trial begins. From the back of the court she waves at Keli, who is sitting in the dock, and then turns sideways to show off her pregnant belly. Keli smiles, and then dabs her eyes with a tissue. Having not said anything to police two years earlier about ever knowing a man named Andrew Norris, Natalie begins her testimony by claiming she may have met Tegan's supposed father. The phone conversation she had with Keli just after giving her statement to police is played to the court, after which Natalie's answers become increasingly defensive. Despite her little digs at Tedeschi, she ends up admitting she can't really remember meeting such a man. She agrees she only claimed she had met Andrew Morris/Norris to police because she read in the media somewhere that Keli claimed this was the man who fathered her missing baby. Her time in the witness box now complete, Natalie takes a few steps then turns to Keli and blows her a kiss, seemingly oblivious to the fact she has just supported the Crown's argument this man, Andrew Morris/Norris, doesn't exist. Keli meets the cheerful expression of her old friend with a blank expression.

Another witness who gives evidence before the trial begins is a man whom the Crown says might have had a one-night stand with Keli sixteen years before. At the time he was visiting from another state to take part in a surf lifesaving competition and had gone to a pub on the Northern Beaches near Manly for a big night out after his team was eliminated. He couldn't identify Keli clearly when police approached him. He could only remember that the girl he had sex with on the grass beside a creek running by a nearby caravan park was athletic with blonde hair and black eyebrows.

The Crown is not suggesting for a moment this man is the father of Tegan – the one night stand happened too early for that. What the Crown wants to suggest is that this chance encounter is where Keli got the name for the fictitious man she claims to have given Tegan to two years later, but they aren't sure yet whether they should put him in front of the jury and the media. This pleasant bloke has the misfortune of being caught up this murder trial because of his name: Andrew Morris. He was one of the forty-one men named Andrew Morris or Norris the police had contacted in their nation-wide search for Tegan, and now he is unlucky enough to be sitting in a courtroom answering questions about a one-night stand he had as a nineteen-year-old after a few too many beers.

Some of the court watchers cluck with disapproval. Justice Whealy, a large, amicable man with round shoulders and a ready smile, knows there is a lot in this trial that is going to stir some of the most deeply-held emotions, moral outrage and prejudices because of the sexual nature of the evidence, and the court system is preparing to deal with it. Observers are perplexed to learn that over two hundred people are being screened to see if they qualify to be on the jury, easily four times the size of the pool from which a jury is normally selected. There are so many people that they can't all fit into the courtroom at once.

Keli's two terminations and two adoption processes, despite being unusual, are perfectly legal, so Justice Whealy is doing everything he can to ensure Keli's trial is held in a court of law rather than a court of morals. As such, jurors must be people who, in their heart of hearts, don't think the fact that Keli had abortions, premarital sex and put children up for adoption make her a bad person. Finding those people will involve ruling out a large number of potential jurors.

'Some people in our community feel very strongly about abortion and the termination of pregnancies. Some people think it is morally wrong and some consider it as against divine law,' he says. 'Now, no one will be critical of any one of you if you are anti-abortion, but because of the need to ensure this is a fair trial, I say to you, bluntly, that if any of you is anti-abortion or has strong religious, moral or other views on the subject, there is simply no place for you in this trial. If any of you has strong moral convictions or views about a young woman becoming pregnant and then putting a child up for adoption, there is equally no place for you in this trial.'

Whealy then adds that if the topic of child murder is too horrifying for any of the potential jurors to contemplate, they shouldn't put themselves forward as jurors, either. 'The fact that this trial will raise highly emotional issues relating to a mother's dealing with newborn children must not interfere with the presumption of innocence, to which Keli Lane is emphatically entitled.'

Justice Whealy then invites people to come up to the witness box and whisper in his ear why they feel they can't be part of a fair trial for Keli. 'I will now ask you to let me know, perhaps just by holding up your hand, if any of you wishes to be excused. Please don't be embarrassed, please don't feel shy about letting me know.' Men and women of all ages and walks of life raise their hands, quietly tell Justice Whealy their deepest, personal views on sex and motherhood and are excused.

Fourteen jurors are selected. As it is to be a long trial, spare jurors need to be empanelled to ensure there are twelve ready to hand down a verdict at the end, even if one or two of them have to quit because of unforseen medical emergencies or the like. They are sent away and told to come back when the barristers are ready to give their opening addresses.

Over the next few days things are relatively quiet. The media can't report on what happens when the jury isn't in the courtroom, so the only people gawking at Keli are the court watchers and young law students visiting to observe the legal arguments. As Keli is not in custody, she walks into the courtroom like everyone else. Initially, she seems timid. Her nearest and dearest can't be in court because they are due to give evidence, so the kindly judge's associate goes out of her way to make sure Keli is comfortable by asking whether she needs water or a cushion to sit on. For much of the time, especially when the two QCs are arguing points of law, no one pays much attention to Keli at all.

On the final day before the media descends on the trial, Justice Whealy muses aloud about the problem of seating the fourteen jurors in a jury box made to hold twelve. 'Do you have any carpentry skills, Mr Crown?' he jokes, using the traditional term to address Tedeschi in his role as the prosecuting barrister.

Everyone smiles, including Keli. But soon a storm will erupt in this courtroom with a ferocity that will dwarf the coronial inquest.

On Monday 9 August, Tedeschi begins his opening address, which is an outline of the evidence he will present to the jury over the next three months. There are four charges in total.

Three of them relate to lies Keli swore to in court documents to do with the adoptions of two of her secret children, the police having added one more since Keli's arraignment in late 2009. The other, and the most serious charge, is that of the murder of her daughter, Tegan Lane, which the Crown alleges occurred by Keli's hand in the few hours between her leaving Auburn Hospital and arriving at her parents' house on Saturday afternoon, 14 September 1996, two days after Tegan's secret birth.

'You won't just be looking at the birth of Tegan,' Tedeschi tells the jury. 'Over the course of seven years – from 1992 to 1999 – the accused became pregnant no less than five times.' Right from the outset, Tedeschi knows he won't be able to explain everything about the case. 'Why on earth would a person in her position, a person who was receiving a tertiary education, a person who came from a solid family life, get pregnant five times?' he asks. 'The evidence will be that she was on the pill, so that immediately raises the question how did she get pregnant five times in seven years?'

It is a question the jury – and ultimately, the rest of the country – will probably never know the answer to, but Tedeschi has to put forward some sort of plausible theory. So he does, and it isn't pretty. 'The answer may be that during those seven years she was drinking very, very heavily,' he suggests. 'She would regularly go out to the pub, and we will hear evidence that she used to keep up with the boys in her drinking. There was a lot of drinking, there was a lot of chucking, and it's quite easy, if somebody is on the contraceptive pill and they are vomiting, that it doesn't get absorbed properly, so it doesn't work and the person gets pregnant.'

Besides painting Keli as a vomiting binge drinker, the question as to why Duncan isn't the father of Keli's first baby is raised. The Crown points out that Keli was sleeping with two men around the time of the child's conception – Duncan and the footy player she was seeing immediately before Duncan. The fact that Keli's first and third secret babies were fathered by two different young men is also revealed.

All of the pregnancies were unwanted, so Keli took action, the Crown's case states, 'to be permanently rid of the responsibility of looking after a child. She did this the first two times by having a termination, the third time in relation to her first baby by adoption, the fourth time in relation to Tegan by killing her, and the fifth time in relation to her third baby by adoption.' Tedeschi goes on to list the three reasons the Crown thinks Keli wanted to be permanently, and secretly, rid of her babies: first, her ambition to play water polo for Australia, especially in the Olympics; second, her desire to maintain her active social and sex life; and finally, her fear of rejection by her family and friends if they ever found out about her pregnancies.

The extraordinary lengths Keli took to hide her secret children are introduced to the jury. Tedeschi outlines how Keli slipped out from the pub after playing a water polo grand final match to give birth to her first secret child that day. He lists in dizzying detail the mountain of lies that she told nurses and adoption agency workers about her family, where she lived, her life story and who the father was for all three babies, lies told so that the real fathers of these children, along with everyone else in her life, had absolutely no idea of their existence.

Tedeschi tells the jury that putting a baby up for adoption was harder than Keli thought. 'The Crown's case is that the accused must have rather naively thought at that stage in her life that the adoption process would be a very simple matter of just handing the baby over, signing a few forms and that would be it. But the reality was quite different.' Besides having to answer a series of probing questions, having the adoption agency try to contact the father so official documents could be properly completed, and having to swear in court documents that everything she had put in writing was true, Keli was also expected to visit her babies in foster care and meet the people who were to adopt them. Tedeschi says Keli found such visits emotionally difficult, and the stress led her to pretend that she was leaving, playing sport overseas for up to a year during the first adoption process, so that she could avoid any more of them.

When Tegan was born the next year, Tedeschi continues, Keli was under even tighter time constraints. He explains that it's the Crown's case that Keli falsely claimed her pregnancy was overdue in an attempt to convince doctors to induce her so she could make Di and Wally's wedding on 14 September. The year before, she had come dangerously close to giving birth in the pool right in front of a crowd that included her mother and Duncan. This time around, she didn't want to risk going into labour in front of wedding guests or at another awkward time, so she did everything she could to give birth as soon as possible. Keli tried to be induced a couple of weeks before the wedding but the doctors at Ryde Hospital kept turning her away. Time was running out as she was only entering the full term of her pregnancy days before the wedding. Finally, she was deemed medically fit for induction, but even after only allowing herself two days to recover, she had literally hours to spare to make it to the wedding.

'Ladies and gentlemen,' says Tedeschi, 'the Crown's case is that because of the delay in convincing a hospital to induce her labour, and because of the unexpected complications that she'd had following the birth of Tegan, the accused's timing to get to this wedding at 4 pm on Saturday the fourteenth became extremely tight. So before the blood had been taken from Tegan for the Guthrie test, before the formal discharge documents had been completed and before the identification of the child had been checked, the accused suddenly left the hospital with Tegan sometime between 11 am and 12 noon on 14 September. She probably left via a fire escape which was almost opposite the room she had been sharing with the other patient. The door had no alarm on it so she was able to leave the ward without having to go past the nurses' station.' Tedeschi then adds that, unlike the year before, Keli didn't have time to put Tegan into foster care.

'We don't know how or where the accused killed Tegan, or how she disposed of the body,' he continues as the jury and media struggle to believe that the nice-looking young woman in the dock could have done all the things the Crown is accusing her of. 'However, Auburn Hospital was just a couple of kilometres away from the Australian College of Physical Education at what was then the Homebush Olympics site which, at that time in 1996, was surrounded by vast swathes of vacant land, a few building sites and deserted roads, particularly at the weekend. So there was an opportunity nearby for the accused to find somewhere that was entirely private, which would have given her an opportunity to kill Tegan and dispose of the body.'

Fear of rejection is perhaps the easiest motivation for murder to understand as it implies some sort of desperation by the then young Keli, even though it was a fear that was clearly baseless given the rock-solid support demonstrated by her family since they'd learned about her secret babies. However, in the eyes of the Crown, Keli has never been any sort of victim. She has been charged with murder, and the motivations for murdering two-day-old Tegan that Tedeschi is inviting the jury to consider are ones of extraordinary selfishness and callousness.

Tedeschi goes on to outline proof of her heartlessness. 'Ladies and gentlemen, there is not the slightest suggestion that the accused was suffering from any form of postnatal depression or other mental disturbance after Tegan's birth. Quite the contrary. At 3 pm she had an appointment to meet her boyfriend, Duncan Gillies, at her parents' home so they could get dressed and go to a wedding. They went to that wedding at four o'clock and they went to the reception after the wedding. The accused was observed having a perfectly good time socialising, drinking, dancing. She was her normal self.'

Even though the Crown states that Keli is a killer, Tedeschi is not claiming she is devoid of emotion. As hard as the adoption process was for her first secret baby, Tedeschi says Keli returned to it when she gave birth to her third secret baby as 'the experience of killing Tegan had been so awful that even the practical difficulties involved in an adoption were preferable to killing another child.'

The Crown's opening address takes more than two days to detail. The judge reminds the jury that what Tedeschi has told them are not the facts, but what the police claim to be the facts. He tells them it's up to them to decide over the coming months what is fact and what isn't after hearing what both the Crown and the defence have to say. By the end of Tedeschi's opening address, the minds of the jury and journalists are swimming in an ocean of dates, names, false addresses, hospital notes, summaries of police inquiries and efforts to imagine how anyone could hide a pregnancy in a bathing suit. The vivid scenario of Keli sneaking out of Auburn hospital and then murdering Tegan at the Homebush site is the one clear message that remains, as well as the insinuation that makes many observers wince – that Keli used to be what every girl fears being branded: a drunken slut.

The core of the Crown's case is the inability of police to find Tegan, to find the man Keli says she gave her to, a man who police say doesn't exist, and Keli's behaviour during the police investigation. Behind the core part of the Crown's case is a mountain of lies Keli told about her three unwanted babies, a mountain so huge it will take months to explain it. For now, the true extent of the police searches and Keli's behaviour and lies are yet to be appreciated by those listening. The idea that Keli was once a young woman who often drank until she vomited and regularly fell pregnant to different men is only a small part of the Crown's case, but it is that insinuation that grates the most. In the early days of the trial many feel sympathy for Keli, who sits with an air of quiet dignity as her character is so brutally attacked. Observers are quick to count up the number of boyfriends behind the parade of unwanted pregnancies. Between the ages of eighteen to twenty-four, Keli is known to have slept with four different guys, five if Andrew Morris/Norris is included. If this number makes Keli a slut, then the average girl feels like she is being called a slut, too. Also, despite the carefully picked jury, many are concerned that the fact she had pregnancies terminated is being used as evidence in a murder trial.

As Keli's barrister Keith Chapple says in his opening address, maybe the difference between Keli and the young men that she slept with, who people may not be so quick to judge, is that Keli can fall pregnant and have babies while they can't. 'People who are unmarried, young and good looking get around,' he tells the jury. 'People sometimes act in ways that you might not have acted or approved of, even when we were younger.'

Chapple ridicules the idea that because of Keli's desire to live her young life unburdened by a child 'she took the extraordinary, criminal and amazing step of killing her second child'. He also expresses his disbelief at the Crown's theory that because committing murder was so horrible and ghastly, she reverted back to adoption to deal with her third child.

'Indeed, the defence's case is that she was actually being very responsible in relation to all her children,' he says. It was kind to put her first and third children up for adoption. 'She did something, you might think, that was even nicer in relation to Tegan . . . because she thought Tegan would have a better chance in life with her natural father and his partner.'

'And do you think that she was so silly, so dense, that when she had to give birth to her third child, she forgot that she'd been to Ryde Hospital?' asks Chapple in relation to Keli's decision to return to the hospital she had attended several times while heavily pregnant with Tegan. 'Or do you think there was nothing that she was really concerned about to stop her from going back?

'She didn't scuttle out of Auburn hospital. She didn't dispose of a body out at the Olympics site. She didn't go and bluff her way through a wedding with the terrible act of murder still in her mind,' he says, before finishing his opening address.

Justice Whealy also has something to say to the jury before the first witness is called. He knows that no one likes a liar, and that the Crown will forcefully show Keli lying about important things in very serious circumstances. But even if Keli is a liar, the judge wants the jury to remember that it doesn't necessarily mean she is a murderer.

20

KELI'S LIES: SAD OR SINISTER?

With the shock of the Crown's opening address still ringing in their ears, the jury begins to hear evidence from the witnesses. Keli's high school boyfriend Aaron is among the first. He's a nice bloke who regrets yelling abuse at her all those years ago on the Corso. He tells the court about the day Keli went off to the city to have an abortion. 'She always loved kids,' he says when explaining how, on top of her Olympic dreams, she wanted to be a teacher.

Next, the hospital records of nineteen-year-old Keli's sudden appearance at hospital in 1995 to give birth to her first secret child are read out. They also detail how polite and grateful she was to everyone. The adoption worker tells the court how emotional Keli was when signing the adoption papers and how Keli, so very anxious that the adoptive parents liked her, bought a huge bunch of yellow roses for her baby's new mother when they met. The evidence surrounding the birth of her first secret baby takes two weeks to get through. Among it are the lies Keli told about her family living in Perth and how she lived with Duncan, the baby's father, who didn't want anything to do with his baby. More than anything, the evidence comes across as being sad. Through it all Keli sits, expressionless.

By the end of the first two weeks the nurses' and doctors' records of Tegan's birth a year later are also read out to the court. The tone of the witnesses gets a little harder. One or two let slip comments about how they thought it was weird that Keli was all alone in the hospital before they are sharply reminded they are not there to give their opinions, only the facts. Much time is spent on where Keli's room in the maternity ward was in relation to the nurses' station and the fire escape, which ran down five storeys and came out at where the ambulances were parked near a quiet road. A doctor from Ryde Hospital, where Keli appeared several times in the weeks leading up to Tegan's birth, including a few hours before she first checked herself into Auburn Hospital, reads out the records of Keli's multiple presentations at the hospital, of her claims that she was about to give birth in a day or so, of ultrasounds being performed and of Keli being sent home. Hours after her last visit to Ryde Hospital, she took herself to Auburn Hospital, where the next day her barely full-term pregnancy was finally induced.

However, evidence is also given that despite Keli's swift and unseen exit from Auburn Hospital with two-day-old Tegan in her arms, all the key medical checks of mother and child had been done and Keli was, in fact, free to go. While staff were surprised to find Keli's bed and Tegan's basinette empty just before lunch on 14 September 1996, they didn't feel the need to raise the alarm or call the police. It was another nurse who took the call two days later from Keli asking for the routine home visit by a hospital midwife to be cancelled, and while this nurse thought it odd, she didn't think to raise any alarm either. Again, Keli sits through the evidence expressionless, save for the occasional eye roll to her solicitor or bout of note taking as she sits in the dock.

The competency of the nurses and doctors is not questioned. It was only when police put all their careful and diligent clinical notes together years later that the strange picture of Keli's behaviour started to emerge, first at the coronial hearing five years earlier and again, here in the Supreme Court. Yes, Keli undoubtedly told lies, gave birth among strangers and hid her babies from family and friends, but people are finding it very difficult to believe that she murdered Tegan.

Many of the journalists observing the trial aren't convinced. Keli sits in front of them in the dock, looking like a perfectly normal person who, by some undeserved misfortune, now finds herself on trial, having to bear the most personal details of her life being read out in open court. Before the jury comes in each day she walks into the courtroom with her lawyers, dressed well and talking with them, animated. While many of her friends and family can't be in the courtroom because they are due to give evidence, she has one or two supporters who jealously guard the seats reserved for them behind her legal team. They smile at her and discreetly signal their support as the jury members take their seats and proceedings get underway. It's hard to fathom that Keli committed the terrible act the Crown accuses her of.

The third week of the trial is full of testimony from people in Keli's life nearly fifteen years ago. Duncan takes the stand, happy to take this chance to show he had no idea that Keli gave birth twice while they were dating. He is also very keen to show what a nice boyfriend he was to her the year she gave birth to Tegan, claiming his relationship with Keli was 'stronger than ever' at that time, despite having agreed eagerly with Coroner Abernethy five years earlier that he and Keli passed each other like 'ships in the night' at that point in their relationship. The game of 'he said, she said' that had been going on for years between Duncan and Taryn is aired in court, much to the delight of the assembled journalists. Days later, Taryn gets her chance to say she never slept with him. Duncan's mother, Julie, and brother, Simon, simmer with fury when they give their testimony. Meanwhile, Keli sits calmly as they talk about what she has dragged them through. The two men who found out they were the fathers of her two other secret children fight back tears when giving their evidence, but Keli remains unmoved. The wedding video showing Keli a few hours after Tegan's disappearance is also played in court. The bride, groom and several guests at the wedding, all of whom had known Keli for years, say they had no idea that Keli had given birth two days earlier. Keli sits stony faced through the evidence of these people, people she'd seen and mixed with hours after the disappearance of Tegan.

However, there are times when Keli gets agitated in the dock. Often it's when her closest friends are in the witness box. Stacy is grilled by Keli's barrister as to why she said nothing to Keli or offered her any help after she and Taryn looked at Keli underwater with their goggles on; but Taryn isn't. Keli's legal team have decided not to take this approach with her, but nonetheless Keli is restless and has an injured expression on her face as her old friend Taryn leaves the stand. In contrast to his prickly performance in the stand five years earlier at the coronial inquest, Brandon is doing his best to answer questions and to be helpful, although his tendency to give his opinions rather than just the facts leads Justice Whealy to tell him off. When he is sent out so that a point of law can be discussed, he and Duncan, who is also in the courthouse that day, sit together on one of the wooden benches in the hall and talk like mates. Having spurned Duncan when Keli's secret children were first revealed, Keli's old inner circle are now reaching out to him. When Brandon finishes giving his evidence and walks out of the courtroom, Keli motions frantically to her lawyers. She tells the junior barrister she wants the judge to stop Brandon from talking about her behind her back.

'I wonder if Mr Ward could be asked not to speak to his wife about his evidence,' says Chapple.

'He's gone now. You would be doing very well if you could stop Mr Ward from talking to his wife,' says Justice Whealy, smiling, before adding that Brandon should be reminded that witnesses shouldn't talk about the case among themselves before giving evidence.

Kati and Melinda both announce they are no longer friends with Keli when they give evidence. Keli sits with her face down in the dock during their respective denouncements of her. But even though she may have lost many of her closest friends, a conviction for murder seems a long way off. 'I don't think Keli's got much to worry about,' says a court reporter for a daily paper as she strides down the hallway outside the courtroom. 'I can't understand why this matter is set down for three months. What else is there to say?'

But as the weeks of the trial roll on and the media interest dwindles, evidence about how Tegan's existence became known to the authorities while she gave birth to and adopted out her third secret baby in 1999 is presented to the jury, often without any media present to report what was said. The jurors learn how Keli flew up to Queensland to try to have her third baby aborted at six and a half months, and even though they have been picked for their liberal views about terminations, they are a little taken aback. They are even more shocked by Keli's lies to nurses that three-year-old Tegan was with her in Sydney and that she had breastfed her for six months.

But it is the testimony of Virginia Fung that makes some curl their lips with disgust. Virginia, who took voluminous notes about her dealings with Keli, is on the stand for three days. Keli's professed inability to consider terminations, her 'love' for her baby and her belief that giving birth is 'a gift', all the while ensuring she didn't mention Tegan, causes several jurors, particularly the females ones, to see Keli in a harsher light. Keli sits in the dock, her head bowed, apparently taking notes, avoiding looking jury members in the eye. Virginia hasn't heard the evidence of Keli's attempt to abort her baby at such a late stage, nor of the lie Keli told nurses just days before she first called Virginia that Tegan was with her in Sydney.

Virginia reads out her notes as asked, recalling her determination to keep Keli involved in the adoption process. The earnest care that Virginia took in writing a life story for Keli's baby born and adopted in 1999 is moving. One female juror, hand over her mouth, holds back the tears as the eight-page story – the story this child will rely on to work out where they came from – is read out. Keli sits serenely, appearing totally unmoved.

John Borovnik, the eagle-eyed DoCS worker who originally flagged the inconsistencies in Keli's stories regarding the births of her babies, has suffered poor health for a couple of years by this time, but is determined to give evidence. Symptoms of his condition include tremors, perspiration and mild deafness, but he wants to see Keli face up to what he thinks she has done, even though he needs a hearing aid to make out the barristers' questions. Afterwards, he sits in the public gallery regularly to watch proceedings.

But even if members of the jury now have a low opinion of Keli, seeking an abortion at six and half months and then being turned away is not proof of murder. Neither is the lie she told nurses about three-year-old Tegan being with her in Sydney. As creepy as it may be, perhaps she told it because she mistakenly thought she had to so that she could give birth again and arrange an adoption with a minimum of fuss.

The media continue to attend sporadically. They take notes as the fax that Keli sent Virginia, once her first secret child and Tegan's existence had been discovered, is read out. Keli begins to cry when she hears the passages about how Virginia was the first person in a long time she felt she could trust and how alone she felt back then. In the morning tea break, Keli walks down the street, flanked by her lawyers and wearing sunglasses, to grab a hot chocolate and take in some air. Keli's tears are reported in the news. The next morning, Keli, clearly elated at the sympathetic tone of the news reports, strolls across the road towards the courthouse, talking excitedly and laughing with her solicitor.

Keli has more cause for celebration when the ex-tenant of the building where she says Andrew Morris/Norris lived during their affair gives evidence about the letters he remembers seeing. Since first approaching the police about these letters after the dig under Duncan's old place in 2008, the ex-tenant has now changed his recollection to not only seeing letters addressed to Andrew Norris back in 1995, but to seeing a couple of letters addressed to Andrew Morris as well. He repeats his explanation that he said nothing about these letters to Coroner Abernethy because he feared being sued by the Lanes, even though he has never spoken to the Lanes or been approached by any lawyer representing them. He tells the court he didn't talk to other tenants in that building much as he generally doesn't trust people. His brother, whom he lived with in that apartment block, had no recollection of seeing any such letters. Whatever the jury thinks of this evidence, journalists report it as possible proof that the man Keli claims to have given Tegan to might really exist.

It becomes apparent that Keli still hasn't told her friends the extent of her lies or which ones she has involved them in. Lisa is clearly surprised to learn that Keli called her from Ryde Hospital not long after giving birth to her third child to chat about their upcoming European holiday and that Keli told Virginia that she was staying with her after claiming she had been thrown out by 'friends' living at Duncan's old place.

The day arrives when Robert and Sandra Lane are due to appear. They sit slightly apart, and silent, as they wait in the corridor outside the courtroom. A TV journalist whispers to colleagues to check whether Keli's mum is in her seventies. It's easy to see why she thinks that. Keli may be fresh faced, but her parents have been physically worn down by the stress of the last six years. Just like her husband, Sandy looks forlorn and crumpled. Both seem twenty years older than they actually are.

The judge sends the jury out so he can talk candidly to Keli's parents. They walk in, holding their heads up high. Keli watches them, and while they aren't ignoring her, they are keeping their eyes on the scarlet-robed judge. They are here to do what they feel is right, and they want to get on with it. Justice Whealy tells them, as Keli's parents, that they have the right not to give evidence, but both say they are happy to answer questions. Justice Whealy calls for the jury to re-enter.

Sandy is the first to take the stand. The older female

jurors have sympathetic looks on their faces as she begins her testimony. Tedeschi asks Sandy a long list of questions. Initially, Sandy is comfortable answering them as they are questions she has answered before. No, she didn't know Keli was pregnant all those times. No, she'd never met Andrew Morris/Norris nor had she heard of him before the police investigation. Yes, the first time she'd seen Keli on the day Tegan disappeared was at around 3 pm when, out of her kitchen window, she saw Keli enter the back gate leading in from the driveway. Yes, this is how Keli normally entered the house if she had driven her car home.

Then Tedeschi begins to ask questions that leave Sandy visibly confused. The questions are the list of lies Keli had told nurses and Virginia Fung around the birth and adoption of her third child and the discovery of Tegan's existence by DoCS. With her voice rising with uncertainty, Sandy answers that, no, she and her husband did not live in London in 1999; no, the family had not disowned Keli. With a look of absolute incomprehension, Sandy denies the claim that Keli had a toddler in her care in 1999. When Rob takes the stand he is asked similar questions, and is obviously confounded. Despite facing a murder trial and despite knowing her parents were about to enter the witness box, Keli still hadn't told her parents all the lies she had involved them in. As they give their evidence, Keli sits in the dock, blank-faced and motionless.

Afterwards, during a break in proceedings, Sandy and Rob stand, confused, in the corridor outside the courtroom. Journalists and lawyers keep their distance, giving them as much space and privacy as possible. Keli walks towards her parents and bursts into tears. Sandy, who is barely taller than Keli's shoulders, stands kissing her daughter's neck. Rob stays close, silent and shell-shocked.

The following weeks are filled with excruciatingly thorough detail of the massive police searches for Tegan and Andrew Morris/Norris. Trollies heaped with folders of search documents are wheeled into court and the jury are provided with colour coded flow-charts to explain how the police went about their search. A female detective, her hand resting on one of three large folders in front of her as she gives evidence, tells Chapple, 'I wanted to find that child.'

The last three weeks of the Crown's case are full of delays. A number of birth certificates of the thousands of girls invest-igated by police are still trickling in from all over the country. The judge is seriously concerned that the defence are being given important evidence at very short notice before it is introduced in open court and Chapple is not being given enough time to think of what questions he might want to ask in cross examination. Days of hearings are abandoned while the court gives the defence more time to pour over the mountains of evidence the police have gathered in their search for Tegan and Andrew Morris/Norris. The defence demand the Crown gathers more evidence on about 150 little girls dismissed as possibly being Tegan without police having obtained birth certificates and other proof of parentage. A large number of these little girls were ruled out on the basis of ethnicity, commonly that they and both parents have, for example, dark-skinned African, Chinese or Thai heritage. However, Keli is facing a murder charge and only the most complete evidence will do.

In a two-day period police undertake an enormous effort to obtain this evidence, including tracking down the parents of a girl born on the same day as Tegan who attends a boarding school in far North Queensland. She is part Torres Strait Islander and her mother lives on a small island with a population of only a couple of hundred off the coast of Papua New Guinea. The little girl's birth certificate, a statement from her mother and proof of her citizenship are all obtained and entered into evidence the same day.

Chapple wants to raise some issues over how thoroughly police investigated two men caught by the Andrew Morris/Norris search, one who lives in South Australia and the other who lives in Victoria. Both are flown to Sydney to give evidence. One spent the 1990s building his own business and arrives in a blue woollen jumper and sneakers. The other, who used the alias of Andrew Norris to falsely claim social security payments years ago, turns up in a suit. Now the men are sitting in front of the jury, the possibility that they had anything to do with Tegan seems far-fetched. After they give their evidence the court breaks for lunch. When Keli returns for the afternoon's evidence she is clearly not happy, banging the gate to the dock.

A couple of days later, a man whose daughter was born on the same day as Tegan and whose mother's name is Mel gives evidence by video link from Brisbane. He is a truck driver, and the defence want to question him about his name changes and the fact his little girl flies in and out of the country a lot. He holds up his daughter's birth certificate showing she was born in the UK. He and his daughter's mother had split up so the little girl now travels between countries to spend time with both her parents. All his evidence does is put another human face on the police's enormous, fruitless search for Tegan. Not a single member of the jury looks at Keli when they leave for the day.

By now, most of the jury are consistently refusing to make eye contact with Keli when she stands as they enter or leave the jury box, as is required by the accused in the dock. Keli generally smiles at them, but sometimes she chooses to ignore them, too, even stifling a yawn or casting an exasperated glance towards her team. While sitting in the dock, Keli is often keen to catch the eye of her instructing solicitor, a young woman with a confident air who dresses in smart pant suits. During one particularly heated debate between Justice Whealy and Tedeschi about the use of lies, Keli tries to roll her eyes at her, but her solicitor is listening intently and isn't looking Keli's way. Keli instead smiles to herself and yawns, as if her rudeness and feigned disinterest will be enough to dismiss those who question her. A shaved headed young male supporter sitting in court that day notices and seems satisfied that the Crown's argument is rubbish. He mistakes one of the judge's comments as an insult and laughs while no one else does. Once the judge has left and Keli is free to leave the dock, she enters a bubble of comfort, chatting casually with her legal team and the young man, who is a member of a Northern Beaches Christian group who have decided to make Keli their cause.

Keli's new boyfriend also begins to make appearances, and Keli arrives at court some mornings with a motorcycle helmet in her hands. In the evenings and on the weekends they are zooming all around the Northern Beaches together, eating out and going to the beach. Sometimes Keli comes to court sunburnt with her hair a little tousled.

However, there are occasions when Keli clearly doesn't feel quite so comfortable. Despite ongoing arguments with the judge, Tedeschi insists there are three lies – Keli's claim to Virginia that she gave Tegan to a couple she barely knew who she thinks now live in Perth; then her claim to Detective Kehoe that she gave Tegan to her natural father named Andrew Morris; followed by her claim to Detective Gaut that she gave Tegan to her natural father named Andrew Norris – that he should be able to use as part of the evidence Keli killed Tegan. These are lies she told once she knew the police were going to look for Tegan. Also, she kept telling the Andrew Norris lie once all her family and friends knew about her secret babies. The first and third babies were safely adopted by that stage and Keli hadn't been rejected by her loved ones like she feared she would be, so Tedeschi argues that what other sensible explanation was there for Keli to keep telling that lie other than to cover up the murder of Tegan?

Justice Whealy is not convinced, even when Tedeschi points out other evidence – namely the police's inability to find Tegan and comments Keli made during the police investigation that he says show she had no expectation that Tegan would be found alive – will also be relied on by the Crown to prove murder. The jury are sent out several times, sometimes for days, as the judge and the Crown fiercely argue whether using a handful of Keli's lies to prove murder is fair. In the end, the Crown wins. Tedeschi will be allowed to invite the jury to view Keli's lie that she gave Tegan to a couple who lived in Perth and her stories about giving Tegan to Andrew Morris/Norris, which police think are also lies, as part of the proof that Keli murdered Tegan.

The television crews have begun to wait outside the courtroom again. Keli had avoided the cameras five years earlier and at the start of this trial, but now she seems comfortable in front of them. She dresses sharply in flattering dresses and high heels. The partner of the firm of solicitors representing her starts to make more appearances. After one long day of detailed and boring evidence, he stands chatting to some journalists.

'Every day is like today,' he says. 'There is absolutely no evidence against her. Once the Crown finish we are going to ask the judge to throw this case out. It just depends on whether he has the ticker to do it,' he boasts.

But the case isn't thrown out. Keli is going to have to face the jury's decision.

21

JUSTICE FOR TEGAN, AGONY FOR THE LANES

Summer has arrived. After so many rainy days there is a series of warm, breezy ones. The jury have now heard everything the police have discovered about Keli's secret babies all those years ago. Keli is not going to take the stand and the defence are not calling any witnesses, so all that is left is to hear each side's final addresses. The jury have looked across the narrow courtroom at Keli since the middle of winter. Sometimes she cried, sometimes she rolled her eyes. She exchanged many glances with her solicitor and supporters, but for the most part she has been expressionless. Keli is a blank canvas everyone projects their feelings onto.

In the eyes of those who think she is guilty, her calmness is strange. As a very young woman she was able to give children away and then spend time with her family and friends as if nothing had happened. Her good upbringing and clean-cut appearance means she was, and still is, always given the benefit of the doubt by those around her, even when her behaviour was highly unusual. It's beyond question that Keli took extraordinary measures to stop family and friends from finding out the truth about Tegan and her other secret children, but it seems clear that her lies about them were never going to stand up to close scrutiny. However, she never seems to have been questioned very closely by anyone in her life, except once by her mother, on the phone. Since then, Keli has benefited from being surrounded by people who are either in denial or determined she not face the full consequences of her actions.

Most of all, she seems oddly untouched by years of pressure from an ongoing police investigation and the associated media exposure that would make most people nervous wrecks, even if innocent. It's as if Keli is merely waiting to see if she is going to be punished, either making the unnaturally cold calculation that she might get away with it if she just lets everyone else do the fighting, or by being in total denial of what she has done. As hard as it was to believe at first, months of watching her have made it possible for people to think she really did kill Tegan and then continue, apparently untroubled, with her life.

In the eyes of those who think she is innocent, her calmness is borne of dignity in the face of the most horrible character assassination and outrageous invasion of privacy. Yes, she kept falling pregnant as a young woman, but now she is paying a price that no one should ever have to pay. It wasn't so long ago that the very real threat of being disowned by family and cast out by society forced pregnant girls to travel to country towns where no one knew them to give birth. Even if Keli didn't actually face such consequences, she may have really believed she did. When Keli was born in the mid 1970s, unmarried mothers were still being pressured to give their children up for adoption, a process that, back then, meant totally cutting all contact between mother and child. How many countless women carry the guilt of giving away their babies, having first suffered bullying from pious hypocrites keen to target any woman soft-hearted, unlucky, misguided or alone enough to find herself pregnant without a husband? How many of those babies, now adults around Keli's age, wonder why their mothers left them?

Even in this modern era, with readily available contraception and legal terminations, women still suffer. The option of termination doesn't come guilt-free for many, even if they choose to take it. The agony of their choice can follow them throughout their lives, sometimes affecting their mental health and emotional well-being. Many people wonder if Keli is being unfairly criticised because she had two pregnancies terminated and sought the termination of a third.

There is also the simple disbelief others have that a woman who looks like Keli and who comes from the sort of family she does could ever kill a child. Would people who hold such a view happily condemn Keli if she came from a more humble background, had tattoos on her neck and wore cheap clothes, or if she came from a solid, supportive Muslim family and sat in the dock with a scarf covering her head?

But beyond anyone's opinion of Keli is the law. Keli told stories that many think are lies and her baby is missing in suspicious circumstances, so a common sense approach might suggest that, unless she is able to say something that leads to her baby's whereabouts or at least something people can find believable, she is guilty. But humans are unpredictable, and the criminal courts know that people lie for many reasons, not all of them sensible. As Justice Whealy has reminded the jury, just because Keli is a liar doesn't mean she is a murderer. Also, for the law to mean anything it has to protect everyone, even people we don't like very much.

This means everyone is innocent until proven guilty, and it is up to the Crown, meaning the police and the lawyers representing the state, to prove that guilt. No one, including Keli, has to prove they are innocent, so they have the right to say nothing if they choose. After all, silence is the ultimate way of saying you have nothing to prove. Exactly what these rights mean in the cut and thrust of a trial is something continuously debated by lawyers, and Keli's case saw some particularly heated debates out of the ear-shot of the jury.

The time arrives for both sides to make their final addresses to the jury, which now numbers twelve as two of the original fourteen have left because of illness. The Crown addresses them first. Keli's family and friends are not in the courtroom, but one or two of her Christian support group are.

'This was not a situation where Keli was prepared to achieve some sort of solution to her problem that meant that in a month's time, in a year's time, in ten years' time somebody would come back to her with a child and say, "Hey, I've looked after this baby for the last however long, it's your turn now." Can you imagine the surprise that it would have been for her family if that had happened?' Tedeschi begins.

Then he states that what Keli was looking for was a permanent solution to the problem of her secret children. Like having a termination, so far as avoiding the prospect of having to look after a child is concerned, adoption is final. 'The adoptive parents couldn't one day appear on Keli's doorstep and say, "We've had your baby for a couple of years, thank you very much, it's been lovely but we would like to hand your baby back",' he says, adding that the relevance of such thinking was when Keli had to deal with Tegan, she chose the most permanent solution of all – murder.

'Keli had two completely separate aspects of her life,' he says, the 'golden girl' image she had among her family and friends, and her hidden life of secret babies. 'Quite clearly the degree to which she went to hide the existence of her pregnancies and the births shows that she never at any time had the slightest intention of taking these babies home,' says Tedeschi. 'And yet she made no arrangements for what she was going to do until after she was in the hospital.'

Tedeschi says that even before Keli left Auburn Hospital there were signs she was thinking of killing her child. 'The filling out of the Medicare membership form shows that the accused never intended handing Tegan over to anyone. It's inconsistent with her giving the baby to anybody. She filled out the form because the hospital were urging her to do so,' says Tedeschi. 'Keli told the police that she filled it in just in case Tegan was in her care in the future. What on earth did she mean by that answer? What, that Andrew Morris/Norris was going to come up one day to Keli's parents' house and say, "Oh, hello Sandra, hello Robert, guess what I've got here? Your grandchild, because I'd like your daughter to take over the child for a little while. The little one's a bit sick, she might need some medical care, but that's all right because Keli's got a Medicare membership for Tegan."'

He goes on to say Keli was a very convincing and succ-essful liar who kept the existence of her three children, including Tegan, completely hidden for many years. What's more, Tedeschi argues, Keli was manipulative. 'She thought she could manipulate Virginia Fung,' he says. 'She sought to play on Virginia Fung's kindness, suggesting to Virginia in her fax that she was now being truly honest with her, finally, and that Mrs Fung would somehow believe her.' He says the true purpose of the fax was to suggest Tegan was now with some unknown couple in Perth and to encourage Virginia to dissuade John from contacting the police.

Then there are the Andrew Morris/Norris stories, which the Crown says are also lies. Tedeschi begins by asking the jury to think about the turn of events surrounding this man's anger at her for being pregnant and his decision to take Tegan, which she asked police to believe. 'This Andrew Morris/ Norris knew Keli had a boyfriend. She doesn't suggest that he even asked her, "Am I the father? How do you know I'm the father and your boyfriend isn't the father?" The idea that a man would say, "Oh, you're pregnant, the baby is obviously mine, I will take the baby over" is quite unbelievable. So, too, is the idea that the man's partner, Mel, would just accept Andrew Morris/Norris is the father of the child and willingly take on the child. It only has to be stated to realise how absurd it is.'

Tedeschi then speaks about the huge search for this Andrew Morris/Norris. 'Ladies and gentlemen, is he the invisible man? We submit to you that Andrew Morris/Norris is a totally fictitious person. There was no man called Andrew Morris or Norris who met her at the hospital car park. There was no man at all.

'If she had had the slightest belief that Tegan was still alive, she would never have sent police on a wild goose chase looking for Tegan living in a household with a nonexistent man called Andrew Morris or Norris and his nonexistent partner Mel,' he says. 'She knew that Tegan was dead, so she had to pretend that she was interested in helping the police to find Tegan.

'We don't know where Tegan died, we don't know how Tegan died. That is not necessary for the Crown to prove. There are many instances in which police or the prosecution is unable to show where a death occurred or how a death occurred. But what we do know, ladies and gentlemen, is that in this particular case the accused had ample opportunity to kill Tegan. Four hours after leaving Auburn Hospital she's at a wedding, acting perfectly normally. She's able to exercise complete control over herself so as not to show any feelings at all,' he says, adding Keli drove herself home to Fairlight after killing her daughter.

Tedeschi then addresses the criticism made by the defence of the search for Tegan. 'Yes, in an ideal world, police would have gone to every school, they would have interviewed every parent, they would have asked for a birth certificate for every one of those tens of thousands of children who had been allowed to enrol in school without a birth certificate. But this is not an ideal world, this is a realistic world where the police have limited resources, so they modified their searches. We submit it was perfectly appropriate for them to do that in the circumstances.'

As to what the schools search did find, he says, 'There is no female child anywhere in Australia whose primary school enrolment shows that she was born on 12 September 1996 who could possibly be Tegan Lane. There is no female child anywhere in Australia whose primary school enrolment is in the name of Tegan Lane who could be the accused's daughter, that is, in the name of Tegan Lane. Finally, there is no child anywhere in Australia whose primary school enrolment lists a father as Andrew Morris or Andrew Norris who could possibly be the accused's daughter Tegan Lane.'

Tedeschi addresses some possible alternative scenarios as to what may have happened to Tegan. Keli's bank account records and the evidence of a couple of witnesses show that Keli didn't receive unusual sums of money or buy anything particularly expensive at the time of Tegan's disappearance. Also, Keli dismissed the idea she sold Tegan herself, as evidenced by police listening devices. Tedeschi adds that if Tegan's death at Keli's hands had been an accident, such as in a car crash, it would have been discovered by emergency services.

'Another fanciful hypothesis is that some unknown person has suddenly come, grabbed the baby from her, and some other person killed the baby. Again, you only have to state it to be able to exclude it. Here is a woman who wants to get rid of her baby and some unknown person comes up to her and causes the death of the baby. Not a reasonable possibility,' he says.

'There is only one person in the world who really knows what happened to baby Tegan between 11 am and 3 pm on 14 September 1996, and that is Keli Lane. She has given many different versions to the authorities about what she did during that time with Tegan, and all of them can be shown to be lies. There is only one reason why she has told all those lies and that is because she was responsible for Tegan's death and she had no other information that could result in Tegan being found alive. The truth was, and still is, dreadful. The accused got rid of her baby daughter Tegan by killing her and then disposing of her body.'

The Crown finishes its final address at 3 pm on Wednesday 24 November. With only an hour to spare before the end of the day, Chapple begins his address. The next morning, Keli's parents, her brother, Keli's ex-husband Peter, his new partner, and several of the Lane's family friends fill the benches behind Keli's legal team. They were free to come and listen to the Crown's closing address but chose not to. Before the judge and jury enter, Keli, her hair done and wearing a flattering, knee length dress, stands at the rear of the courtroom, discussing seating arrangements with a young court officer. She delays entering the dock till the very last minute, pausing to thank several of her family's friends for coming.

'What is the Crown's suggestion?' asks Chapple. 'That Keli is so stupid that she doesn't know what is involved with the murder of her own child; that she went ahead and did it and, to her shock, found out it was dreadful, so she reverted back to adoption? The Crown's argument seriously seems to be that Keli thought she had to murder Tegan to get to the wedding. How selfish would you have to be if that's the plan you come up with? The motive that you want to be free to pursue your sporting dreams and so on is a motive for adoption,' he says, adding in the case of Tegan, most likely an informal and illegal adoption if she gave Tegan to someone who wasn't her natural father.

Besides, Chapple goes on, going to the wedding that day wasn't such a big deal for either Keli or Duncan. It was just another social event out of the many they went to. Additionally, Chapple asks whether Keli really thought she would be missed if she didn't make the wedding. 'Nobody seems to care two bits about Keli not being there at the 1995 grand final celebration when she goes off to give birth to her first secret baby,' he says. 'Nobody seems to bat an eyelid.'

Keli maintains that she gave Tegan to the child's natural father Andrew Morris/Norris, and Chapple says there is evidence to support the notion he exists. Besides the ex-tenant's recollection of seeing some letters addressed to both Andrew Morris and Norris, Chapple says Keli knew a lot about the interior of Andrew's apartment without having to enter it. He also says she spoke about him to Peter and her mother in intercepted phone conversations and conversations caught by listening devices. 'He is referred to in the way you would refer to a real person,' says Chapple. 'If the Crown case is right, Keli must just be an actress.'

As to why Andrew Morris/Norris isn't coming forward to prove that Tegan is alive, Chapple says, 'The Crown can't rule out that Andrew decided to pass the child on to someone else. Not a particularly laudible thing, you might think' but it's an explanation why nonetheless.

During and after the birth and adoptions of her secret children Keli told lies that 'mucked people around a bit and wasted some effort and time' but Chapple suggests they were an effort to maintain her privacy and to keep her secrets safe. Besides, Keli didn't always lie. She used her real name, gave her real date of birth and provided her Medicare number when she checked into hospitals. Chapple says the fact that Keli went back to Ryde Hospital in 1999, having been there three years earlier when heavily pregnant with Tegan, meant she had nothing serious to hide from the nurses and doctors there. 'You might think it would dawn on somebody that if you went to Ryde Hospital one year and you turned up again a bit later on, that there would be records there about your earlier visits,' he comments.

Next, Chapple addresses Keli's explanation for filling out the Medicare form and why there have never been any rebates for Tegan. 'She says, "I've never used it because she has never been in my care." What is so strange about her answer?'

He also addresses the possibility that Keli might be lying about having given Tegan to a man named Andrew Morris/Norris. 'Even if it is a lie, and we don't submit to you that it is, we submit that she is trying to conceal the fact that she has given her child to a man or a couple she does not want to identify.' He adds that Keli might still be protecting this person's or couple's identity to this day. As to why this man or this couple have not come forward to prove that Tegan is alive and well, Chapple again says it may be simply because they are ashamed.

The defence's main case is that the police can't prove Tegan is dead. 'If you are looking for a needle in the haystack, and you're looking for the wrong name, the schools search is useless,' he says, adding the police were also 'slavish' in their search for a girl born on 12 September 1996. However, even if Tegan is dead, Chapple says it isn't because Keli murdered her. The people or persons she gave Tegan to may have caused her death. Or, just maybe, Keli killed Tegan by accident.

'You heard from a detective that Keli Lane has no criminal convictions. Why on earth would Keli Lane even think of murdering her baby, let alone do it?' asks Chapple about the Crown's attempts to cast Keli as a person who 'would stoop to murder her own child'.

'Everything Keli does and says is looked at by the Crown in the blackest possible light,' concludes Chapple.

The jury, exactly half of whom are women, are left to make their decision. They start their deliberations at 11.15 am on Monday 6 December 2010. The whole week passes without a verdict being reached. Clearly there is serious debate going on in the jury room.

Monday, 13 December begins with difficulties and delays. The jury has been called into court, but the judge, Keli, Sandy Lane and everyone assembled inside are asked to wait. Debate within the jury room has become so intense that jurors have to calm down before they can enter the court. Finally they file in, sullen, their arms crossed, looking exhausted. They have reached unanimous verdicts for the lesser charges relating to lies Keli swore to on adoption documents, but they can't reach a unanimous verdict on the murder charge.

Keli shakes and weeps as she stands in the dock. By now her brother has come in and is sitting next to Sandy, cradling his mother in his arms. Rob Lane isn't present as he is at home with Keli's young daughter, Macy. The family friends, who have made a few short appearances since first showing up en masse, are not present. Keli's boyfriend wanders in wearing a t-shirt and shorts, looking like he is ready to go to the beach. The judge tells the jury they can still reach a verdict if eleven out of the twelve of them can agree that Keli is either guilty or not guilty. Court is adjourned so the jurors can see if eleven of them can agree.

With the judge out of the courtroom, Keli is free to leave the dock. She walks over to where her mother is sitting. The gallery is on a raised platform, so when Sandy leans over the banister she is able to envelop the head and shoulders of her daughter in a hug. Keli sobs on her shoulder and her legal team gather around her as everyone else leaves the courtroom for lunch.

Everyone tries to guess what the jury is thinking. Is the jury split right down the middle? Is there just one or two who feel differently to the rest? None of them looked happy to speak to each other, so it's hard to tell who was agreeing or disagreeing with whom. By the time lunch is over, many in the courtroom think it might be a hung jury, one unable to decide if Keli is guilty or not guilty. This would mean the whole trial would have to be heard again the next year.

However, they do reach a verdict.

The judge asks what it is.

The foreman whispers, 'Guilty.'

While few in the courtroom can hear the foreman, everyone

hears Sandy scream, 'Oh no, oh no!' Keli gives out a low, guttural moan and then falls to the ground with a loud bang, like a tree that has been felled.

Court officers rush into the dock, tending to her. 'Keli, Keli, open your eyes. Can you hear me?' they ask. A paramedic is called for. Meanwhile, Sandy begins to fall apart.

The courtroom is cleared while the paramedic attends to Keli, who is lying motionless on the floor of the dock. When everyone re-enters fifteen minutes later, Keli is sitting upright, with a few tears trickling down her face. Her female solicitor sits in the dock with her, holding Keli's hand as Keli glances reproachfully at the jury. Her boyfriend has gone. He walked out of the courtroom just after the verdict was read out, ran across the road, hopped onto his motorbike and drove away. Sandy and Keli's brother are now sitting in different seats. They are in the section of the public gallery that is close to the dock, but blocked from seeing into it. Sandy is crumpled into a ball, rocking, then is motionless. Her son, dressed in a beautiful pin-striped suit, holds her close. Everyone else in the courtroom is watching Keli's every move, but his eyes are fixed on his mother.

The barristers start discussing the date for the sentencing hearing. Keli looks a little taken aback at her barrister and the Crown conversing in such a businesslike manner, with very little regard for the drama that has just unfolded. She looks with widened eyes at the judge, but this kind, fatherly man can't help her. A date three months away is settled on. Keli is denied bail. Justice Whealy, aware of the fact that Keli's daughter is at home waiting for her, knows that Keli now faces many years in jail. To allow her to go home to wait for the sentencing hearing would fill her and her family with false hope. Her prison sentence begins now.

There is no triumph in the courtroom, not from the detectives, not from the DoCS worker John Borovnik, not from anyone. All that is left is the fact that Keli murdered her baby. Everyone silently leaves as the court officers prepare Keli for the arrival of the prison truck. Sandy and her son hold each other. Cameras snatch images of Keli being led to prison, sobbing and handcuffed. But there is no image of Tegan for the evening news – her picture was never taken. The reporters and cameras descend on Borovnik as he steps outside. Emotionally drained, the only comment he makes is that the verdict is correct. 'Justice for Tegan,' he says quietly. 'Justice for Tegan.'

Ex Chief Coroner John Abernethy sits in his black leather easy chair at home. In the hallway a fluffy white cat lies in the middle of the floor, confident that anyone who comes through the front door will step around him. With his scratching post and other toys nearby, it's clear who rules the house. Happily dozing, the cat doesn't even bother to open his eyes if anyone approaches.

Before he retired, John spent decades ruling on suspicious deaths, including that of Tegan and many other children. 'I always think the kids who have died have gone to a better place,' he says.

The devastation that Keli's murder of Tegan has caused in the lives of those around her is extraordinary. What Keli really thinks or feels is a mystery. Who knows if she is aware of what she has done, or if she cares? But out of the dark confusion has come love.

It was in the eyes of Sandy Lane when she gave evidence at Keli's trial. On one of the worst days of her life, she was asked about her granddaughter Macy. At the mention of her name, not used in this book, Sandy's eyes lit up like only a proud grandmother's can. It was also in the notes of Virginia Fung, who arranged for the adoption of Keli's third secret baby, and the adoption agency that found Keli's first secret child's family. Both children are growing up in happy, loving families.

But the mystery remains as to how Keli could have been surrounded by so many people, sometimes while in her swimming costume, with no one noticing or caring that she was about to give birth. The fact that she shared her bed with Duncan while pregnant with her first secret baby and Tegan without him knowing still baffles Detective Gaut. However, police are satisfied that the people in Keli's life had nothing to do with Tegan's death, and no lawyer representing Keli is yet to suggest otherwise.

The sunny, privileged life in Manly that Keli was so desperate to hold on to has gone forever, but there is still a future, as bleak as it is for her. Macy remains in the care of family who have surrounded her and loved her all her life. And Keli's parents are people who love their children and granddaughter more than anything in the world. And when all is said and done, who wouldn't want to belong to a family like that?

ACKNOWLEDGEMENTS

I am particularly grateful for the help of two people while researching and writing this book: Mark Tedeschi QC, Senior Crown Prosecutor for New South Wales, and John Abernethy, retired New South Wales Chief Coroner.

I would also like to give my special thanks to Alan Stokes, whose considerable journalistic expertise guided me through the early drafts.

A big thank you to my agent, Sophie Hamley, and my publisher, Tina Gitsas, for believing in this book. Thanks also to my editor, Roberta Ivers, to Andrew Spitzer, to Lisa Prior for tossing ideas around with me over the years, and to the many people who spoke to me on an anonymous basis about their experiences with Keli Lane, her family and friends.

I am grateful to Mark Patterson, General Manager, Glebe Department of Forensic Medicine, for showing me the workings of Glebe Morgue in 2008. A description of the morgue didn't make the final edit, but it was a privilege to have him explain the extraordinary service carried out there every single day.

I also wish to acknowledge my reliance on several chapters of Chris Masters's book, *Jonestown*, for descriptions of some events in the early to mid 1980s.

Rachael Jane Chin